The Spanish Tragedy

ARDEN EARLY MODERN DRAMA GUIDES

Series Editors:

Andrew Hiscock
University of Wales, Bangor, UK and Lisa Hopkins,
Sheffield Hallam University, UK

Arden Early Modern Drama Guides offer practical and accessible introductions to the critical and performative contexts of key Elizabethan and Jacobean plays. Each guide introduces the text's critical and performance history, but also provides students with an invaluable insight into the landscape of current scholarly research, through a keynote essay on the state of the art and newly commissioned essays of fresh research from different critical perspectives.

A Midsummer Night's Dream edited by Regina Buccola

Doctor Faustus edited by Sarah Munson Deats

King Lear edited by Andrew Hiscock and Lisa Hopkins

1 Henry IV edited by Stephen Longstaffe

'Tis Pity She's a Whore edited by Lisa Hopkins

Women Beware Women edited by Andrew Hiscock

Volpone edited by Matthew Steggle

The Duchess of Malfi edited by Christina Luckyj

The Alchemist edited by Erin Julian and Helen Ostovich

The Jew of Malta edited by Robert A. Logan

Macbeth edited by John Drakakis and Dale Townshend

Romeo and Juliet: A Critical Reader, edited
by Julia Reinhard Lupton

Julius Caesar: A Critical Reader, edited
by Andrew James Hartley

Richard III edited by Annaliese Connolly

Twelfth Night edited by Alison Findlay and
Liz Oakley-Brown

The Tempest edited by Alden T. Vaughan and
Virginia Mason Vaughan

Further titles in preparation

The Spanish Tragedy

A Critical Reader

Thomas Rist

Bloomsbury Arden Shakespeare
An imprint of Bloomsbury Publishing Plc

B L O O M S B U R Y
LONDON • OXFORD • NEW YORK • NEW DELHI • SYDNEY

Bloomsbury Arden Shakespeare

An imprint of Bloomsbury Publishing Plc

Imprint previously known as Arden Shakespeare

50 Bedford Square	1385 Broadway
London	New York
WC1B 3DP	NY 10018
UK	USA

www.bloomsbury.com

BLOOMSBURY, THE ARDEN SHAKESPEARE and the Diana logo are trademarks of Bloomsbury Publishing Plc

First published 2016

Editorial matter and selection © Thomas Rist, 2016

Thomas Rist has asserted his right under the Copyright, Designs and Patents Act, 1988, to be identified as author of this work.

All rights reserved. No part of this publication may be reproduced or transmitted in any form or by any means, electronic or mechanical, including photocopying, recording, or any information storage or retrieval system, without prior permission in writing from the publishers.

No responsibility for loss caused to any individual or organization acting on or refraining from action as a result of the material in this publication can be accepted by Bloomsbury or the author.

British Library Cataloguing-in-Publication Data
A catalogue record for this book is available from the British Library.

ISBN: HB: 978-1-4725-3275-6
PB: 978-1-4725-2895-7
ePDF: 978-1-4725-2773-8
ePub: 978-1-4725-2284-9

Library of Congress Cataloging-in-Publication Data
A catalog record for this book is available from the Library of Congress.

Series: Arden Early Modern Drama Guides

Cover image taken from 1615 title page of *The Spanish Tragedy*, by Thomas Kyd

Typeset by Fakenham Prepress Solutions, Fakenham, Norfolk NR21 8NN
Printed and bound in India

CONTENTS

Series Introduction vii
Notes on Contributors viii

    Introduction   *Thomas Rist* 1
1   The Critical Backstory   *Edel Semple* 21
2   'Look on This Spectacle': *The Spanish Tragedy* in Performance   *Peter Malin* 53
3   *The Spanish Tragedy*: State of the Art   *Stevie Simkin* 83
4   New Directions: Seneca and *The Spanish Tragedy*   *Gordon Braden* 111
5   New Directions: Geopolitics and *The Spanish Tragedy*   *Eric Griffin* 131
6   New Directions: *The Spanish Tragedy* and Virgil   *Tom Rutter* 153
7   New Directions: Female Mourning, Revenge and Hieronimo's Doomsday Play   *Katharine Goodland* 175

8   *The Spanish Tragedy*: Resources for Teaching
    Leslie Drury   197

Notes 227
Select Bibliography 271
Index 295

SERIES INTRODUCTION

The drama of Shakespeare and his contemporaries has remained at the very heart of English curricula internationally and the pedagogic needs surrounding this body of literature have grown increasingly complex as more sophisticated resources become available to scholars, tutors and students. This series aims to offer a clear picture of the critical and performative contexts of a range of chosen texts. In addition, each volume furnishes readers with invaluable insights into the landscape of current scholarly research as well as including new pieces of research by leading critics.

This series is designed to respond to the clearly identified needs of scholars, tutors and students for volumes which will bridge the gap between accounts of previous critical developments and performance history and an acquaintance with new research initiatives related to the chosen plays. Thus, our ambition is to offer innovative and challenging guides that will provide practical, accessible and thought-provoking analyses of early modern drama. Each volume is organized according to a progressive reading strategy involving introductory discussion, critical review and cutting-edge scholarly debate. It has been an enormous pleasure to work with so many dedicated scholars of early modern drama and we are sure that this series will encourage you to read 400-year-old play texts with fresh eyes.

Andrew Hiscock and Lisa Hopkins

NOTES ON CONTRIBUTORS

Gordon Braden is Linden Kent Memorial Professor of English Emeritus at the University of Virginia. He is author of *Renaissance Tragedy and the Senecan Tradition* (1985), *The Idea of the Renaissance* (1989; with William Kerrigan), and *Petrarchan Love and the Continental Renaissance* (1999) and co-editor (with Robert Cummings and Stuart Gillespie) of the Renaissance volume of *The Oxford History of Literary Translation* (2010). He is currently at work on a study of English Petrarchism.

Leslie Drury received her PhD in English from the University of Aberdeen. Her research focuses on old wives' tales and the female storyteller in early modern literature and drama, exploring topics which include childbirth, alehouse culture and witchcraft. She also explores the interplay between oral cultures and literature in various periods, with a current collaborative project on the use of Walter Scott's *The Minstrelsy of the Scottish Border* in current day storytelling. She has previously published 'Neil Gaiman: The Teller of Tales and the Fairy Tale Tradition' in *The Mythological Dimensions of Neil Gaiman* (Kitsune Books, 2012).

Katharine Goodland is Professor of English at City University of New York's College of Staten Island. She is the author of *Female Mourning and Tragedy in Medieval and Early Modern English Drama* (Ashgate 2006) and co-editor with John O'Connor of *A Directory of Shakespeare in Performance*, 3 Volumes (Palgrave, 2007 and 2011). Her articles have appeared in *Early Theatre*, *Medieval and Renaissance Drama in England*, *The Journal of Religion and the Arts*, *SB: The Journal of Early Modern Drama and Performance*, and several edited collections on gender and emotion.

Eric J. Griffin is Janice B. Trimble Professor and Chair of English at Millsaps College. The author of *English Renaissance Drama and the Specter of Spain: Ethnopoetics and Empire* (University of Pennsylvania Press, 2009), among his other publications are several essays on *The Spanish Tragedy*. With additional research interests in the Colonial Americas in comparative relationship, Griffin directs the Millsaps Latin American Studies Program and contributes regularly to the college's interdisciplinary Living in Yucatán curriculum. He is currently writing a book on Anglo-Spanish relations in Jacobean drama, c. 1604–25.

Peter Malin is an independent scholar with a particular interest in the performance of early modern drama. A retired school-teacher, his educational publications include A Level study guides on *The Winter's Tale*, *The Alchemist*, *'Tis Pity She's a Whore*, *The Duchess of Malfi* and *The White Devil*. He has contributed theatre and book reviews to *Early Theatre*, *ROMARD* and *Cahiers Élisabéthains*. His article, '"Entertaining Strangers": 50 Years of Shakespeare's Contemporaries at the RSC' appeared in *Shakespeare* (2012). He is currently working on a post-1900 performance history of plays in the John Fletcher canon.

Thomas Rist is Senior Lecturer in English at the University of Aberdeen in Scotland. He is author of *Shakespeare's Romances and the Politics of Counter-Reformation* (1999), *Revenge Tragedy and the Drama of Commemoration in Reforming England* (2008) and chapters and journal articles on early modern drama, religion and poetry. He is co-editor (with Andrew Gordon) of *The Arts of Remembrance in Early Modern England: Memorial Cultures of the Post Reformation* (2013).

Tom Rutter is Lecturer in Shakespeare and Renaissance Drama at the University of Sheffield. He is the author of *Work and Play on the Shakespearean Stage* (Cambridge, 2008) and *The Cambridge Introduction to Christopher Marlowe* (2012), as well as numerous journal articles and book chapters on Renaissance drama, and he is a co-editor of the journal *Shakespeare*. He is currently completing a book on Shakespeare and the Admiral's Men.

Edel Semple is Lecturer in Shakespeare Studies at University College Cork. Her research interests include early modern drama and prose, sexuality and gender studies, and adaptations and appropriations of Shakespeare, and she has presented this research across Ireland, Europe, and Canada. She is co-editor of *Staged Transgression in Shakespeare's England* (Palgrave, 2013) and she has recently written on Shakespeare's bawds, prostitution in Elizabethan drama, early modern travel literature, and Shakespeare's *Pericles* on film. Edel is also a regular contributor to 'Shakespeare in Ireland', a scholarly blog on early modern research and events in Ireland.

Stevie Simkin is Reader in Drama and Film at the University of Winchester. His most recent book is *Cultural Constructions of the Femme Fatale: from Pandora's Box to Amanda Knox* (2014). Previous publications include *A Preface to Marlowe* (2000), *Analysing Texts: Christopher Marlowe* (2001), *Revenge Tragedy: A New Casebook* (2001) and *Early Modern Tragedy and the Cinema of Violence* (2005). As well as Renaissance theatre, Stevie teaches and researches screen violence and censorship. He is co-editor of Palgrave's *Controversies* book series, to which he has contributed studies of *Straw Dogs* (2011) and *Basic Instinct* (2013).

Introduction

Thomas Rist

> *No sooner had we spoke but we were here*
> *I wot not how, in twinkling of an eye.*
>
> THE GHOST OF ANDREA, *THE SPANISH TRAGEDY*, 1.1.84–5[1]

When we come to *The Spanish Tragedy*, we bring an idea of its genre and content from our knowledge of *Hamlet*. Yet the idea of revenge tragedy as a 'distinct species' of play relating to *Hamlet* was an invention of 1902, when the critic A. H. Thorndike sought formally to define what he termed 'The Relations of *Hamlet* to Contemporary Plays'.[2] When audiences first heard the Ghost of Andrea open *The Spanish Tragedy*, by contrast, there was neither any idea of *Hamlet*, by William Shakespeare, nor any idea of the cultural prestige Shakespeare or *Hamlet* would accrue. To define and categorize *The Spanish Tragedy* as a revenge tragedy echoing Shakespeare, as Thorndike did, would have meant nothing. No such bearings existed for Thomas Kyd or his audience. Bearings were something Kyd would have to create.

That is what Kyd is doing when he makes the Ghost of Andrea introduce the play. He is setting a scene from which a narrative can develop. Yet he is also shrouding his scene in mystery, since it comes from a ghost; and enhancing the mystery by complicating the ghost's origins. Andrea hails from an afterlife preceding the present. Though focused on Christian 'sins' (1.1.71), his afterlife is classical; and while purporting to be dead, he seems alive. Variously, the Ghost of Andrea also hails from Spain (1.1.4), Portugal (1.1.15), and the Elizabethan England where we find him: the only place we shall see him and also the only theatrical place in which Spain exists. Paradoxes of setting and identity abound, creating an intriguing but also unstable scenario. To the confused Ghost who 'wot not how', Revenge has a proposal: 'Here sit we down to see the mystery' (1.1.90). As it will be repeatedly in *The Spanish Tragedy* (see 1.4.139 and 3.15.28), theatre, now and 'here', is the mystery awaiting.

The intrigue, developed in conspiracies of justice and politics, points to the play's huge popularity in its day. Yet the mystery of Kyd's play also points to its disappearance from English theatre from the mid-seventeenth century.[3] For when, in the wake of the Puritan closing of London's theatres (1642–60), critics eventually rehabilitated Shakespeare in the eighteenth century, they canonized him as 'the poet of nature'.[4] Accommodating Kyd to this natural ideal is not simple. It requires rationalization even beyond what A. C. Bradley would manage for Shakespeare: 'although this or that *dramatis persona* may speak of gods or of God, of evil spirits or of Satan, of heaven and of hell, and although the poet may show us ghosts from another world, these ideals do not materially influence his representations of life'.[5] Bradley's example from 1904 helps illustrate how extensively the ideal of a non-supernatural, Elizabethan drama took hold in English aesthetic discourse. In Bradley's view it is not just Shakespeare who confines himself to 'non-theological observation and thought', but also, confidently: 'The Elizabethan drama was almost wholly secular'.[6] There is no place for Kyd in this erroneous construal. The critical and also theatrical history of *The Spanish Tragedy* belies a long thread of secular wishful thinking.

Happily, the thread is broken. Already in Bradley's era some scholars, and later some theatre groups, were beginning to discover *The Spanish Tragedy*. Edel Semple and Peter Malin document the development, and the prejudices that beset it, in these pages. Yet the 'turn to religion' in Elizabethan theatrical study is a largely twenty-first century development: the prejudice that would prove most enduring was the secular.[7] Only recently has criticism acknowledged Elizabethan theatre and the supernatural firmly inseparable.[8]

For *The Spanish Tragedy* as for Kyd, the development is momentous. Recognizing a supernatural theatre, we need no longer be troubled that, as its Arden editors observe, Kyd's 'main plot, enacted by human characters' is 'a second-level story mediated by ... supernatural entities [the Ghost and Revenge]'.[9] Today we can celebrate in *The Spanish Tragedy* the Elizabethan theatre's fullest expression of its supernatural type; and the play's equally large claims for a spiritual humanity.

This recognition places *The Spanish Tragedy* in the very good company of *Dr Faustus*, by Kyd's friend Christopher Marlowe, as well as alongside Shakespeare's later *Macbeth*, *The Tempest* and *A Midsummer Night's Dream*. Of these, *The Spanish Tragedy* is unique in presenting its human story at a second level consistently, but like them, it foregrounds the mediation of spirits in human inter-action.[10] The philosophical result is an explanation of how characters move, according to the classical idea that nothing comes from nothing.[11] The force of this adage for the ancients – as for many in modernity – lay in the thought that things that exist must come from somewhere, meaning they must have a cause. The existence of this cause implies some kind of force, or animating energy, at work in the universe, including in human actions. Theological and sociological implications can follow. According to Emile Durkheim, 'man feels that he has a soul, and consequently a force, because he is a social being'.[12]

The Spanish Tragedy constantly illustrates the spiritual causes of action along these social lines. When Pedringano addresses Fortune regarding the action of shooting a pistol, for example, he says: 'Give but success to mine attempting spirit, / And let me shift for taking of my aim' (3.3.4–5). As the 'attempting' agent, the spirit's action is crucial here. First the spirit, and only then the person, move; and only from both movements can aiming follow. Larger passages present similarly spiritual causation:

> Now in his mouth he carries pleasing words,
> Which pleasing words do harbour sweet conceits,
> Which sweet deceits are limed with sly deceits,
> Which sly deceits smooth Bel-Imperia's ears,
> And through her ears dive down into her heart,
> And in her heart set him where I should stand.
> Thus hath he ta'en my body by his force,
> And now by sleight would captivate my soul ...
> (*The Spanish Tragedy*, 2.1.124–31)

The soul, here, is the subject of suffering, but the developing lines detail the production of this suffering as matters of cause-and-effect between words and the anatomical body. As so often in the play, the implication is that words, body and soul (a metonym for 'spirit' in early modernity's mingled medical and religious analysis) continually interact.[13] Yet there are disconnections between 'her heart', 'my body' and 'my soul', which the ostensible cause of suffering, Horatio, does not account for, not least because he is not present. The gaps imply invisible, animating agencies at the interstice between characters; or, lest we miss it, not so invisible. Filling the gaps between every character, the ever-present Ghost and Revenge loom supernaturally large.

Addressing action and speech, these examples of the play's spiritual physiology declare its intense theatrical awareness in complex ways. According to the standard idea that drama functions through examples, one of these is a view of drama as illustrative of life. 'For instance, lordings, look upon your King', says the Viceroy, making himself a life-lesson (3.1.12). 'But thus we see our innocence hath saved / The hopeless life which thou, Villuppo, sought', says Alexandro, similarly extrapolating (3.1.82–3). Above all, following the claim to be 'soliciting their souls', so that 'poor Hieronimo / Cannot forget his son Horatio' (3.15.19–20), there is Revenge's overarching claim:

> Behold, Andrea, for an instance how
> Revenge hath slept, and then imagine thou
> What 'tis to be subject to destiny.
> *(The Spanish Tragedy*, 3.15.25–7)

Each of these examples puts theatrical seeing at the heart of the drama, implying the action illustrates the world. Implying they are real (so Revenge affirms) the dramatic world illustrates the retributive agency of souls.[14]

Seeing also in these cases means absorbing, remembering, drawing the lesson. Linked to the grief of Hieronimo for his son, it signals an un-Reformed discourse of early modern remembrance for the dead variously explored in this volume by Stevie Simkin, Tom Rutter and Katharine Goodland.[15] Simultaneously, it develops the mediation of theatre. While Revenge and Ghost are spectators of the play, the Ghost is also spectator to Revenge (waiting on and responding to his actions, disappointed when he sleeps, encouraging him to action). The pair illustrate theatrical action in microcosm.

One result is the opportunity to see what a model early modern tragedian hoped for from his audience. To dramatic purpose, Revenge clarifies what the spectator must initially 'know' (1.1.86), but that extends only to seeing 'the author of thy death, Don Balthazar … Deprived of life by Bel-imperia' (1.1.86–9). Other events transpiring by the Ghost's next speech, the spectral spectator needs direction again: 'Be still, Andrea, ere we go from hence, / I'll turn their friendship into fell despite' (2.1.5–6). When they talk next, this pattern recurs. Revenge tells the unhappy Ghost to 'Be still' (2.6.10). Requiring direction one last time, the Ghost remains unhappy and confused in Act 3, Scene 15. He only accepts Revenge's instruction, this time to 'Content thyself' (3.15.19), when the developing drama is clarified: 'Sufficeth me; thy meaning's understood' (3.15.35).

With stillness and content established as his necessary demeanour, the note of change in the Ghost's last scene is marked: 'Ay, now my hopes have end in their effects ... Aye, these are spectacles to please my soul' (4.5.1, 12). At long last, the spectator is 'pleased', in a transformation emphasizing that however rough, the justice satisfies. Rather than relying on direction in anguish, moreover, this Ghost is active: 'I'll lead my friend Horatio to those fields ... / I'll lead fair Isabella ... / I'll lead my Bel-imperia... / I'll lead Hieronimo .... / Let me be judge ...' (4.5.17–30). Contrasted with his previous speeches, this is electric.

What the newly-energized Ghost illustrates is catharsis, which from Aristotle meant a medical cure for theatrical audiences, but which meant purgation and Purgatory in early modern England.[16] Dramatizing a medico-spiritual scenario requiring patience, Revenge has made a patient of the Ghost before curing him. As a paradigm of external audiences, for whom patience with delayed revenge in tragedy will soon become normal, *The Spanish Tragedy* concludes in theatre's benefit to health, spiritual and embodied. Following allusion to 'Saint Jeronimy', Shakespeare would trumpet:

> For so your doctors hold it very meet,
> Seeing too much sadness hath congealed your blood,
> And melancholy is the nurse of frenzy.
> Therefore they thought it good you hear a play
> And frame your mind to mirth and merriment,
> Which bars a thousand harms and lengthens life.[17]

Yet we need not reach to Shakespeare's recollection of Kyd for parallels to the audience-cure enacted in *The Spanish Tragedy*. As an axiom, 'melancholy is the nurse of frenzy' captures the trajectory of Hieronimo, the second-level story mirroring the first as the play presents living and dead in community. The Ghost's last 'Ay, now my hopes have end in their effects / When blood and sorrow finish my desires' (4.5.1–2) speaks for Hieronimo, who through blood finds the remedial purge Isabella, in her own, ghostly parallel, seeks helplessly:

> So that you say this herb will purge the eye
> And this the head,
> Ah, but none of them will purge the heart!
> No, there's no medicine left for my disease,
> Nor any physic to recure the dead.
>
> (*The Spanish Tragedy*, 3.8.1–5)

In the final scene, the purged dead are 'recured' in *The Spanish Tragedy*: the sought-after physic is found. Through a bloody purging of the 'heart', the spectator's 'eye' and 'head' find solace. Above all, *The Spanish Tragedy*'s simultaneous purgation in the temporal and spiritual planes affirms an imagination of its outset: there is a Purgatory.[18] This is not the 'spiritual instruction and corporeal correction' advanced as catharsis by contemporary, moderate Protestants.[19] Nor is it the demonized catharsis of Protestants less moderate. *The Spanish Tragedy* ends in spiritual correction in the land of the dead as the means to justice for the living.

Toward that end, the play explores the relation of corporeal to spiritual correction. Royal and civic execution scenes display the 'theatrical elements' and 'spectacle' Michelle Foucault has highlighted in early modern punishment rituals.[20] Yet *The Spanish Tragedy*'s places of execution are also places of the dead, according to the theological inflection of Peter Marshall and Bruce Gordon.[21] A focus also of twenty-first century archaeology, the connection of execution to theology receives lengthy treatment in Act Three, where Alexandro is wrongly suspected of the death of Balthazar:[22]

> VICEROY: Why linger ye? Bring forth that daring fiend
> And let him die for his accursed deed.
> ALEXANDRO: Not that I fear the extremity of death,
> For nobles cannot stoop to servile fear,
> Do I, O King, thus discontented live.

> But this, oh, this torments my labouring soul:
> That thus I die suspected of a sin
> Whereof, as heavens have known my secret thoughts,
> So am I free from this suggestion.
> VICEROY No more, I say! To the tortures! When!
> Bind him, and burn his body, in those flames
> *(They bind him to the stake.)*
> That shall prefigure those unquenched fires
> Of Phlegethon prepared for his soul.
> (*The Spanish Tragedy*, 3.1.38–50)

Even as Alexandro is pronounced 'fiend', civic execution here explicitly prefigures the afterlife.

Since Alexandro is innocent, the implied theology of execution might look faulty. Yet the fault serves two theological purposes. According to the drama's exemplary style, first, it allows Alexandro's claim that 'My guiltless death will be avenged on thee, / On thee, Villuppo, that hath maliced me' (3.1.51–2) to receive demonstration. The drama eventually shows the discovery of Villuppo's guilt and it is he, not Alexandro, who goes to the torture. Standing for sin, execution is here distinguished from its mere threat. While royal authority prefigures the spiritual, it is also more fallible.

Second, the fault provides a dramatic space, between the seeming absolutes of guilt and innocence, where Alexandro will not suffer and die, but rather will suffer and live. The space highlights a different kind of suffering from civic, which Alexandro elucidates: 'this torments my soul: / That thus I die suspected of a sin / Whereof ... / ... I am free'. There is, this implies, a suffering even for the apparently guiltless, which will not persist but which may be inevitable. Its purgation is made visible in Alexandro. Having previously 'menace[d]' (3.1.54) Villluppo, Alexandro finally '*seems to entreat*' (3.1.100 SD) for him. Implying he has been purged, and perhaps entailing kneeling iconography, Alexandro's forgiveness is saintly.[23]

Alexandro's scene of public execution contrasts with that of Pedringano. Here too the place of execution as a place of the dead is evident, but discourses of spiritual health are greater. To 'Methinks you should rather hearken to your soul's health', Pedringano replies: 'Why, sirrah hangman? I take it that that is good for the body is likewise good for the soul; and it may be, in that box is balm for both' (3.6.77–81). Here, too, the possibility that a reprieve will come exists, but Pedringano is guilty and the box, on which he has relied for pardon, is empty. The parody of pardon presents the spiritual drama materially:

> PEDRINGANO I prithee, request this good company to pray with me.
> HANGMAN Ay, marry, sir, this is a good notion. – My masters, you see here's a good fellow.
> PEDRINGANO Nay, nay, now I remember me, let them alone till some other time, for now I have no great need.
> (*The Spanish Tragedy*, 3.6.88–93)

Prayer for the dead was key in the Purgatorial cult of Catholicism rejected by Reformers. Yet the association of the box void of pardon with the avoidance of prayer – compounded by the villainy of Pedringano – claims prayer for the dead as necessary in spiritual health. The list of souls punished at play's end uniquely remembers Pedringano for blasphemy (4.5.44).

Just as scholars now elide early modern spectacles of theatre with those of punishment, so *The Spanish Tragedy*, whose varied influence on subsequent drama this volume explores, conflates both spectacles with Catholicism's imaginative purgatories. Figuring the Christian catharsis of redemption in England's religious drama, the bloodshed at the close of *The Spanish Tragedy* testifies to this; as does the play's image of the sword: both 'this cross' (2.1.87) and 'thy tragedy' (2.1.93).[24]

That figuration is significant for the execution scenes. At the point of death, part of what troubles Alexandro is that his audience fails to hear his confession of innocence. Pedringano, on the other hand, refuses the spiritual confession of prayer. Both broken confessions enrich the genre's Senecan dynamic, in which authority's deafness to a subject's complaint turns him to violence. Gordon Braden explores the theme in these pages.[25] Yet secular authority is not the only basis of confession in *The Spanish Tragedy*. The arrest of Pedringano highlights this:

> PEDRINGANO Now by the sorrows of the souls in hell,
> *(He strives with the Watch.)*
> Who first lays hands on me, I'll be his priest.
> 3 WATCH Sirrah, confess, and therein play the priest.
> Why hast thou thus unkindly killed this man?
> (*The Spanish Tragedy*, 3.3.36–9)

Connoting the last rites, the primary sense of confession here is the sacrament, where a malefactor speaks to religious rather than secular authority. As Marlowe's Friar Barnardine illustrates in *The Jew of Malta*, the sacrament was well-known in Elizabethan England:

> Know that confession must not be revealed,
> The canon law forbids it, and the priest
> That makes it known, being degraded first,
> Shall be condemned and then sent to the fire.[26]

Pedringano has no interest in this confession. Yet his exchange with the Watch highlights the sacrament's purgative 'machinery for the regulation and resolution of offences' as the era's death-avoiding alternative to secular power.[27] Private confession excluding secular interference, the subversion is twofold; and it develops in the act of salvation haunting Pedringano's box. When that proves void, secular confession proves unforgiving, enhancing the sacrament's alternative appeal.

Their contrast resonates in the box until Pedringano's death. Charles Borromeo introduced confessional boxes to Europe in 1575, as those with continental connections in

England knew. Marlowe, with whom Kyd shared lodgings in 1591, was in Europe at least once in his life. On the testimony of Richard Baines, in 1592 he was deported from Holland. A Catholic apostate, Baines would later state Marlowe claimed 'if there be any God ... it is with the Papists'; and the Privy Council itself denied Marlowe visited a Catholic seminary in France in 1587.[28] Irrespective of the truth of the claims, many around Kyd were equipped to recognize the confessional satire of *The Spanish Tragedy*.

Yet it is the rationale of confession in Act Three, Scene Three that speaks widely for the play. Fearing he is 'Betrayed' (3.4.13), less than thirty lines later Lorenzo moves from the universals of axiom to the particulars of plot:

> A guilty conscience urged with the thought
> Of former evils easily cannot err.
> I am persuaded – and dissuade me not –
> That all's revealed to Hieronimo.
> And therefore know that I have cast it thus. –
>
> (*The Spanish Tragedy*, 3.4.14–18)

It is Lorenzo's 'guilty conscience' that persuades him he is found out. Yet a 'conscience' causing a secret to be 'revealed' before leading to action describes religion's confessional process. In the confessional's spiritual scheme, it seems, thus, and only thus, is the secret out of the box. For Lorenzo, who operates below the radar of the state even while part of it, the confessional's alternative to state-power resonates in every action. His box of tricks proving as empty as his servant's in the end, his confession is a parody. For Hieronimo, however, the confessional process presents the paradigm of spiritual over state confession at its most defiant. It begins in conscience; leads to outraged disclosures the state will or cannot see; ultimately produces the reveal of Horatio's corpse and the accompanying, purging annihilation of the state. The defiance kills the confessor. Yet in the spiritual tragedy the catastrophe is not final, as the last scene shows.

The paradigm of theatre as spiritual confession also works for Andrea, who is self-evidently outside state (though not spiritual) power, and whose opening confession produces action and revelation in its widest frame. Yet positioning the audience as receivers of confessions kept from civil authority – indeed, positioning them as confessors, in the sense of a confession's receiver: priests – the subversion of the play comes home to Elizabethan England. Although the content of the heretical papers for which Kyd was eventually arrested and tortured may never be known, Lukas Erne is just one of today's critics to wonder if Kyd was a Catholic.[29] *The Spanish Tragedy* points to such sympathy.

This is a far cry from the secular theatre of A. C. Bradley. It is also far from the mid-twentieth century views of S. F. Johnson and Ronald Broude. They argued the play's depiction of defeated Spanish corruption reflected Elizabethan Protestantism.[30] Yet history has moved on. Though Johnson and Broude assumed a 1580s England of anti-Catholicism and Hispanophobia, today we know the prejudices had little purchase.[31] For Johnson and Broude, the mistake was costly: Hieronimo's means of revenge, the playlet 'Soliman and Perseda', was a multilingual figure of Babylon; spelling, they argued, the Catholic Babylon of Protestant Revelation. Yet beside the uncertainty of whether 'Soliman and Perseda' was in many languages or in English; beside the historical error and beside, as we have seen, that its revelation – far from requiring apocalyptic exegesis – conforms to the mechanics of confession pervading the play, the Protestant approach contains another difficulty. Of the playlet, Hieronimo distinguishes between what, generically, 'all tragedians do' (4.4.77) and what he intends:

> Here break we off our sundry languages,
> And thus conclude I in our vulgar tongue:
> [...]
> *([Draws the curtain and] shows his dead son.)*
> See here my show, look on this spectacle.

> Here lay my hope, and here my hope hath end;
> Here lay my heart, and here my heart was slain;
> Here lay my treasure, here my treasure lost;
> Here lay my bliss, and here my bliss bereft.
> (*The Spanish Tragedy*, 4.4.73–92)

Whether 'sundry languages' is truth or a fiction, this passage makes clear they were not the dramatic centre. The nine privacy-foregrounding iterations of 'my' following the revelation of Horatio's corpse make it the centre of 'my show'. The lines preceding the revelation ('Here break we off …') produce a dramatic refocusing on the mourned corpse as the centre of action. If there are Protestant echoes (even, faintly, in an English-only performance), the corpse and Hieronimo's remembrance of it displace them. Anticipating the procedure is the burning of Alexandro at the stake. Recalling the execution of Reformers under Mary Tudor and Henry VIII, the scene displaces that punishment for heresy by making Alexandro's burning a matter of treason (3.1.29; 57). Yet since it was treason for which Catholics were executed in London from 1581, the scene shifts its Protestant martyrology to a Catholic one. Following Alexandro's exoneration, it underscores this by evoking for Villuppo 'not so mean a torment as we here / Devised': one 'that yet may be invented for thine end' (3.1.98–9; 101). Calling being burnt at the stake 'mean' hardly compliments the Reformed martyrs. Looking forward in martyrological contexts to new and allegedly greater torments, on the other hand, evokes the 'Tyburn Tree' (known also as 'The Triple Tree' or simply 'The Tree') erected in London in 1571. Here from 1581, and so contemporaneously with Kyd's play, Catholics were hung, drawn and quartered. The play never shows this Elizabethan torment. Yet the parody of justice Horatio suffers, hung from a tree and then stabbed, followed by the commemorations of Hieronimo and Isabella, points to its martyrdom. The preservation of Horatio's corpse evokes reliquary practices the Counter-Reformation renewed.[32]

Looking to the organization of chapters to come, *The Spanish Tragedy*'s ritual meanings bear comment. In the spectacles of execution of Pedringano, Alexandro and Horatio, the play juxtaposes rival examples of state and religious power, making exemplarity complex and meaning associative. In the association of execution scenes with its dramatic parodies – including the 'executions' of the penultimate scene by Knight Marshall Hieronimo – the play layers its meanings further. The richness of the layers emerges when recalling C. L. Barber's observation – recalled by Stevie Simkin and Katharine Goodland in these pages – that hanging Horatio from a tree evokes Christ hanging on the cross. The site of Elizabethan martyrdom, Tyburn's Tree (indeed the 'Triple Tree', since Christ died in a triptych) looks emblematic from this perspective, but the play looks dazzling.[33] From the punished but salvific Christ; through images of Protestant and Catholic martyrdom; past secular punishments for persons more and less innocent; including a kaleidoscope of parodies, the play's developing intrigue of spirits and bodies simultaneously tests subjects and their means of trial. Like Andrea's opening 'passage through […] wounds' (1.1.17), the passage of *The Spanish Tragedy* is complex.

The present volume presents it in layers. It moves from chapters on the history of criticism and performance, through four chapters of New Directions in criticism, to conclude with resources and means to teach the play. In 'The Critical Backstory', Edel Semple considers the reception of *The Spanish Tragedy*, charting how quickly it became a 'cultural reference point' (p. 22). Writers appropriating it included Ben Jonson, Thomas Dekker, James Shirley and Thomas Rawlins. In the early recollections, Hieronimo and Don Andrea stand out: the former as a 'verbal and visual image of extreme passion, grief and madness'; the latter as a 'courtier, a soldier and lover, and an otherworldly figure of retribution' (p. 23). Though evocations can be tongue-in-cheek, they testify to how ingrained the play became 'in the public consciousness' (p. 22). 'To get the joke or reference, or to fully appreciate the imitator's reworking of the text, the audience must already have some degree of familiarity with the original' (p. 22). Moreover, Semple shows that the play had social as well as literary uses. For the anti-theatrical William Prynn, for example, it stands for 'the base pleasure of theatre' (p. 28). Yet in Richard Braithwaite's tale of a dying woman, 'vehemently calling on Hieronimo' stood in for pious reflection on death (p. 28).

The play's reputation suffered in the eighteenth and nineteenth centuries, but in the twentieth century, a 'balanced eye', 'less likely to set out to cast a moral judgement on the play's action' (p. 50), began its critical recovery. Cautious of any 'simplified evolutionary critical trajectory' (p. 50), Semple nevertheless shows how valuable the attention of serious critics including Frederick Boas, William Empson and T. S. Eliot was in the process. By the 1960s, there is a 'notable upswing in ... books, chapters, articles and doctoral theses' (p. 39). Concluding the development with Gordon Braden's *Renaissance Tragedy and the Senecan Tradition: Anger's Privilege* (1985) is telling. There is a long tradition of associating Kyd with Seneca. Yet in Braden's later twentieth-century view, Seneca's 'influence' has developed into a European history of tension between despots and their repressed subjects we have touched on. From a twenty-first century vantage-point, Braden reimagines the perspective in a later chapter in this collection.

Approval, contempt and a renewed appreciation also characterize *The Spanish Tragedy*'s performance history, as Peter Malin shows in '"Look on This Spectacle": *The Spanish Tragedy* in Performance'. Yet while the mockery by Samuel Pepys of a performance in 1668 'can be taken to herald the theatrical silencing of Kyd's tragedy for over 250 years' (p. 60), simple, evolutionary perspectives are again misleading. Roughly a decade after its opening, the play's acting style already created uncertainty. Malin theorizes the style was one of 'gestural hyperbole', which was 'parallel to the rhetorical elaboration of the dialogue' (p. 58). In the seventeenth century, it could denote 'emotional falseness'

(p. 59). Yet early modern like modern revivals faced similar challenges: 'The balance between historical reconstruction and contemporary relevance; the handling of the Revenge framework; the interpretations of the characters and delivery of their rhetorical modes' (p. 75). In a challenge of his own, Malin argues modern productions have yet to master each of these in a single performance. Nevertheless, combining 'rhetoric with … spontaneity and naturalism' (p. 76), in a performance where actors seemed to be coming to their parts from 'some purgatorial ante-room' (p. 77), the 1997 RSC production at The Swan in Stratford-upon-Avon came close. We are not far, then, from the great performance *The Spanish Tragedy* 'deserves' (p. 79).

The history of modern revivals being entwined with scholarship, as Malin shows, critical approaches to *The Spanish Tragedy* following the 'advent of critical theory' (p. 83) is the subject of Stevie Simkin's '*The Spanish Tragedy*: State of the Art'. The burgeoning understanding of the play culminating, in Semple's account, in the literary analysis of culture, soared in the 1980s, as cultural criticism newly emphasizing the theory took hold. Scrambling canons of taste with narratives of subversion and *différance*, in asserting 'no end of subversion' the age's new varieties of historical criticism made drama in the era of Kyd illustrative of early modern conditions and mentalities.[34] Yet it also made it evasive and polyphonic. Simkin illuminates the ensuing, wide divergences in criticism of *The Spanish Tragedy* through a series of categories: 'Authorship, date, sources and influences' (p. 88); 'Protestantism, Catholicism and anti-Iberian Prejudice' (p. 93); 'Class politics' (p. 96); 'Cosmology' (p. 100); 'Revenge' (p. 104); 'Legacy' (p. 107). The last of these highlights through examples from film to 9/11 'the enduring appeal of the revenge theme in contemporary culture' (p. 107). The overriding effect of the chapter is to demonstrate that, stemming from culture, the hallmark of criticism of *The Spanish Tragedy* today is 'profound meditation' (p. 110).

In the first of four chapters presenting New Directions in critical thinking, therefore, Gordon Braden welcomes in 'Seneca and *The Spanish Tragedy*' a moment ripe for looking at Kyd's 'whole landscape' of revenge 'afresh' (p. 113). Versed in Seneca's literature and translation, Braden finds Seneca's 'aggressive' voice, 'propulsive ... for the [dramatic] speaker's emotional state' (p. 116), linking this to Hieronimo's self-evocation as a 'spectacle of ... woe' (p. 127). As for Seneca in imperial Rome, so Hieronimo becomes this spectacle in an 'age of tyrants' (p. 118), from whose 'unrestrainable savagery' (p. 118) the identities of revengers derive. Rejecting oppositions of 'Christian' and 'pagan', the chapter concludes with historical and ethical meditations for the future: 'what we want to know about Seneca's "influence" is how much of it involves an active appetite for harshness beyond Christian recuperation' (p. 126).

Observing that in Renaissance Iberia 'Senecan stoicism was enfolded within a widely observed habitus of "honour"' (p. 141), Eric Griffin offers bearings on this question. The focus of 'Geopolitics and *The Spanish Tragedy*' is early modern Europe's 'culture-wide' (p. 138) emulation of imperial Spain. A Spaniard prophesying Spanish imperial dominance, Seneca is one of several cultural indices, including Miguel de Cervantes, which in *The Spanish Tragedy* expound 'Empire's beautiful and warlike compulsions' (p. 137) to an England between admiration and envy. Exploiting the ambivalence, Kyd wrote 'against the reductively Hispanophobic currents that increasingly dominated the era' (p. 141). Revivals after his death diminished the play's 'utterly different quality' (p. 142) from the Black Legend of Spanish Cruelty.

Classical translation becomes the focus in Tom Rutter's '*The Spanish Tragedy* and Virgil'. This Roman poet afforded a 'touchstone for successful translation' (p. 165) for contemporaries and the 'period of personal contact between Kyd and Marlowe may be connected to the points of contact between their most famous plays' (p. 168). *The Spanish Tragedy* and *Dr Faustus* excavate a 'literary tradition imaginatively located' (p. 170) in Virgil's underworld. Evoking religious and personal rituals, this gave life to England's drama. In the 'broader cultural sense' (p. 163), Kyd's 'less self-disabling' (p. 173) resurrection of Virgil is triumphant. One generation after *The Spanish Tragedy*, the English stage 'has a classical tradition of its own' (p. 174).

In the Bible of St Jerome 'crucial' (p. 168) to Marlowe and Kyd, Latin translation collides with commemorations of sainthood. In Katharine Goodland's 'Female Mourning, Revenge and Hieronimo's Doomsday Play', it is the translation of English Slaughter and Corpus Christi plays producing the sanctity. Yet this 'encompasses an ethos of justice' (p. 176) conscious of class, gender and suffering. 'Kyd understood the dramatic power of the *Planctus Mariae* [Marian lament], especially its ability to engender in an audience not only compassion for the victim, but also a sense of moral and emotional outrage wherein reparation feels necessary and urgent' (p. 184). Vengeance, here, is nested in 'devotional purpose' (p. 189). In the last word from the New Directions chapters on the place of harshness in Christianity, distinctions between 'revenge and justice' which 'might be possible' collapse in *The Spanish Tragedy* and Corpus Christi 'in the theatrical performance' (p. 195).

Concluding the volume with 'online features, academic articles, and group discussion topics' (p. 197–8), in '*The Spanish Tragedy*: Resources for Teaching' Leslie Drury makes Kyd's discourses of revenge, violence and justice accessible to 'educators and students' (p. 197). Through structured exercises and analogies with modern film and TV, students can find *The Spanish Tragedy* 'meaningful' (p. 211) and close to 'their own preferred entertainment' (p. 209). For readers of the volume as a whole, 'contemporary relevance' (p. 65) and historicism may clash productively. What relation exists between the 6,160 persons hanged at Tyburn during Elizabeth's reign, the hundred priests and fifty-three lay persons who experienced its 'makeshift vivisection', and the pleasures of *Game of Thrones*?[35] What relation exists between *The Spanish Tragedy* and its sources? While critics today speak of ghosting and 'hauntology', Kyd, whose play puts the *animus* in animation, said a Ghost.[36] It is in that spirit of causation noticed at the outset that *The Spanish Tragedy*, more than the sum of its parts, comes magically to life as a 'mystery': if 'I wot not how', nevertheless 'in twinkling of an eye' (1.1.90; 85).

1

The Critical Backstory

Edel Semple

The beginnings

The critical history of *The Spanish Tragedy* is bookended by popularity. Kyd's play was an instant success in the late 1580s and was widely known to audiences for decades after its first performances. However, with the closure of the theatres in 1642 and with changing tastes, the play slipped into relative obscurity and received only sporadic critical attention. Indeed, the limited interest in the play is evinced by the fact that its author was unidentified until the mid-eighteenth century, when scholars unearthed a comment by Thomas Heywood which quoted 'M. *Kid* in the *Spanish* Tragedy'.[1] Gradually rediscovered in the early twentieth century, *The Spanish Tragedy* is now celebrated as one of the most ground-breaking and influential dramas of the Elizabethan era.

Written between 1582 and 1589, *The Spanish Tragedy* proved to be a lasting commercial success on the stage and in print. Henslowe's *Diary* records a remarkable twenty-nine performances in five years (1592–7), while between 1592 and 1633 the playtext went through eleven editions.[2] The variety of likely performance venues is also notable: as well as the Rose on Bankside, *The Spanish Tragedy* may have been staged at the Cross Keys Inn, Newington Butts, the Fortune, the Theatre and the Curtain in Shoreditch, the Globe, and the second Blackfriars. It also possibly toured the provinces and may even have been performed at court in 1619–22.[3] That Kyd's tragedy remained a valuable theatrical product is demonstrated by the expansion of the play through Additions, printed in 1602,[4] and by the appearance in 1605 of *1 Hieronimo*, an anonymous play that takes as its subject Don Andrea and Bel-imperia's romance and that may be a burlesque of or prequel to Kyd's play.[5] The number of performances, the range of venues (inns, private and public theatres), the steady sequence of printings, the Additions, and the staging of a prequel, all attest to the play's enduring popularity with a heterogeneous audience over several decades. Moreover, *The Spanish Tragedy* was no less admired abroad. Over the next century, in various forms, the play made its way around mainland Europe. It was performed by English actors in Frankfurt in 1601, by an English company in Dresden in June 1626, in Prague in 1651, and in Lüneburg in 1660. The play was also adapted and printed in German (in 1618, c. 1662–6, and 1680) and in Dutch (in 1615, 1621 and 1638); so popular was this last Dutch adaptation that reprints were issued well into the eighteenth century.[6]

Despite and perhaps because Kyd's play was popular, original, and memorable, it became an established cultural reference point and was quickly imitated and parodied. The prevalence and permanence of allusions, homages, echoes, and mockeries further demonstrate how quickly *The Spanish Tragedy* firmly established itself in the public consciousness. The play was appropriated in a myriad of ways for diverse purposes but, to get the joke or reference or to fully appreciate the imitator's reworking of the text, the audience must already have had some degree of familiarity with the original. In turn, the echoes and imitations of the play's most memorable scenes, lines, and characters, then reaffirm and intensify popular knowledge of Kyd's work. From the beginning,

Hieronimo and Don Andrea were key figures for authors and audiences and four speeches were commonly parodied: Don Andrea's opening speech (1.1.1–85); Balthazar's rhymed lover's complaint beginning 'No, she is wild' (2.1.9–28); Hieronimo's soliloquy when he discovers Horatio's body 'What outcries' (2.5.1–33); and Hieronimo's grandiloquent 'O eyes no eyes' (3.2.1–52).[7] In a variety of texts, Hieronimo stands as a verbal and visual image for extreme passion, grief, and madness; Balthazar is remembered as a euphuistic jilted lover; while in the ghost of Don Andrea early modern authors and audiences saw a courtier, a soldier and lover, and an otherworldly figure of retribution. References to and parodies of *The Spanish Tragedy* are widespread in sixteenth- and seventeenth-century literature, as a sample of representative examples serves to show.[8]

In his 1589 preface to Greene's *Menaphon*, Thomas Nashe mocks Kyd's blank verse and his alteration of the Virgilian underworld (in 1.1.73) by ridiculing unlearned writers who ignorantly 'thrust *Elisium* into hell'.[9] Andrea's prologue also appears in Heywood's late Elizabethan comedy *1 The Fair Maid of the West* (c. 1597–1603) when the clown Clem, a drawer arrived in Morocco as a privateer, marvels at his rise in status and proudly identifies with Andrea as a peer:

'It is not now as when Andrea liv'd,' – or rather Andrew, our elder journeyman. What, drawers become courtiers? Now may I speak with the old ghost in *Jeronimo*
    When this eternal substance of my soul
    Did live imprisoned in this wanton flesh,
I was a courtier in the court of Fez.[10]

As was typical in many dramatic appropriations, the original tragic bent of Kyd's play is replaced by humour and levity. The bombast and pretensions of Andrea's speech are also deflated in *The Knight of the Burning Pestle* (c. 1607). In his role as the eponymous knight, Rafe enters to give his dying speech; with an arrow lodged in his head, he begins: 'When I was mortal, this my costive corpse / Did lap up figs and raisins in the Strand'.[11] Here, the absurd demise of the lowly grocer's apprentice and the scatological wit – Rafe describes himself as a constipated cadaver – are used to poke fun at the play's lofty rhetoric and to undercut the seriousness and permanence of death.

The play proved to be a favourite target of scorn for Ben Jonson. Throughout his career, he frequently used Kyd's tragedy as a marker of outmoded drama favoured only by the unsophisticated spectator.[12] When, in *Every Man In His Humour* (c. 1598), Matthew excitedly praises *The Spanish Tragedy*'s 'fine speeches' and recites parts of the 'O eyes' soliloquy, it exposes him as an pretentious gull with coarse tastes.[13] The Praeludium to *Cynthia's Revels* (1600) ridicules an imaginary play-goer with 'more beard than brain' who 'swears down all that sit about him "that the old *Hieronimo*", as it was first acted, "was the only best, and judiciously penned play of Europe"'.[14] The Induction to *Bartholomew Fair* (1614), with tongue-in-cheek, states that it will say nothing of the 'constant' (old-fashioned) tastes of the play-goer who will 'swear *Hieronimo* or *Andronicus* are the best plays', even though this conviction is 'ignorance'.[15] Hieronimo's aside as he is denied access to the King – 'Hieronimo, beware; go by, go by' (3.7.30) – became a stock catchphrase in early modern drama, so much so that even forty years after the first performances of *The Spanish Tragedy*, Jonson's *New Inn* (1629) includes the phrase as an expression of impatience and dismissal.[16]

Like Jonson, Nathan Field employs *The Spanish Tragedy* as revelatory of character in his comedy *A Woman is a Weathercock* (c. 1609–10). Full of hope and not a little vanity, Sir Abraham Ninny recites parts of Balthazar's euphuistic lover's complaint, but the rhymed responses of his companions show that he is an unattractive buffoon who cannot win the lady Lucida.[17] The melodrama of Horatio's murder and Hieronimo's histrionic response become the target of Lording Barry's satire in *Ram Alley* (c. 1611); finding Boutcher, a broken-hearted suitor, attempting to hang himself, William delivers a parody of Hieronimo's 'what murderous spectacle is this' speech (2.5.9–33). William's performance of grief goes unappreciated, however, as he discovers there is indeed 'yet life' in the would-be Horatio when Boutcher revives only to complain of the clamour caused by William's recital.[18] This reworking of the scene not only deflates the excessive emotion aroused by Horatio's death, but it also halts and reverses the tragic momentum of the original, for, Boutcher lives and goes on to marry his faithful mistress. The university comedy *Albumazar* (1615), presented before James I at Trinity College, Cambridge, burlesques Hieronimo's 'O eyes' soliloquy by channelling Balthazar's ardour for Bel-imperia. In Act 2 the foolish farmer Trincalo, who notably has learned much from attending plays at the Fortune and the Red Bull, expresses his passion by travestying Hieronimo's speech as an ineloquent lover's lament beginning 'O lippes, no lippes, but leaves besmear'd with mel-dew'.[19]

The Spanish Tragedy also proved to be popular off the stage, with allusions and adaptations in seventeenth-century prose, song, and poetry. Like the dramatic references to Kyd's tragedy, the allusions in these forms are helpful in determining how the play was received (what caught the attention of its first audiences?) and why it was appropriated (how did the play become so engrained in the fabric of popular culture?). To begin with, Thomas Dekker references *The Spanish Tragedy* in two of his prose pamphlets. The first of these, *The Wonderfull Yeare* (1603), which reflects on the events of 1603, includes a tale of a cobbler's wife who confesses her infidelities on her deathbed. Her husband is counselled by their neighbours to 'be not horne mad: thanke heauen that the murther is reueald: study thou *Baltazars* Part in *Ieronimo,* for thou hast more cause (though lesse reason) than he, to be glad and sad.'[20] The cobbler is asked to imagine himself as another Balthazar, betrayed by his mistress; as a married man he has more 'cause' for complaint, in the legal and sexual sense, than Balthazar, but, with the 'murder' of his honour out in the open and his wife dead, he also has more 'reason' (rational judgement and motive) to not seek vengeance. While Dekker's tale may be a fabrication, it shows how the play and its characters had become familiar, shared images, of use and interest to the urban community. This vignette also demonstrates how Kyd's work could be imaginatively reworked into a shorthand to illustrate a point and prompt a particular response. Writing on 'Cruelty' in the second pamphlet, *The Seven Deadly Sinnes of London* (1606), Dekker criticizes pitiless creditors and wishes that a law be instated that a 'miserable debtor' be buried at his creditor's door so that he may torment the creditor by seeming to '[rise] up (like the Ghost in *Jeronimo*) crying Revenge'.[21] Although no such scene directions are extant, this image may point to Andrea and Revenge's first entrance as staged in the public theatres: rising through the trapdoor from the underworld and howling for revenge, their identities would have been quickly established and an atmosphere set.[22]

The Spanish Tragedy was also appropriated in poetic works. In Thomas Andrew's 'The Unmasking of a Feminine Machiavell' (1604), the speaker dreams of meeting '*haplesse* Andrea' '*wofull wight ... Whose heart with sorrowes deepe was gal'd*'.[23] This Andrea is in part a cipher for the author; he is both a lover and a soldier (but is an Englishman), and he recounts how he has been betrayed by his unnamed mistress and reports on his experience of the Battle of Nieuwpoort in 1600 by imitating parts of the General's speech (1.2.22–86).[24] In another poem of the same year, Anthony Scoloker's 'Daiphantus, or the passions of love' (1604), Hieronimo functions as a reference point for grief and high-blown oration. Here, the tormented lover 'mad Daiphantus' dons only a shirt like Hieronimo in 2.5 and, overcome by his ardour, he patchily imitates three of Hieronimo's declamatory speeches: 'O eyes, no eyes', 'What outcries pluck me', and 'I'll down to hell'.[25]

Hieronimo also features in the broadside ballad 'Hockley in the hole' (c. 1620), which appears to borrow from both *The Merchant of Venice* and *The Spanish Tragedy*. In this song, young love triumphs as a daughter escapes from the clutches of her miserly father to live happily with her beloved in Hockley.[26] Like Hieronimo, the father, a usurer, 'loses' a child, and he goes on to commit the suicide by hanging that Hieronimo only threatens:

> Her father having mist her, grew heavy and sad,
> But the losse of his money did make him stark mad
> Like to *Jeronimo*, raging he goes,
> The losse of his golde was the cause of his woes ...
> and urgd to dispaire ...
> he hanged him selfe

Once more, then, Hieronimo is a reference point for paternal grief and lunacy; however, the auditors' sympathies are diminished as the usurer's anguish derives from his avarice, rather than the death of his child.

One notable spinoff of the play comes in the form of the ballad 'The Spanish Tragedy, Containing the lamentable Murders of Horatio and Bellimperia: With the pitifull Death of old Hieronimo' (c. 1601–40). This song ventriloquizes Hieronimo, who calls on the audience to listen to his '[great] woes'.[27] The ballad omits the frame narrative and some of the play's events, but other memorable incidents such as Hieronimo's dipping the handkerchief in blood and his organization of the playlet, are retained. Hieronimo's family tragedy is at the heart of the ballad and the final verses suggest that he gains some satisfaction from vengeance: he embraces death to be reunited with Horatio and sees the kings, who were unsympathetic to him, suffer similar losses. The song ends with a neat moralistic conclusion:

> Here have you heard my Tragicke tale.
> Which on Horatio's death depends,
> Whose death I could anew bewayle:
> But that in it the murtherers ends,
> For murther god will bring to light:
> Though long it be hid from mans sight.

In contrast to the play, then, the ballad is unequivocal in its support of Hieronimo's actions, and it suggests that his suffering had a clear purpose. Through him, the murderers have been punished and providential justice has been served. Furthermore, whereas Revenge promises the enactment of an 'endless tragedy' (4.5.48) in the afterlife, in the ballad death provides Hieronimo and his audience with closure.

Frequent references to the play in Caroline and Restoration literature attest to the continuance of what one recent critic has termed the '"Hieronimo phenomenon"', though interest in the play did decline in the later seventeenth century.[28] In *The English Gentlewoman* (1631), while criticizing women who devote themselves to pleasure, Richard Brathwaite relates a curious anecdote of a theatre aficionado who, on her deathbed, refused to reflect on her imminent death but instead shockingly ended her life 'with a vehement calling on *Hieronimo*'.[29] True or not, this story not only testifies to the endurance and significance of *The Spanish Tragedy* in the public's mind, it also demonstrates the varied uses the play could be put to. Hence, for Brathwaite, and William Prynne after him, the play stands as representative of the base pleasure of theatre, and so it is recycled to suit their didactic purpose. Even so, for the dying woman in this anecdote, Hieronimo may stand as a sympathetic vision of death, loss, or grief, or even operate as a kind of *memento mori*.[30]

A scene in Thomas Randolph's satirical comedy *Hey for Honesty* (1627) recalls the alarming appearance of Kyd's ghost. In Act 2 Penia-pennilesse, the goddess of poverty, enters in such a ragged state that two men cannot resist mocking her; the first notes that she resembles a creature from tragedy, to which the other replies: 'By *Jeronymo*, her looks are as terrible as *Don Andrea* or the Ghost in *Hamlet*'.[31] As in *Albumazar*, James Shirley's *Changes, or Love in a Maze* (1632) has a foolish lover bungle Hieronimo's 'O eyes' speech. Displeased with the lady Chrysolina, the wealthy booby Sir Simple declares 'Oh eyes no eies but Mountaines fraught with teares?' and scorns the lady by passing her while saying 'Goe by,

Jeronymo, goe by, goe by'.[32] Recalling the mechanicals' play in *A Midsummer Night's Dream*, Thomas Rawlins's tragedy *The Rebellion* (c. 1636–40) has four tailors meet to discuss what play they should perform before the King of Spain. Showing their pedestrian preferences, the tailors settle on '*Jeronimo*' and note of the titular character that 'he was a mad rascall to stab himself'.[33] Like Shakespeare's Bottom, the tailor Vermin ambitiously wishes to play several roles; he begins with Andrea, but then decides he should also play Hieronimo, Horatio, Balthazar, and the King. To prove his suitability for this virtuoso performance, he rehearses Andrea's prologue but, comically, fudges its ending: 'I was a Tayler in the court of *Spaine*'.[34] The play is also briefly referenced in 1675 in the prologue to *The Scoffer Scoffed* and, once again, it is representative of an affected style and old-fashioned tastes.[35] Thus, while *The Spanish Tragedy* endured as an iconic narrative alive in the collective cultural memory, as it had been in the first decades of the seventeenth century, it also continued to be a common butt and references to it were frequently divorced from their original meaning.

Late in February 1668, Samuel Pepys attended a performance of *The Spanish Tragedy* at the Nursery, a relatively new playhouse in Hatton Garden. Pepys declares that the actors' 'play was a bad one, called "Jeronimo is Mad Again," a tragedy. Here was some good company by us, who did make mighty sport at the folly of their acting, which I could not refrain from sometimes, though I was sorry for it.'[36] Frustratingly then, Pepys has little to say on Kyd's play beyond its being 'bad'. Moreover, this fleeting judgement is the last record of a performance of the play until the twentieth century. As the Nursery operated as both a playhouse and training school for young actors, we might speculate that the play's heightened rhetoric and dramatic action appealed to a fledgling company learning its craft, but their poor performance did little to revive the failing reputation of Kyd's tragedy. In his *An Account of the English Dramatick Poets* (1691) Gerard Langbaine does not even connect Kyd's name to his greatest work. Listing the play as *Jeronymo*, Langbaine observes only that 'This Play has been divers times acted, and several Lines have been quoted out if it, by several Authors'.[37] By the late seventeenth century, then, the star of *The Spanish Tragedy* had fallen considerably.

The eighteenth and nineteenth centuries

Post-Restoration audiences and readers found little to please them in *The Spanish Tragedy*, and thus the play suffered from critical neglect for much of the eighteenth and nineteenth centuries. Scholarly discussions of Kyd and his play were frequently confined to positive or negative evaluations. Critics saw the play as a puerile spectacle of gratuitous violence replete with poetic excess designed to please the masses, and they cited the parodies of earlier writers as evidence of its inferior quality. For instance, writing in 1748, Peter Whalley's opinion of *The Spanish Tragedy* is scathing and, perhaps drawing on Revenge's closing line, he predicts a kind of textual 'endless tragedy' for Kyd's play: 'The Author has had the Happines to be at this Time unknown ... yet though his Name is saved, his Work will continue to suffer Life with perpetual infamy'.[38] The prominent Shakespearean Richard Grant White, writing in 1865, views *The Spanish Tragedy* as a juvenile work that is a necessary but embarrassing step in the evolution of revenge tragedy, a development which will reach its apotheosis only with *Hamlet*.[39]

The play was, however, printed for the first time in over a century when it was anthologized in 1744 as part of Robert Dodsley's neat pocket volume set *A Select Collection of Old Plays* and Kyd was correctly identified as the play's author by the literary historian and critic Richard Farmer.[40] Late in the century, the seeds of a scholarly recuperation of *The Spanish Tragedy* can be located in Thomas Hawkins's multi-volume work, *The Origin of the English Drama* (1773). Basing his edition on Q1 and collating it with three later editions of the play, Hawkins ultimately produced a fine version of the text that would be reprinted several times over the next century.

In 1815 the German Romantic critic August Wilhelm von Schlegel describes the play as inane and compares it to the hastily made 'drawings of children'.[41] According to him, Kyd's 'want of power' is everywhere in evidence and, most damningly, the play is designed 'for popular effect'.[42] Schlegel does concede however that there is a lightness of touch in the scene changes and some naturalness to the dialogue. More definitive praise comes from John Payne Collier's *History of English Dramatic Poetry* (1831). Unlike his predecessors, Collier champions Kyd as an author and he offers a reassessment of *The Spanish Tragedy*; while it is not without its flaws, its potency and pathos are particularly impressive and overall it may be described as 'a very powerful performance'.[43] It would take some time, however, for the wider scholarly community to see the play in such a positive light.

On the whole, however, the fate of Kyd's play was relatively healthy at the close of the nineteenth century. Two scholarly editions of *The Spanish Tragedy* appeared in the late 1890s – John M. Manly's old spelling edition and Josef Schick's carefully modernized edition in the Temple Dramatists series – and these would soon be followed by the publication of Kyd's collected works early in the new century.[44]

The twentieth century

After two centuries of relative neglect, *The Spanish Tragedy* underwent a critical and performative revival in the twentieth century.[45] A steady recuperation of Kyd's tragedy is in evidence in scholarly studies, although earlier judgements of Kyd and his masterpiece were sometimes reiterated. For instance, some critical studies continued to regard *The Spanish Tragedy* as inchoate and destined to be mere provender for later, greater, artists; in particular, Shakespeare's shadow looms large over the career of his predecessor. However, there were considerable developments in critical approaches to and understandings of the play in this period. And notably, since the 1910s *The Spanish Tragedy* has consistently formed part of the canon of early modern drama.[46]

1901 saw the publication of Frederick S. Boas's *The Works of Thomas Kyd*, a valuable and seminal work of scholarship, but not one without its flaws.[47] Boas includes a lengthy critical commentary to his edition exploring Kyd's biography, influences, reputation, drama and prose. In addition, he considers the Additions to *The Spanish Tragedy* and its relationship to *1 Hieronimo*, and provides ample notes on the play (which rely heavily on Schick's), along with supplementary documents of interest such as 'The Spanish Tragedy' ballad and Ayrer's 1615 German adaptation of the play. Like his predecessors, Boas feels compelled to comment on the fame of Kyd's play: it was the most popular drama of its day 'because it was the work of a man who, though not a great poet, thinker, or moralist, was a born dramatist, with a genius for devising impressive situations and flamboyant phrases, and for exploiting to the full the technical resources of the contemporary stage'.[48] Kyd, it seems, was the right man in the right place and time.

According to Boas, Kyd's success comes from his blending of popular elements with lofty classical traditions. At the same time, Boas is clearly more interested in the classical aspects of the play. He discusses, for instance, Kyd's use of Seneca, Lucan, and Sophocles, and observes the hitherto unrecognized influence of *The Aeneid* on Andrea's prologue, noting that the worthy auditor would no doubt detect an air of the Virgilian throughout the play.[49] Of the 'Sophoclean irony' behind Hieronimo's plotting of 'The tragedy of Suleiman', Boas writes: 'Here Kyd is classic in a higher sense than he sought or knew, and attains effects which were novel at the time, and have remained rare throughout the history of

English theatre'.⁵⁰ While Boas does much to advance Kyd as a dramatist worthy of critical attention, he also does not spare the criticism. Hence, when Kyd excels at crafting scenes that draw on but surpass classical models to form something striking and original, it seems to Boas that his achievement is merely intuitive, rather than reasoned or intellectual; in effect, he is accidentally clever and unconscious of his artistry.

Boas, like other twentieth-century critics, found that the central flaw in the play is Hieronimo's dilatory revenge, a rationale for which is not satisfactorily supplied; for all his remarkable achievements Kyd, again, is deemed an inchoate tragedist incapable of handling 'so subtle a dramatic problem'.⁵¹ Elsewhere though, Boas praises Kyd's skill. Although he considers Bel-imperia's haste to revenge her soldier-lover 'well nigh grotesque', he is impressed by her combination of 'masculine strength of will and intellect ... [and] polish and charm' and places her alongside Lady Macbeth as one of the great tragic heroines.⁵² He judges Act 2 to have several virtues; the scene of the lovers in the bower shows Kyd's artistry at its best, and Hieronimo's entrance half-dressed and his distress at finding his son's body leaves a lasting impression. This moment 'so full of natural pathos, still keeps much of its affecting power', but our sympathy is curbed by Hieronimo's 'instant determination upon revenge'.⁵³ Assessing the use of and rationalization for violence, Boas declares that, until the fourth act, the play can clearly be categorized as a tragedy (rather than a gory melodrama). However, Hieronimo's savage removal of his own tongue and murder of Castile, and Andrea's gleeful plans for eternal torture, are evidence that Kyd's 'finer instinct' has failed him.⁵⁴ The only saving grace to the calamitous violation of the grand dénouement of tragedy is that Virgil's influence emerges once more so that 'glimpses are given us of Hieronimo and his loved ones amidst the Elysian fields – glimpses that help to make us less forlorn'.⁵⁵ Whether, however, we are to be 'forlorn' because of Kyd's disappointing abuse of the venerable genre of tragedy, or because of the never-ending torment of his characters, is unclear.

The play was published again in 1911, by Harvard professor William Allan Neilson, who judged its significance to be that it was Kyd's landmark contribution to the 'Senecan tragedy of revenge'. In his biographical note on Kyd, 'a man of gloomy temperament', Neilson presents a viewpoint that is broadly representative of early-twentieth-century attitudes to Kyd and *The Spanish Tragedy*:

> In spite of tendencies to melodrama that, to the modern taste, border on the ludicrous, Kyd rises at times to the utterance of genuine passion, and even his sensationalism is frequently impressive. But his historical importance in the development of the type of tragedy of which *Hamlet* is the climax must be granted to be greater than his intrinsic value.[56]

Once again, Kyd's play is assessed as a text of historical merit, its poetic worth indefinite, especially when compared to Shakespeare's preeminent achievements. In a number of scholarly studies then, Boas and Neilson included, it seems that, however 'good' the play is – original, ground-breaking, popular, the progenitor of a genre – it could always have been better. From the vantage point of retrospection, it is viewed as a prototype destined to be succeeded and superseded by greater works.

In this context, T. S. Eliot turned his attention to *The Spanish Tragedy*'s contribution to English tragedy. Kyd appeared on Eliot's syllabus in 1918–19 and was introduced to his students as 'The First Important Dramatist'. In the lectures, he analysed the play as part of the genre of the 'tragedy of blood' and touched on both its popularity and connections to *Titus Andronicus* and *Hamlet*.[57] In his essay 'Hamlet and His Problems' (1919), Eliot describes Kyd as an 'extraordinary dramatic (if not poetic) genius'.[58] Like other critics of the twentieth century, Eliot also discussed the impact of Seneca on Kyd; thus, in an essay of 1927, he grants that *The Spanish Tragedy* was the 'most significant popular play under Senecan influence', but he argues also that the play is '[allied] to something more indigenous', and that its material is generally dissimilar to Senecan material.[59] The play evidently made some impression on Eliot as a seminal historical text, but also and significantly as a work of art. Indeed, Hieronimo is referenced in the closing lines of *The Waste Land* (1922), a poem that collects and curates the fragments of great literature.[60]

In the next decade, Howard Baker's *Induction to Tragedy* (1939) questions the contention that the play is Senecan, a judgement that is by then a critical commonplace, and instead argues that Kyd's sources are closer to home. Firstly, Seneca and Kyd's treatment of ghosts and revenge are wholly dissimilar.[61] Baker follows Boas in emphasizing the Virgilian elements of the play, and he proposes that medieval drama and non-dramatic poetry, such as *The Mirror for Magistrates*, are instead central influences on Kyd's tragedy. For instance, Don Andrea and Revenge 'are adaptations of stock characters in the medieval metrical "tragedies"' of England.[62] The influence of the Induction of *The Mirror for Magistrates* can also be seen in Isabella's speech before her suicide. In a brief but astute reading, Baker argues that Isabella implies that she is going on a marvellous journey with 'sorrow and despair' (4.2.27) as her personified guides, much like Andrea who is led by Revenge.[63] Although, overall Baker somewhat underestimates Seneca's influence on *The Spanish Tragedy*, his arguments have recently been re-examined and the list of Kyd's influences has broadened considerably.[64]

Elizabethan Revenge Tragedy, written in 1940 by the bibliographer and editor Fredson Bowers, proved to be an influential study of the genre. For Bowers, *The Spanish Tragedy* was the progenitor of revenge tragedy, the first play to popularize retribution as 'a tragic motive on the Elizabethan popular stage'.[65] Indeed, so successful was the 'Kydian formula' for the genre (which Bowers outlines in twelve points), and such was the impact of *The Spanish Tragedy*, that the 'golden era of the true Kydian revenge tragedy' would last for almost two decades.[66] (Nonetheless, Bowers still cites *Hamlet* as the superlative revenge play.)[67] In contrast to criticism in the vein of nineteenth-century scholarship, Bowers appears to see the attraction in Kyd's subject: 'Sensational though the central motive proved, it was a universal one, appealing to all classes of people and to all time.'[68] Like Boas, Bowers overlooks the significance of the multiple (but different) descriptions of the battle and Andréa's demise.[69] For Bowers, Kyd's early dilemma is how to satisfy Andrea's desire for revenge for his (just) death and engage the audience in the action. Having thoughtfully examined the options (Bel-imperia as revenger, Horatio as Bel-imperia's tool of vengeance, etc.), Bowers concludes that Kyd's solution, although it renders Andrea and Revenge superfluous, forms a weighty core for the play: 'the strength of the opposing force' is enhanced as Lorenzo emerges as the arch-villain while Bel-imperia and Horatio embark on a love affair, motivating Balthazar and Lorenzo to vengeance, and so enabling the emergence of Hieronimo as the play's true revenger.[70] Notably, Bowers reads Hieronimo's initially deferred revenge as necessary (there would be no plot without it) and entirely plausible.[71] But, the Marshal's decision to delay and carry out his revenge through secret means (in 3.8.20–44) 'marks the turning point from Hieronimo the hero to Hieronimo the villain'.[72] To this moral degradation in character, the early modern audience could only have responded with abhorrence; Hieronimo's calculated turn to unchristian violence and Machiavellian deception in his 'Vindicta mihi' speech is in fact clear evidence that 'Kyd is deliberately veering his audience against Hieronimo'.[73] Such motivation and actions doom Hieronimo; as a disingenuous intriguer and a murderer it is 'absolutely necessary for him to die'.[74] The rationale for Bel-imperia's suicide lies not in her morality but her antecedents, and so Bowers asserts that the audience most likely looked on her with some leniency; moreover, she dies, not because she is a villain, but to satisfy the conventions of the tragic heroine of romantic fiction.[75] Concerning the final massacre, Bowers concludes that Hieronimo's self-mutilation is pointless except as a crowning horror, and the murder of Castile is either the climax of Hieronimo's villainy or an example of Kyd's bloodthirstiness.[76]

In Moody E. Prior's *The Language of Tragedy* (1947), Kyd's play is declared a work of remarkable innovation that greatly advanced the development of blank verse, style, and diction in tragedy. During a careful close reading of some of Hieronimo's speeches and a thoughtful discussion of his character, Prior also considers the play as an ur-text of early modern tragedy and herein, it seems, lies much of its worth: 'That Hieronimo is not one of the great dramatic figures is chiefly due to the technical immaturity of Kyd; the brilliance of the conception, not wholly apparent in Kyd's play, is to be seen in its progeny.'[77] Such an originary view not only burdens *The Spanish Tragedy* with the weight of dramatic history, it also impedes a reading of it as accomplished or mature. From this view, it can only ever be seen as a starting point, the locus of tragedy's embryonic potential rather than its realization. Later, Prior situates Kyd's play as a mid-point on the evolutionary trajectory of tragedy when he asserts that 'the transitional nature of the play is therefore to be seen in the retention of the older style [of tragedies such as *Gorboduc*] in spite of the original advances'.[78] Kyd was caught, then, between the competing demands of maintaining the style of his tragic forebears and instituting a new style to suit his plot. His 'ingenious' solution is to employ 'a variety of styles through a kind of principle of decorum which suited the style to occasion or person', but Prior ultimately deems this inadequate as both poetic skill and originality are compromised in the process.[79] Weaknesses aside, Prior asserts that, along with *Tamburlaine*, *The Spanish Tragedy* helped to move English tragedy 'in the direction of its artistic destiny – toward the final integration of proper means to proper ends without which no art can realize its possibilities'.[80] Overall, Prior's analysis of *The Spanish Tragedy* is useful and he contributes to a growing, if sometimes reluctant, appreciation of the play.

In an article of 1956, William Empson, one of the leading lights of New Criticism, sets out to explain some key issues in the play, which has 'been under-rated through misunderstanding'.[81] Empson sets himself against the play's detractors but, contradictorily, at times he presents the play as crude and worthy of censure: the play's first audiences 'had laughed at [it] even before they decided it was out of date', the Portuguese subplot is ridiculous, and the first dumb show is a clumsy piece of theatre.[82] In part, the play appears to Empson like a murder mystery in need of solving, and previous critics have missed some vital clues that indicate its intricacies. Drawing on the fact that Andrea enters knowing 'no reason for revenging himself', Empson offers a 'bold conception'; although it is unstated in the play, the audience are aware that Castile and Lorenzo have collaborated with Balthazar and plotted Andrea's death in battle, and they gain pleasure from watching Andrea's Ghost 'to see whether he has guessed the point yet'.[83] Andrea is thus aligned with the audience in terms of knowledge and so its view; as Andrea is ignorant, he and Revenge sit on the stage as 'part of the audience' to learn as the action progresses.[84] (The placement and influence of these two characters comes to be a frequent topic of discussion for later critics.) Empson's personal opinions and fanciful conjectures occasionally slip into his more sober critical analysis, especially when he considers the responses of the play's original audiences. Of Bel-imperia, he judges that the first audiences were likely to have been shocked by her clandestine sexual affairs, but would come out on the side of right; the audience, he is certain, would be against the oppressive royal marriage of the Spanish Bel-imperia and Portuguese Balthazar, which recalled the proposals from foreign princes to Queen Elizabeth, who 'had been quite right to refuse'.[85] For much of the article, Empson treats of the psychology and actions of Hieronimo, the rightness (or not) of revenge, and the audience's response to these. He proposes that, like Hamlet, Hieronimo is 'both mad and not mad', and his biting out of his tongue is evidence that he has become completely insane.[86] In contrast to Bowers, Empson argues that the play showcases a diverse range of attitudes towards vengeance and that the audience likely had differing opinions on its morality.[87] In fact, this 'early play gave a more profound treatment of Revenge than the later ones', and a key element in this achievement lies in Kyd's handling of the notion of Fate. On this point, Empson proposes that, through his circumlocutory scheming, the mad Revenger is determined to 'show that he is acting *as* or *like* Fate'; this is 'the doom of Old Hieronymo', but Andrea is spared such pains and he can instead view revenge with the audience, from some distance.[88]

Critical analysis of *The Spanish Tragedy* took some substantial leaps forward in the 1960s. From this point on, there is a noticeable upswing in the number of books, chapters, articles, and doctoral theses on the play, and the scholarly understanding of Kyd progresses considerably, but, occasionally, the old anxieties do emerge. For example, in 1963 Alfred Harbage proposes that Kyd's great innovation is his borrowing of intrigue from comedy 'to employ comic methods with tragic materials', such as is the case with Pedringano's hanging.[89] However, Harbage finds such moments distasteful, and so he barely tolerates the play as an obligatory precursor to *Hamlet*, and deems Kyd too weak a talent to handle this cross-genre borrowing with sophistication.[90] Of the play's darkly farcical moments, he notes with chagrin: 'We are dealing with a pervasive feature of the tragedy of the age with which we must come to terms', and he asserts that Hieronimo's actions and the play as a whole 'fail to win our approval'.[91]

In the same collection as Harbage's essay however, is S. F. Johnson's '*The Spanish Tragedy*, or Babylon Revisited', which presents some insightful and original arguments. Firstly, Johnson attends to the political implications of 'The tragedy of Suleiman'; his central contention is that Kyd uses Hieronimo's play as an analogy for 'the confusion of tongues wrought by the Lord at Babel ... and [for] the horrible destruction of both the historical and symbolic Babylons'.[92] With Spain equated with Babel and Babylon, and with its political system essentially ruined by the close of the play, Kyd's English audience would have no doubt relished this 'wishful discomfiture of the Spanish enemy'.[93] Significantly, Johnson's discussion also calls for a reassessment of Bel-imperia – albeit in a lengthy footnote – who has been harshly judged by earlier critics. From this view, Bel-imperia is an essential link to all of the play's intrigues and 'between the super-natural and human worlds', and her loyalty, spirit, and sagacity were sure to have impressed the early modern audience.[94] In opposition to Bowers, Johnson asserts that Hieronimo's dilemma – he is a public judge forced to seek justice by his own hand – is a piece of genius on Kyd's part, and that the audience's understanding of revenge is more complex than has hitherto been realized.[95] Strikingly, Johnson treats Hieronimo's last bloody actions with seriousness and critical acuity; his auto-glossectomy arises from a true fear of breaking his vow to Bel-imperia and is a 'symbolic refusal to participate in the confusion of the world after Babel'; moreover, his murder of Castile unknowingly fulfils Andrea and Revenge's desires.[96]

Like many critics of the twentieth century, Eleanor Prosser focuses on Hieronimo and the morality of revenge in her brief survey of the play. Writing in *Hamlet and Revenge* (1967), she sets out the by now standard critical views of Hieronimo (he is either a hero whose actions are valid, or he is a good man turned villain), and traces the trajectory of the audience's sympathy. It is at a high, for instance, when Hieronimo places his faith in Heaven or in the King, but it is diminished when we see Hieronimo invoke Hell and abuse his son's corpse to feed his passion.[97] Comparing Hieronimo at his last to a maleficent medieval Vice, Prosser finds, like Bowers, that it is 'extremely doubtful that Kyd's audience viewed Hieronimo as justified'.[98]

Three full-length studies of Kyd appeared in the latter half of the 1960s: Philip Edwards's *Thomas Kyd and Early Elizabethan Tragedy* (1966); Arthur Freeman's *Thomas Kyd: Facts and Problems* (1967); and Peter B. Murray's *Thomas Kyd* (1969). Edwards's slim volume follows his excellent scholarly edition of the play for Revels, which had appeared in 1959 and was reprinted throughout the 1960s and 1970s.

Edwards opens by making a case for the exceptionality of *The Spanish Tragedy* and by comparing Marlowe and Kyd, a comparison which he fears 'may seem rather comic'. According to him, Marlowe's 'originality and genius do not need to be established', but apparently the value of the minor playwright Kyd still needs explication.[99] Here, it is clear that Edwards feels the weight of a critical tradition that has often presented an uncomplimentary picture of Kyd's play.

Edwards begins his discussion by helpfully positioning *The Spanish Tragedy* in relation to a range of sixteenth-century plays, including *Cambises*, *Horestes*, *Gorboduc* and *Arden of Feversham*. Both *The Spanish Tragedy* and *Arden* are free from the easy 'moral clichés of the tragedies of [their] time', and their authors are interested in the 'complexities of life'.[100] Kyd in particular eschews simple Christian moral judgement and, therefore, he has successfully 'written a tragedy and not a tract'.[101] Noting the alternating of styles in *The Spanish Tragedy*, Edwards speculates that this may have been 'a deliberate attempt to fuse the two worlds of tragedy, classical and popular, thus familiarizing the elevated, and elevating the familiar'.[102] While such a range of tone is commendable, Edwards proposes that, had Kyd 'forged a single style' encompassing the formal and naturalistic, this would be an even finer achievement.[103] Of special note in Edwards's study is his fruitful engagement with the play's metatheatrical aspects and treatment of divine will, and his fresh take on the closing scenes. In his consideration of whether the characters are subject to providence, Edwards observes that the executions of Pedringano and Villuppo are not simply contrasts to Hieronimo's frustrations, but are in fact used to 'confirm the extremely capricious way in which justice works'; rather than showing a divine will at work, repeatedly *The Spanish Tragedy* shows human justice 'in a very ironic light'.[104] The audience are further encouraged to reflect on life's mysteries through the events of the finale. When the deaths in Hieronimo's playlet are shown to be 'real on the level of the reality of the play-world', Edwards suggests, then the fabricated reality of

The Spanish Tragedy becomes 'so much more real for the spectators'.[105] Kyd's aim here is 'to impress on us that human life *is* a play', and a complex one at that.[106] Like Bowers before him, Edwards deems Hieronimo's final bloody acts to be mere 'meaningless savagery', but overall his reading of the finale is more progressive. He finds that 'there is a kind of triumph, a kind of victory, but no one feels it except the dead man who has been watching from the shadows, for whom the whole of Hieronimo's strivings have been only as inset within a larger story'.[107] At the close of the play we possess a kaleidoscopic view of Hieronimo and revenge, but we have a clear vision of an individual struggling in a complex world; the play's open-endedness is valued by Edwards: 'What we are certain of is our uncertainty.'[108]

As the title of Freeman's volume suggests, his interest lies in the facts, uncertainties, and questions surrounding Kyd's biography and literary output. In his opening thoughts, Freeman sums up a common preoccupation of twentieth-century critics when he asks: 'Has Kyd a claim to our consideration beyond his unquestioned originality, historical "importance", and theatrical debt owed to him by Shakespeare and other eminent successors?'[109] (Freeman's answer is that Kyd is indeed worth attention; not too much, but also more than he has garnered heretofore. This response is reserved but overall Freeman's study champions Kyd and his work.) *The Spanish Tragedy* is the focus of two of the chapters in this study and, in both, Freeman's exploration of the play's sources, date, afterlives, and its style and structure, is invaluably detailed. Freeman is struck overall by Kyd's mastery over his material; he draws on, but is not subservient to, a diverse range of influences. In employing historical events and classical and contemporary literary sources, Kyd demonstrates 'a fine sense of selection, imagination and ability to conflate separated details with dramatic possibilities into a fluent and homogenous whole'.[110] Freeman begins his analysis of the play proper by distinguishing himself from his critical predecessors with a bold declaration:

> For all the gusto and sensationalism of the climax of Kyd's popular play, the manner of *The Spanish Tragedy* is essentially patient and graceful. For all that it has been called bombastic, crude, and rhetorical, Kyd's style is actually rather reserved, unimposing, and delicate.[111]

The subsequent discussion supports these claims, exploring issues such as Kyd's use of high rhetoric, reportorial speeches, and Latin, and finds much of merit in these. Weak points in Kyd's writing are also identified; the love scenes between Bel-imperia and Horatio, for instance, are clunky, Kyd's skill lies not in climaxes but in creating a steady tempo, and Hieronimo's 'O eyes' soliloquy is overdone.[112]

In Freeman's observations on the play's theme, 'justice and injustice', we can detect a shift in, or rather, broadening of, the critical focus on revenge; this scholarly trend is also perceptible in Johnson, Edwards, and in Murray (discussed below).[113] While Freeman sees the play as being 'about' Hieronimo and in particular the evolution of his desire for revenge – a subject he spends some time on – he redresses a gap in criticism when he attends to the Portuguese sub-plot.[114] In contrast to critics such as Empson and Edwards, Freeman views the sub-plot as purposeful; it is connected fully to Kyd's central interests (adjudication, justice and injustice) and he uses the episodes involving Villuppo and Alexandro to explain 'why Hieronimo cannot rush into the matter of punishing the villains without true proof'.[115] Some other characters and scenes are passed over rather swiftly however (Isabella is dismissively labelled 'Horatio's somewhat ineffectual mother', for instance, and her suicide is deemed a 'superfluous episode'.)[116] Attending to Kyd's finale, Freeman proposes that Castile's death is not mere sensationalism; rather, it has multiple aims which include tempering the audience's pleasure at the villains' downfall as revenge has destroyed both the guilty and the innocent. Furthermore, Hieronimo's self-mutilation may be a final dig at his captors or be the Marshal's ironic 'countering [of] the physical tortures threatened by the King with psychological tortures of his own'.[117] On Andrea and Revenge's concluding speeches, Freeman urges a charitable reading; this scene is not tacked on by a poor artist, rather it is Kyd pressing 'us to feel pity while we exult, to modify our self-righteous blood-lust with horror at wanton punishment, and furthermore to recognize the super-human characters for the cold fish they are'.[118]

Despite its all-encompassing title, Peter B. Murray's *Thomas Kyd* is in fact a focused eight-chapter study of *The Spanish Tragedy*. Murray's tome is comprehensive: over five chapters, he carefully sifts through the play's four acts, offering meticulous close readings of every character and scene, and identifying recurring themes. One of the strengths of Murray's volume is that he consistently shows how *The Spanish Tragedy* operates as a unified whole; of Kyd's structure, Murray argues that the main plot and sub-plot 'combine as a single action, and each must always be considered in relation to one another'.[119] The acknowledgement of such dramatic unity is a noticeable trend in twentieth-century criticism. Central to Murray's thesis is the idea that the play's tragedy arises because the characters fail to perceive that they are related 'as images of each other, or, most deeply of all, as forms of each other'.[120] For example, Balthazar is a form of Andrea, and Hieronimo and Castile are forms of each other; the failure to recognize this leads to the isolation of the tragic individual (who cannot comprehend the world and his place in it), and in the end, to his destruction. This problem even extends to the nations of Portugal and Spain, who are unable to see they are interdependent.[121] And, like Freeman, Murray proposes that the audience are called on to engage their sympathies and rational faculties.[122] As spectators in the theatre, we are detached from the action and occupy a position of greater knowledge and understanding than Hieronimo and the other characters; from this superior vantage point we may see that Hieronimo's actions accord with a tragic fate and 'that he acts ironically and becomes the thing he hates'.[123] However, we must also take care to try to comprehend and pity Hieronimo's situation, to 'put ourselves in [his] place', and to avoid judging him severely because, ultimately, Hieronimo is 'a form of ourselves'.[124] Although we are aware, Murray argues, that Hieronimo's revenge causes him to become a version of the murderous Lorenzo, he 'never becomes a villain, for the great strength of his feelings makes us sympathize with his deeds at the same time that we see them as flawed'.[125]

In an original reading, Murray interrogates Horatio's character, action, and motives. Parallels between Horatio's tale of Andrea's death in battle and Villuppo's false tale of Balthazar's death encourage us to question whether Horatio is a guileful social-climber 'playing for Bel-imperia's favor' in 1.5.[126] Murray concludes that the audience may be unsure 'what to think of Horatio'; we see him both from the perspective of his enemies and his father, and our reservations mean that, while his murder was undeserved, we may begin to 'question the justice of seeking revenge for Andrea or Horatio'.[127] Throughout Murray's study, and in many discussions of the play from this period, audiences and metatheatricality are of recurrent interest. Developing some of the arguments found in Edwards, Murray proposes that when the royal audience realize that the events in 'The tragedy of Suleiman' are:

> a real part of Spain, we may suddenly see that events in Spain are part of our world, that the characters have been made to work on our emotions because Kyd wants us to feel their passions directly, and not only as part of an esthetic whole from which we maintain a large degree of detachment.[128]

Reflecting further on the play-within-the play, the reveal of Horatio's corpse, and the ensuing bloody events, Murray detects a potential political critique. In their actions and response in this final scene, the King, Viceroy, and Castile, and even Hieronimo, show that 'people of high rank think themselves to be above the action of those around them, and they try to act as puppeteers or as an audience having little human responsibility or concern for what is going on among *others* who are *lower* than themselves and not *forms* of themselves'.[129] In the end, even Revenge forgets himself; in his plans to personally escort the villains to hell and begin their punishment, 'perhaps we are to see that he has deluded himself into thinking he is the supreme power in hell'.[130]

The 1970s and early 1980s saw the stock of Kyd's tragedy rise considerably and scholarly discussions of *The Spanish Tragedy* abound; a few studies must suffice to give an impression of the preoccupations and growing diversity of this material. Writing in 1970, Harriett Hawkins explores the metatheatricality of Kyd's play, *A Midsummer Night's Dream* and *The Tempest*. Implicit in Hawkins' early observation that *The Spanish Tragedy* 'introduced on the English stage the multiple levels of dramatic action and the multiple perspectives on dramatic action which Shakespeare explores throughout his career' is the familiar notion that Kyd's work is immature and doomed to be surpassed.[131] Like Murray before her, Hawkins suggests that the play's layering of audiences is intended to remind the Elizabethan audience of the limitations of its knowledge; gaining privileged access to all that goes on in the play world prompts us to recognize that 'this total insight into the motives of others is no more available to us in our own everyday lives than it is available to the vulnerable characters on the stage'.[132] Linking Hieronimo's play, the 'real' tragedy of the finale, and the 'endless tragedy' in hell, Hawkins makes the perceptive observation that 'these tragic realms involve the same actors and the same audiences, while the action and outcome of one is dependent on the action of the others'.[133]

Ronald Broude explores the topos of 'Time as the revealer of truth and bringer of justice', which finds expression in a number of places in the play, and proposes that some of Kyd's innovations are connected to 'the intellectual activity generated by the tense situation' caused by the Catholic threat to England in the 1580s.[134] Broude offers a fresh perspective on the 'Vindicta mihi' soliloquy, arguing that it demonstrates that Hieronimo has 'quite rightly, always considered himself a just revenger' and that Kyd uses it to show the audience that the Marshal realizes fully that he must wait patiently for the right time to act.[135] He concludes his consideration by noting that, through staging the destruction of a corrupt Spanish state, the play would have surely provided the nationalistic English audience with some comfort that 'Divine Providence would punish their enemies' wickedness and time would vindicate the truth and justice of the English cause'.[136] Kyd's consideration of the 'function of the poet and the relationship of art to life' is central to Donna B. Hamilton's 1974 analysis of *The Spanish Tragedy*. Focusing on Hieronimo, Hamilton proposes that Kyd depicts ceremonies, allegiances to family and state, and art 'as [varieties] of man's attempts to come to terms with experience [including the experience of injustice, incomprehension, and death] through ritual and pattern'.[137] Despite his efforts to grapple with the worst of human experience, Hieronimo dies because 'he exchanges the release possible through art's presentation of universal truth for the desire of a particular event, the death of his son's murderers'.[138]

In an article of 1976 Eleanor M. Tweedie offers a lively consideration of the staging of Kyd's play, attending to setting, action, props (such as letters, which are markers of truth), and the 'rich visual imagery' which is everywhere in evidence.[139] She reminds the reader that it was as a 'master of stagecraft that Kyd captured the admiration of contemporary audiences' and encourages us to appreciate how skilfully 'the deepest concerns of the play' are conveyed both visually and aurally.[140] Whereas Tweedie explores Kyd's dramaturgy, Carol McGinnis Kay focuses on the failure of language in *The Spanish Tragedy*. Identifying the differing reports of the Spanish-Portuguese battle, 'The tragedy of Suleiman', and Hieronimo's auto-glossectomy, as the play's most problematic incidents, McGinnis Kay persuasively argues that these three events are connected in order to underline one of Kyd's central themes: words are untrustworthy and deception is frequently the intention behind human interaction.[141] Through these key incidents, 'Kyd makes a strong statement about what happens to man and society when honest and open communication is not the essential aim of everyone'.[142]

Pivotal to Joel B. Altman's 1978 analysis of *The Spanish Tragedy* is the idea that Tudor plays were 'fictional realizations of questions' that aimed to progress their audiences 'toward some fuller apprehension of truth'.[143] Altman thus suggests that Kyd's play raises questions about justice and judgement, and offers multiple perspectives on revenge through 'a frame that points in one direction and an action that points in another'.[144] For Altman, unlike earlier critics, the three versions of Andrea's death are constructive; each account encourages the audience to become more and more discerning, so that, when the revenge plot is introduced, they will be fully cognizant of 'what is involved in any act of adjudication'.[145] In the end, Hieronimo fails to obtain 'judgment in understanding' from the royal spectators; the theatre audience are the only ones who can fully comprehend his experience and pity and 'judge him in the light of all circumstances'.[146]

In his 1982 study of the staging practices and performance conditions of the Elizabethan theatre, Michael Hattaway offers an engaging exploration of the play that is at times speculative, but always useful. In many ways, *The Spanish Tragedy* marks a break from the moralistic and allegorical medieval drama: 'Kyd was one of the first to learn how the physical arrangement of stage and tiring-house, the spatial relationship between the players and spectators, made possible that combination of history and tragedy, the particular and the universal'.[147] Hattaway expressly singles out Kyd's 'sense of theatrical space' as a 'distinctive contribution' to stagecraft.[148] Echoing Boas, Hattaway finds that Kyd's blending of courtly forms, such as masques, with folk entertainments, is also worthy of recognition.[149] Much pleasure is to be had from the elements of the everyday and the popular in *The Spanish Tragedy*; critics may disparage the scenes which recall the dumb show, the ceremony of the court, or the urban drama of executions, but these 'images are the stuff of popular drama' and underpin the play's achievements.[150] Following centuries of criticism, here, the popularity of the play and its use of the popular is a cause for celebration. Interestingly, in examining the play's expanded titles and the woodcut to the 1615 edition, Hattaway convincingly contends that 'these descriptions ... do not imply only a single hero but see the tragedy as that of a family or dynasty, and suggest that what would sell the play would be a reminder of those great *scenes* in the play that had caught the imagination of the audiences'.[151] Like Freeman and Murray, the play's frame and layering of audiences, who have varying degrees of detachment from the action, suggest to Hattaway that Kyd is 'not addressing himself primarily to the morality of revenge' and that the play discourages an easy, one-sided response to its events.[152] In the end, what is most notable about the play 'is the assured shape of its action, Kyd's skill in contriving a strong dramatic rhythm', and his dexterous guiding of the audience to that tragic recognition that 'turns theatrical convention into an image of life'.[153]

Hieronimo's selfhood and Seneca are the focus of Gordon Braden's 1985 exploration of Kyd's tragedy. Whereas earlier scholars had often sought to chart the influence of Seneca on Kyd only to then denigrate his use of the classical philosopher, Braden argues that *The Spanish Tragedy* adds to and enriches the depiction of the Senecan autarkic subject.[154] In Hieronimo's complaints to the King, Braden proposes, there lies the potential for a moral ending that would support the political hierarchy; but Kyd forgoes such an easy conclusion.[155] Hieronimo's frustration and wrathful actions are in fact a response to the moral condition of the Spanish court; injustice abounds and the political system is oppressive. Hieronimo's 'knowledge of guilt in the Court' and his grasp of 'primal terrors', such as the absoluteness of loss, isolate him from normal society and drive him to act against the play's ruling families.[156] Distancing himself from humanity, suppressing his emotions and hiding his intentions, Hieronimo forms an outward appearance of acquiescence; however, as Braden persuasively shows, this façade shields and conceals 'a new and more powerful self, [that speaks] with the voice of Senecan rage'.[157] Like Hamilton, Braden perceptively notes the resistance of the royals to the truth offered by Hieronimo: 'He brings a knowledge [of man's tragic condition] they do not want to have and that, intentionally and otherwise, they band together to refuse as long as they can.'[158] In his thoughtful reading of the Marshal's final bloody acts, Braden suggests that what emerges in the closing scene of the play is the clear sense that 'Hieronimo's success, however complete, has not changed the central truth of his condition: the hostile discrepancy between the self and its surroundings'.[159] Thus, for Braden, what Kyd's masterpiece ultimately stages is 'the drama of a selfhood separated from the world by the passion of its involvement in it, of a selfhood conscious that all such involvement is in some important dimension distant and incomplete'.[160]

While *The Spanish Tragedy* has had a chequered critical history, in the latter half of the twentieth century the play stood on firmer ground than it had in almost four hundred years. We should be cautious, however, about imagining a simplified evolutionary critical trajectory for Kyd's tragedy, where it is popular in the early modern period, disappears into obscurity, and suddenly bursts back onto the scene in the twentieth century. Broadly such an image has some veracity, but in focus, in the particulars, the picture is more complex. Though often in the shadows, Kyd's play features in important ways in older studies and, looking past the value judgements and subjective opinions, there is much to be learned from earlier enquiries. Although twentieth-century scholarship is not free from the oversights or imperfections of earlier criticism, in general, we can perceive a willingness to cast a more balanced eye on *The Spanish Tragedy*. Later twentieth-century critics are less likely to set out to cast moral judgement on the play's action; to approach the play from a position where they assume it is inferior; and to take as writ that its popularity is a stain on its artistry or on Kyd's career.

All this has enabled a diversification of the subjects available for critical discussion and has led to fresh perspectives on old preoccupations, such as Hieronimo's revenge, and a broadening of approaches to Kyd's play. Thus, we can safely say that, by 1985, Whalley's prophecy that *The Spanish Tragedy* would 'continue to suffer Life with perpetual infamy' had been thankfully disproved, and the study of Kyd's masterpiece continued apace.

2

'Look on This Spectacle': *The Spanish Tragedy* in Performance

Peter Malin

On Friday 9 November 1921 at Birkbeck College, the first known performance of *The Spanish Tragedy* since the seventeenth century began with a rhyming prologue written for the occasion by the poet Alfred Noyes. F. S. Boas thought this 'admirable' and hoped to see it in print.[1] It was not published, however, and has eluded all efforts to trace a copy; lost forever, perhaps, down the back of history's capacious sofa. All we know, from contemporary reviews, is that Noyes characterized the play as 'a boyish penny dreadful of the period', and explained its interest as its 'manifestation of the state of mind of the theatre into which Shakespeare was born'.[2] Thus began two of the wearying conventions associated with the play's irregular modern performance history, of denigrating its quality and assessing it primarily on the basis of its relationship to Shakespeare – an exercise that invariably concludes to Shakespeare's advantage.

J. H. Lobban, the Birkbeck lecturer who directed the production, was responsible for a commendable run of early modern drama revivals at the college for over ten years. When he restaged the play in 1931 he wrote his own prologue, which on this occasion was printed in the programme. In this fascinating piece, Lobban identifies the play's enduring strengths while acknowledging its stylistic limitations.

> With all the crudeness of an earlier age,
> Its artless borrowings from the Roman stage,
> Its noisy rhetoric, its uncertain touch
> Hovering betwixt too little and too much,
> With verse unkindled by the fire divine
> That glows and leaps in 'Marlowe's mighty line',
> Our tragedy, with more prosaic art,
> Finds a sure entrance to the human heart,
> Tracing relentlessly, without relief,
> The poignant anguish of a father's grief.[3]

Since Lobban is writing here on the basis of having previously directed the play, his 1931 prologue may be regarded as the first modern critique of its qualities to be informed by the practical experience of mounting a production.

Despite its status as part of the contextual and comparative discourse contingent on Shakespeare's iconic position, Kyd's extraordinary drama stands at one remove from the more familiar corpus of early modern plays whose performance history has grown over the last hundred years or so. Its particular qualities are not easily subsumed into the generalizing tropes that colour our understanding of revenge tragedy, lacking as it does the overwhelming ambience of decadence and moral corruption that modern directors have found so rewarding in their explorations of the genre. In its stern grandeur, *The Spanish Tragedy* feels somehow remote, monolithic, strange; like the grey slab of Stanley Kubrick's *2001: A Space Odyssey*, it remains mysterious and aloof, both icon and enigma, functioning as the instigator of unpredictable cultural productivity yet largely unrevealing of its own origins.

The play's alien, and perhaps alienating, quality can be ascribed to various causes, from the framing of its action within the gazes of Andrea's Ghost and the not-always-attentive Revenge, to its historically unspecific representation of the Spanish and Portuguese courts. Mainly, though, it is the play's language, particularly its formalized rhetorical structuring, that distances it from what we might consider drama's essentially mimetic function. Even in its own time it soon felt archaic. Barely a decade after its first performances it was subjected to modernizing revisions, printed in 1602, that lent greater naturalism to both dialogue and characterization. Clara Calvo and Jesús Tronch suggest that one of the four main questions faced by modern directors is 'whether to [...] incorporate, in full or in part, the 1602 "additions"', but the decision should surely be informed by a recognition that to do so is, for better or worse, not true to the original.[4] Though Lobban included the Painter scene in both Birkbeck productions, his 1931 prologue noted that the 1602 revisions 'Added new passages without apology | That well nigh broke the back of Kyd's psychology'.

The other issues identified by the Arden editors as demanding significant directorial choices relate to the onstage presence of Revenge and the Ghost, the language(s) in which Hieronimo's play of Suleiman and Perseda should be spoken, and the placing of the courtly audience for its performance. I believe these are far outweighed by the need to determine how the actors can most effectively deliver the play's rhetoric in a theatrical culture that seems increasingly wary of formally patterned dramatic language. First, however, I shall consider how the play was performed in the late sixteenth and early seventeenth centuries, as far as this can be deduced from the limited evidence.

'See here my show': Early stagings

From Tuesday 14 March 1592, when Lord Strange's Men presented it at the Rose, to Saturday 19 September 1626, when it was performed by an English company at the Court of Saxony in Dresden, over thirty performances of *The Spanish Tragedy* are recorded, most of them before 1600.[5] The play passed from company to company, theatre to theatre. Edward Alleyn may have originated the role of Hieronimo, and Ben Jonson probably played it on tour during the 1590s. It almost certainly featured in the repertoire of the Chamberlain's or King's Men, with Richard Burbage as its star. Just as the play's text was altered to conform to changing notions of dramatic characterization and language, we can assume that both its staging and the style in which it was acted were continually in flux, responding to particular performance venues and increasingly sophisticated theatrical taste. Perhaps the additions were crafted to give scope to Burbage's apparently subtler, more naturalistic style, and in view of later accounts of barnstorming actors hamming up the main part, it would be fascinating to know how it was played by its earliest practitioners. Unfortunately, a notional early modern staging of the play is irrecoverable, each performance being determined by its particular theatrical and historical circumstances.

One element that seems to have persisted in early productions, however, is the presentation of the characters as recognizably Spanish. The Q7 title-page woodcut (1615), for example, shows Bel-imperia in mantilla and hooped skirt: the stereotypical Spanish lady as impersonated by Wittipol in Jonson's *The Devil Is an Ass* (1616). And in the frontispiece to the anonymous Dutch play, *Don Jeronimo, Marschalck van Spanjen* (1662), the court figures sport the traditional 'cloak, ruff, and hat' ascribed to Hieronimo by Face in *The Alchemist* (1610) and mocked in Surly's Spanish disguise ('He looks in that deep ruff, like a head in a platter'; 'Thou look'st like Antichrist, in that lewd hat').[6]

Other clues, many of them embedded in the early quartos, provide us with tantalizing glimpses of the mechanics and aesthetics of the play's earliest performances. The printed texts are rich in stage directions, though modern editors have found it necessary to supplement these in order to fill surprising gaps in the notation of important staging practicalities. It is unclear, for example, how Andrea's scenes with Revenge were originally presented. Since Revenge invites the Ghost, 'Here sit we down to see the mystery' (1.1.90), Kyd's intention is clearly that they should remain on stage throughout. But where is '[h]ere'? We can only guess. More interesting, perhaps, is the non-specific entrance that begins the play: '*Enter the* GHOST of Andrea *and, with him,* REVENGE' (1.1.0 SD). Those relishing dramatic spectacle might wish to see them rise melodramatically through the stage trap, and there is some evidence to suggest they originally did so. The play ends with an invitation from Revenge to Andrea: 'Then haste we down to meet thy friends and foes' (4.5.45). 'Down' seems specific enough, though the subsequent direction '*Exeunt*' is frustratingly vague. There may be a clue in Dekker's pamphlet, *The Seven Deadly Sins of London* (1606), which refers to a debtor buried at the door of his creditor who 'might think he still rises up (like the Ghost in *Jeronimo*) crying "Revenge"'.[7] This intriguing allusion seems fairly assertive about the 'rising up', which would logically demand a subsequent 'descent'.

In other respects, the texts of *The Spanish Tragedy* are richly provided with indicators of stage action and gest, from which we can draw tentative conclusions about the performance styles adopted by the play's early modern actors. Many of the directions seem essentially descriptive: '*He cuts him down*' (2.5.12 SD); '*They bind him to the stake*' (3.1.48 SD); '*Shoots the dag*' (3.3.32 SD); '*He turns him off*' (3.6.108 SD); yet they raise questions about how the performers might play such moments. In the Portuguese court, for example, when the Viceroy, in desperation at his country's defeat and his son's apparent fate, '*Falls to the ground*' (1.3.8 SD), the action demands to be read in conjunction with the tenor of his language: 'This better fits a wretch's endless moan | [...] Here let me lie, now I am at the lowest' (1.3.9–14). As readers, we can thus extrapolate from his spoken words the exaggerated self-pity of the action. Such exaggeration is typical of many of the acting clues in the text.

Hieronimo's and Isabella's madness are conveyed partly through physical actions indicating lunacy. '*She runs lunatic*' (3.8.5 SD); '*He diggeth with his dagger*' (3.12.70 SD); '*Tears the papers*' (3.13.122 SD); '*staring him in the face*' (3.13.129.3); '*makes signs for a knife to mend his pen*' (4.4.194 SD): all these suggest a performative mode we might define as gestural hyperbole. More elaborately, the directions often add a robust physical comedy to the representation of madness, with Hieronimo popping in and out of the stage doors like a character from a Whitehall farce.[8] For the Elizabethans, such comically exaggerated actions and gestures were aspects of what Duncan Salkeld calls 'the spectacularity and strangeness of madness', in a culture increasingly influenced after 1598 by the popularity of public visits to the Bethlem Hospital.[9]

Elsewhere, the text apparently demands similar gestural exaggeration from characters not afflicted by madness: '*Balthazar starts back*' (2.1.78 SD); '*Alexandro seems to entreat*' (3.1.101 SD); Lorenzo '*whispereth in her ear*' (3.10.77 SD). Even the apparently neutral description in which Bel-imperia '*in going in, lets fall her glove*' (1.4.99.1) is hedged about with acting demands. '[L]*ets fall*' suggests agency rather than accident, requiring some movement, gesture or facial expression from the boy actor, perhaps no more than a glance at the incoming Horatio. This tiny moment is hugely significant to Bel-imperia's developing motivation and needs pointing by some slight artificiality of body language.

The acting style I am proposing runs parallel to the rhetorical elaboration of the dialogue, and the evidence suggests that both soon seemed archaic. Many later references to the play offer affectionate parodies of old-fashioned performers. In Thomas May's *The Heir* (1620), for example, Polymetes comments on an actor's playing of Hieronimo.

> I have seen the knave paint grief
> In such a lively colour, that for false
> And acted passion he has drawn true tears
> From the spectators. Ladies in the boxes
> Kept time with sighs and tears to his sad accents,
> As he had truly been the man he seem'd.[10]

This is complex, and Polymetes's critique is ambivalent. He pinpoints the actor's artificiality in both the metaphor of painting and the emphasis on his emotional falseness, and apparently satirizes the ladies in the audience who are taken in by the performance. His analysis, though, suggests a grudging admiration for the effectiveness of the actor's histrionics.

In Thomas Rawlins's *The Rebellion* (1634), written for the King's Revels, there is an entertaining suggestion of how Shakespeare's Bottom might have played Hieronimo.

> 2 TAILOR Who shall act Jeronimo?
> [VERMIN] That will I:
> Mark if I do not gape wider than the widest
> Mouth'd Fowler of them all, hang me!
> 'Who calls Jeronimo from his naked bed? haugh?'
> Now for the passionate part –
> 'Alas! it is my son Horatio.'[11]

As Rebekah Owens observes, Vermin here 'makes the distinction between two modes of speaking, breaking up the lines to demonstrate that he can easily change the tone from bewilderment to grief'.[12] Bottom-like, he is also eager to demonstrate his versatility by offering to play the Ghost, Horatio, Balthazar and the King. His 'gaping', in which his mouth is compared to a fowling-piece or blunderbuss, is more than just a signifier of his bad acting and amateur status, being crafted to remind the audience of Richard Fowler's performance as Hieronimo for the rival company at the Fortune. As Andrew Gurr notes, Fowler was 'the noisiest and most physical' of the Fortune's actors, who were recalled by

Edmund Gayton as 'terrible tear-throats'.[13] Most interesting, perhaps, is that May's and Rawlins's parodic critiques are directed not at the play itself but at an acting style associated with the role of Hieronimo, implying an awareness that Kyd's drama may not, after all, be best served by such performative exaggeration.

Even so, the overripe acting style associated with the play seems to have survived decades of change in theatrical fashion. In 1668, roughly eighty years after its first performance, Samuel Pepys's verdict on *Jeronimo Is Mad Again* at the Nursery Theatre in Hatton Garden was that it was a bad play, badly acted.[14] Pepys's participation in the mockery directed at the actors can be taken to herald the theatrical silencing of Kyd's tragedy for over 250 years.

'Acted by gentlemen, and scholars too': Student productions

For over fifty years after the first Birkbeck production, *The Spanish Tragedy* remained the preserve of student companies until its professional revival in 1973 at London's Mercury Theatre. Since then, only three major companies have tackled it: Glasgow Citizens in 1978, the National Theatre in 1982 and the RSC in 1997. Nevertheless, it has acquired a burgeoning performance history, growing in popularity with university groups and small professional companies across the UK and USA, with at least one production in Ireland and one in Australia.

Charting a course through nearly a century of performances is a problematic but fascinating activity. The extant records carry vast, often incompatible cargoes of cultural freight. How might one balance the polite scholarly reservations of Kyd's first modern editor, F. S. Boas, about the inauthenticity of the 1932 production at Christ Church, Oxford against the cluster of banal, sometimes impolite tweets that haunt the online presence of the 2012 production in King's College Chapel, Cambridge? I make no judgements about the relative validity of these responses, nor of those that fall between, from press reviews and academic analyses to anecdotes and personal recollections. All, however, reveal as much about the cultural circumstances of their historical moment as about Kyd's play.

Roughly half the play's modern productions were mounted in academic institutions. This is hardly surprising; it features prominently on university and college syllabuses, inevitably attracting the interest of performance-minded students and their teachers. Since *The Spanish Tragedy*'s performance history owes so much to the persistent championing of the play by academic practitioners, these amateur productions deserve attention.

In the first half of the twentieth century, the inspiration for staging Kyd's play seems to have been largely its status as an archaic but influential curiosity. The presentational methods applied to it were generally backward-looking, striving for that elusive sense of Elizabethan authenticity that was being explored elsewhere by practitioners such as Poel and Granville-Barker. The Birkbeck programmes quoted the *Daily News*'s praise of the college's 'excellent work in reviving antique plays', and 'antique' sums up the ethos of Lobban's productions. Such an approach was probably inevitable in reviving the play after its long absence from the stage. Strikingly, however, the 1921 staging seems to have drawn no contemporary resonances from its post-war context, despite the play's vivid descriptions of battle, which must surely have struck a chord with many of its performers and audiences. Unlike the famous London productions of Webster's tragedies in the late 1940s, Kyd's great arias of conflict, bloodshed, loss, grief, commemoration and revenge seem to have functioned paradoxically as an escape from the realities of recent history into a folksy antiquity, emphasized by the use of the play's old-spelling title and the inclusion of Elizabethan music and dance.[15] Audiences apparently responded unsympathetically to both play and production. Birkbeck's in-house reviewer called it 'a very bad play' and 'an ugly piece of worthless sensationalism' (Watters, *Lodestone*, 82, 85). The evening's principal redeeming feature was Mr Nixon's Hieronimo, a performance of 'power and intensity [that] retained all the "bombastic fury" and yet made the part human and convincing' (p. 83).

In 1931, though the spelling of the title was modernized, the presentation remained explicitly Elizabethan. Production photographs show actors posed awkwardly in elaborate period costume, English rather than Spanish, on a bare, black-draped stage furnished only with a wooden bench and a primitive scaffold.[16] In language echoed time after time in reviews of early modern tragedy, the *Morning Post* reported that the 'crowded audience found Kyd's glut of ghastliness and murder a theme for uproarious mirth'.[17] Whether the mirth was directed at the play itself, its representation by the student actors, or both, is unclear.

Midway between these Birkbeck productions, *The Spanish Tragedy* was performed by younger students, at Winchester College in 1926. Though superficially more 'authentic' in having an all-male cast, in other respects the staging was more original than at Birkbeck. The college magazine's reviewer describes in detail the production's striking design, which employed hanging tapestries and painted backcloths. The night-time discovery of Horatio's body was played in a black-and-white setting, while the Ghost and Revenge, 'in white and red respectively, sat motionless in a dim light beside symbolic globes, celestial and terrestrial'. Authenticity is melding here into a more interpretative vision of the play, a striking achievement for a school production.

Unfortunately, the staging was 'static' and the acting 'uneven', though Hieronimo, played by Richard Crossman – later a Labour cabinet minister and controversial diarist – 'excelled the rest […] and was a living figure of tragic intensity'. Elsewhere, the reviewer's witty understatement affectionately delineates a series of typical schoolboy performances. Kenneth Knowles's Bel-imperia 'was no doubt hampered by the formalities of court etiquette; but a little more encouragement to her lover would surely not have been unmaidenly'. Henry Kingdon's Horatio, doubtless maximizing his histrionic opportunities, 'was better dead than alive, and best of all dying'. Kyd's tragedy, in only its second production of modern times, seems a bold choice for a school play, but the reviewer found it instructive. Though he acknowledged the play's 'power, emotion [and] poetry', it was 'episodic, unsustained, and rather elementary in form'. He concluded by judging it against the inevitable touchstone, declaring that the performance 'added something valuable to our appreciation of the genius in Shakespeare'.[18]

John Izon's 1932 Christ Church production shifted the focus of 'authenticity' towards the college's own dramatic tradition which, according to Claude Burgess's programme note, dated back to the sixteenth century and boasted at least three monarchs among its spectators, along with 'three people in the audience [...] killed by the fall of a wall near the entrance door'. 'Great occasions,' quipped Burgess.[19] Boas, who did not see the production, noted in a good-natured letter to *The Times* that traditional college practice had been ignored in the choice of a professional-theatre play rather than one written for undergraduates, and the use of the library rather than the dining-hall, adding a witty comment on the casting of women in the female roles.[20] As for the production, the *Manchester Guardian*'s reviewer liked 'the simplicity of its settings and the beauty of its lighting effects'. The costumes, in a rare nod to 'Spanishness' as a marker of performative authenticity, were 'in the fashion shown by Spanish painters of the period', while the '[c]ontemporary music, transcribed from manuscripts in the British Museum and the Christ Church Library', was essentially English, though it included John Bull's 'Spanish Paven'. Burgess himself 'scored a great personal success' as Hieronimo.[21]

In 1937 Nevill Coghill, then a young Fellow of Magdalen College, collaborated with the Poet Laureate, John Masefield, on the Oxford Summer Diversions, a short-lived festival of music, poetry and drama. Coghill's was the first modern production of *The Spanish Tragedy* to be presented outdoors. It was performed in St Edmund Hall's intimate Front Quad, and the Hall magazine contains a striking photograph of the final scene in performance. Three bodies lie on the grass near the college well, under the spreading branches of an overhanging tree from which a noose is suspended, while Hieronimo, dressed as the pasha, confronts the bowed and baffled court. The magazine reports that Brian Cave-Brown-Cave, the only Hall member in the cast, 'received very favourable criticism' as Hieronimo.[22]

The production's programme demonstrates a tension between academic respectability, the vocabulary of marketing and the awkward practicalities of staging. Coghill recommends the play for its language, its sensationalism and its historical significance: an 'ancient and famous poetic melodrama', 'noble and vivid', 'presenting a ghost, a spectre, two maniacs, five murders, three suicides and two hangings'. He praises the added Painter scene, 'one of the most affectingly tragic in all Elizabethan drama', which perhaps 'no hand could have written [...] but Shakespeare's'. The venue, however, presented some practical difficulties, and audiences were advised that 'owing to the fact that no one exit connects with any other, scene-divisions will be marked by the ringing of a bell, to facilitate continuity in making entries. Pauses will be filled by music.'[23] Similar problems were undoubtedly faced by Elizabethan touring companies playing in non-theatrical spaces.

The post-war performance history of *The Spanish Tragedy* began in 1951, with productions in Oxford and Edinburgh. The Oxford production, at St John's, has left only a passing, unhelpful mention in the college bulletin: 'There have been no special events to record. The Mummers gave a lively performance of Ford's *Spanish Tragedy* [sic], which ends with the stage littered with corpses.'[24] The most notable feature of the Edinburgh University production was its renewed striving for authenticity, to which end it was performed on a reconstructed Elizabethan stage, accompanied by period music played on virginals, recorders and violins. A photograph of the final scene shows an imitation half-timbered construction with a musicians' gallery linked by wooden stairs to the main stage. The court audience are seated beneath the gallery, being harangued by Hieronimo amidst the scattered bodies. Other observers occupy every level, creating an impressive if rather sentimentalized reimagining of an Elizabethan theatre.[25] As with the 1921 Birkbeck staging, the records of this production suggest nothing of its post-war context. In neither presentation nor critical reception did it reflect the revelatory responses to the West End revivals of *The Duchess of Malfi* in 1945 and *The White Devil* in 1947.

Even as late as 1968, in a production by Glynne Wickham at Bristol University, the play's status as an Elizabethan curiosity was prioritized. A programme note by Douglas Halstead explained that it would be 'presented in a manner approximating to conditions prevailing at Court performances in Elizabethan times'.[26] For fifty years, then, audiences lucky enough to see *The Spanish Tragedy* were offered distancing presentations of it, often directed by university academics or scholars of early modern theatre such as Lobban, Coghill and Wickham, which preserved it as an artefact intelligible only within an approximation of the cultural accoutrements of its early performances. The play's first professional production, at London's Mercury Theatre in 1973, did nothing new with it. It was a university production later that year that dragged Kyd's apparently intractable text into the modern age and the ambiguous territory of 'contemporary relevance'.

By the 1970s, student productions were becoming more self-consciously 'experimental', emulating companies such as the RSC in offering challenging interpretations of classic drama. These qualities were evident in Francis Matthews's staging for Oxford University's Experimental Theatre Club at the Oxford Playhouse. The production was widely reviewed and subjected to much analysis of its *Clockwork Orange* ambience, its elaborate visual effects and what Michael Billington called its 're-inforced concrete music' suggestive of '*Dr Who* and the

Droogs'.[27] Its typically 'student' quality, however, is encapsulated in an anecdote recounted by Alan Halliday, who recalls that when Jon Plowman's Pedringano met his end 'he was left swinging on a noose like a pendulum from one side of the stage to the other for a whole scene'.[28] This, together with the setting of the play in a fascistic dystopia, suggests that Kyd's text was partly an excuse for these Oxford students to demonstrate their irreverent theatricality. Yet the production marks an important shift from historicism to presentism in the performance of early modern drama. Though in 2010 Emma Smith noted that she had 'not read any academic criticism of a non-Shakespearean play of the period linking it explicitly with our own moment', productions such as Matthews's have explored such connections for over half a century.[29]

Frank Dibb, veteran reviewer of *The Oxford Times*, was habitually dismissive of what he termed 'relevant-for-our-times' productions. On this occasion, he wearily noted the professional antecedents of the show's presentational choices: the 'badly worn' Fascist uniforms, he growled, were 'a hoary Guthrie gimmick'. But Dibb was also a champion of language, and was interested in the play's acting demands. Performances of the necessary 'force and scale', he suggested, were 'seemingly no longer a workable proposition in Oxford' – unfortunate for a play with 'language well worth the speaking and, if properly spoken, well worth the hearing'. He commended the 'musical and intelligent' delivery of Jacinta Peel as Bel-imperia and praised Crispian Cartwright's efforts as Hieronimo, while advising him that his voice needed 'more variety[,] and to be strengthened in its lower register'.[30] Dibb's commendable concern for an actor's handling of dramatic language has particular relevance for *The Spanish Tragedy*, but the issue has generally been ignored by the play's reviewers.

By the time of the 2009 Oriel College production, the presentation of early modern drama had progressed considerably.[31] Will Maynard's staging, moved from the Quad to the Chapel for the performance reviewed by Rebekah Owens, was notable for two features that typify its twenty-first-century credentials. Gender-blind casting was by now common practice in student groups; here, unusually, it generated a female Hieronimo and a male Bel-imperia, though for Owens this 'yielded no fresh readings of the play'.[32] Concept-driven productions were also gaining ground, though audiences were frequently unable to access the concept without reading the programme. The intention here, signalled by Maynard's programme note on bipolar disorder, was to present the play as a surreal reflection of Hieronimo's mental disturbance. This entailed a remoulding of Revenge's role, with four actors designated as Fate, each doubling with significant characters in the main action while pushing Hieronimo towards the execution of his vengeance. According to Owens, the production's psychological grounding was inconsistently realized, and it was not clear which characters were 'part of Hieronimo's psychosis' (p. 138). Though she observed that 'the performances were notable', she made no comment on the delivery of the play's rhetoric or the quality of the leading actors. The *Daily Information* website, however, reveals that Rob Hoare Nairne as Bel-imperia had 'mastered some wonderful feminine mannerisms'; and that 'the booming Kate Lewin' as Hieronimo and 'the delicately nuanced Naomi Webb' as Isabella 'brought a large proportion of the audience to tears with their laments' (KLew, 03/06/09).[33] There is a naïve freshness in these comments that is generally absent from professional reviews, and in this, of all plays, it is useful to be given some indication of the actors' vocal qualities.

After six Oxford productions, Cambridge caught up with the play in 2012, in a 'site-specific' staging in King's College Chapel. The setting, thought Nancy Napper Canter, was 'fantastic' and 'awe-inspiring', but the Chapel's acoustic generated an overpowering echo. '[W]hile all this booming is thrilling if you're at the front,' Canter observed, 'if you're at the back it drowns out the dialogue.'[34]

From a gentle swing at college tradition to a wildly swinging Pedringano; from a booming Oxford Hieronimo to a booming Cambridge echo: can these university productions tell us anything useful about *The Spanish Tragedy*, or do they merely offer an insight into the development of student drama? Hieronimo proudly claims that his tragedy of Suleiman and Perseda was 'determined to have been acted | By gentlemen, and scholars too' (4.1.98–9), a conjunction of theatre, privilege and scholarship that reads as wryly ironic in one of the most popular plays ever written for the public stage's rough and tumble. It is a conjunction that remains culturally sensitive, however, and to a non-academic audience perhaps nothing could seem more remote from everyday reality than Oxbridge students staging an obscure Elizabethan tragedy built around long speeches in high-flown language. Responses to the Cambridge production posted on the *Tab* website included a salutary reminder of the social divisiveness implicit in Oxbridge drama: 'A bunch of elitist rich kids with nothing better to do. Crap and badly performed' (cambridge. tab). Perhaps this is why so many student productions aim for a certain street-smart irreverence, emphasizing the play's current siting at that awkward junction between its historical significance and the need for it to 'live' for a modern audience.

'Author and actor in this tragedy': Staging Revenge

I suggested at the start of this chapter that *The Spanish Tragedy*'s quality of antique strangeness is partly attributable to its framing conceit. What are we to make of a dramatic narrative that unfolds within the scrutiny of a supernatural entity and a personified abstraction? Modern productions have persistently attempted to make sense of this device, which simultaneously focuses and distorts our viewing of the play's action. The problem is compounded by the nature of the Ghost's extended accounts of his passage through the underworld, which are linguistically, topographically and theologically alien to a modern audience. Theatre reviewers rarely have space to consider the dramatic effectiveness of these pseudo-Virgilian set-pieces, though they occasionally offer insights into the acting skills needed to animate Andrea's role. Reviewing the 1921 Birkbeck Ghost, B. D. Watters commended the actor's 'real distinction' in a part which 'requires most careful restraint for it is so easy to overdo' (p. 84). The benefits of restraint are also implied in Emrys Jones's account of Stephen Hattersley's 1982 performance at the National, his opening speech 'taken straight, with no hurrying and no gimmicks, but delivered [...] with such weighty clarity and conviction that we absorb the situation with no effort'.[35] In the 2014 Baltimore production, Amanda Gunther noted that '[Megan] Farber's opening monologue is delivered from a hallowed place within her; a silence radiating through her figure that creates a vocal stillness in her woeful tale'. Though the precise meaning of these words evaporates under close scrutiny, they nevertheless capture something about the performance that 'sets the tone for the play and invites the audience to the perilous journey of revenge that lies ahead'.[36] Andrea's establishing prologue, then, can work effectively in the modern theatre if directors and actors trust their material.

In his 1986 New York production, Ron Daley cut the Ghost/Revenge framework entirely. 'Frankly, that sort of thing isn't acceptable here,' he asserted; 'in the twentieth century, there's a certain kind of dramaturgy we insist on.'[37] In other words, perhaps, Kyd needs some 'dumbing down' to reach audiences with narrower expectations of dramatic etiquette and limited knowledge of classical mythology. Most directors, however, have chosen to retain the play's outer frame, subsuming it into a presentational concept considered more accessible to a modern audience, as in the Oriel production already discussed. At its least intrusive, this approach incorporates Revenge into the play's main action, enhancing his agency at key moments, most commonly in making him the deliverer of Bel-imperia's mysteriously dropped letter. At the National, Peter Needham's cheroot-smoking Revenge, in studded leather, was 'the initiator of all the play's many vindictive actions', including 'providing

Lorenzo with the empty box which will trick Pedringano to his death; placing an open Seneca on Hieronimo's chair and gently abstracting his prayer-book' and cueing speeches 'with a glance or a gesture'.[38] Revenge thus becomes 'author' of the play's events – an author who, Hardy-like, revels in piling unnecessary suffering on the characters *en route* to the narrative's pre-ordained outcome.

Directors have engineered such interventions principally, I think, to satisfy a modern notion of dramatic structure in which the play's constituent parts are coherently integrated; Kyd, after all, requires Revenge and the Ghost merely to 'sit' and 'see' events as they unfold. Frequently, though, casting, characterization and doubling have been used to endow Revenge with a more weighty significance. The 1951 Edinburgh production was the first of many to present a female Revenge. In student productions, such de-gendered (or re-gendered) casting may be as pragmatic as it is interpretative, yet audiences are still likely to read it as a statement – though of what is not always clear. Calvo and Tronch's comment on the Edinburgh casting is simply that it was 'innovative' (p. 68).

The 1978 Glasgow Citizens adaptation of the play began an intermittent fashion for casting children in the role of Revenge. Here, he was 'a dapper pageboy in white who spoke most of the servants' lines and magically dropped in every letter needed to draw the characters towards their nemesis'. He was also the boy with the box, extending that character's relish of mischief by observing Hieronimo's pain 'with detached pleasure, at one point shining a torch full into his face for a closer view'.[39] Even more disturbingly, at the Arcola in 2009 Revenge was a 'grimy young girl', 'deliciously disturbing' according to Kevin Quarmby;[40] she was represented in the promotional material in a party dress, clutching a bloody axe. Eoin Price, after running through a selection of '[c]reepy children' tropes from modern horror films, suggested that the juvenile casting raised interesting questions about Revenge's role: 'Is the child as Revenge a symbol of lost innocence, of the corruption of something essentially good; or does it suggest that revenge is an innate human desire[?]'[41] Similar questions were raised by the 2013 San Rafael production, in which an older child, 'seventh-grader' Julia Schulman, embodied Revenge as 'a little goddess[,] pert, and magnetic if at times unintelligible'.[42] The principal impact of these 'creepy children', however, was surely to invest Revenge's role with a sinister frisson designed to counteract the likelihood of sceptical laughter directed at a mere morality-play abstraction.

Sometimes, Revenge has provided the focus for a more politicized interpretation of the play. Alex Robson's New South Wales production of 2010 opened with a blood-soaked panorama of violence presided over by Revenge costumed as 'a torture victim from the U.S. controlled Iraqi prison of Abu Ghraib'. Taking his cue from the King's line at the end of the play, 'What age hath ever heard such monstrous deeds?' (4.4.198), the director, according to his subsequent website, 'argued through this production that the human race is always exacting some new horror on itself in retribution for some old one'.[43] Perhaps the time is ripe for further productions to investigate the play's contemporary resonances, demonstrating that its apparently archaic rhetoric of retribution is, in fact, frighteningly in tune with the modern world.

Most of the productions considered so far in this section prioritized theatrical impact over fidelity to the play, often to striking effect. More academically orientated stagings have also experimented with the portrayal of Revenge, albeit more conservatively. At Boston in 1994, Andrew Hartley played Revenge in his own production, which he subsequently wrote about in *Cahiers Élisabéthains*.[44] Operating as both prompter and stage-manager, Hartley's Revenge was costumed in conventionally 'sinister' fashion, in 'a hooded, wine-red robe and [...] a white, featureless mask' (p. 8). Most significantly, he was doubled with Bazulto, which Hartley justified on the grounds that 'Bazulto's words and appearance prompt Hieronimo's move towards the act of vengeance itself' (p. 9). Few directors have the opportunity to explain so fully the rationale behind their staging decisions, and few among their audiences will read such explanatory analyses. It is therefore not always clear how particular staging details contribute to the director's interpretative vision. Reviewing the 2010 Minneapolis production, Matthew Everett was struck by the moment 'when Ariana Prusak was peeled out of her Revenge costume [...] and underneath was the white nightgown of Horatio's grieving mother Isabella'. For Everett, this was merely a 'bit of costuming magic'; 'an instant scene and character change'.[45] How else, though, might we interpret it? A casting convenience? The supernatural possession of a human character? Or a gendered reading suggestive of female empowerment in a patriarchal society?

Perhaps it doesn't matter. Like *Macbeth*'s witches, Revenge offers directors an enormous creative challenge. Too often, however, there seems to be a patronizing belief that modern audiences are incapable of taking an imaginative leap into the theatrical and cultural assumptions of a previous age. While presentational decisions about the supernatural framework can go some way towards alleviating this perceived cultural timidity, the play's language poses a more intractable problem for the actors charged with speaking it.

'Such as can tell how to speak': Delivering rhetoric

Kyd's rhetorical strategies in *The Spanish Tragedy* have elicited much scholarly analysis. Frequently, this takes the form of a spirited defence of the play's language in the face of what Lukas Erne defines as 'superficial and uninformed critical opinion' that sees only 'rant, conventional rhetoric, mechanically patterned speech and other alleged rhetorical absurdities' in it (p. 68). Writing about his Boston production, Andrew Hartley addresses the modern actor's difficulties in locating 'consciousness' in Kyd's 'problematic language' which, he asserts, 'can strain the patience and understanding even of an audience used to Shakespearean diction'. Hartley's conclusions are worth reading in full for his attempts to reconcile Kyd's text with a modern notion of dramatic characterization. He suggests that '[i]f there is any "self" or "psyche" to these characters [...], it exists not in the language but in fissures within the rhetorical modes [they] utilize' (pp. 2–3).

Repeatedly, reviewers of the play have disparaged its linguistic qualities. In 1973, Michael Billington found it 'bereft of poetry' and nine years later observed that 'the verse is undistinguished'.[46] More forcefully, John Barber noted in 1982 that the characters 'declaim a rhetoric so emphatic as to be ridiculous',[47] while Nicholas de Jongh castigated 'the ponderous, faked grandeur of the verse' and its 'metrical lethargy'; he neglected to suggest how 'faked grandeur' might be distinguished from the genuine article.[48] Given the exigencies of reviewing, one cannot expect more substantial analysis. Yet when Billington finds no 'poetry' in the play, he is clearly begging at least two questions: what is poetry, and is it a valid component of drama? The answers to both questions are complex. Sheldon Zitner argues that Kyd's language is neither poetic nor dramatic but theatrical, and that 'poetic drama is an oxymoron'.[49]

How Kyd's rhetoric should be delivered is another question, to which reviewers of the two Birkbeck productions were confident they had the answer. In 1921, the *Observer*'s critic castigated the actors for their slow and sometimes indistinct speaking in what amounted to 'a ranting, roaring melodrama of superhuman bombast'. The play's blank verse, he declared, 'should not be spoken: it should be declaimed. And where it should not be declaimed, it should be shouted' (H. G.). Ten years later, the *Telegraph* reviewer praised the 'fine dignity' achieved by the anonymous actor of Hieronimo, 'even in those passages which were, most properly, "ranted"'.[50]

Frequently, it is the player of Hieronimo who suffers from such misconceptions, not just about the language, but about the nature of the role. De Jongh thought Michael Bryant's performance at the National showed 'an actor whose talent is stretched to breaking point'; his gift for 'phlegmatic control and irony' meant that the 'heights of anguish and the peaks of rage are never scaled' (p. 25). Barber thought Bryant's 'dry, precise naturalness [...] so ill-suited to the vengeful father that he has to make a joke of his most terrifying speeches'. There seem to be two parallel assumptions in the comments of these and other reviewers: firstly, that Hieronimo's status as tragic hero requires the casting of a conventionally 'heroic' actor; secondly, that the character's rhetorical flights demand a matching degree of vocal extravagance and emotional display. Neither assumption quite fits the role. Hieronimo is neither king, nobleman nor warrior but an ageing, albeit respected, functionary of pointedly inferior status in Spain's rigidly hierarchical court. The language articulating his grief and anguish already carries in its rhetorical grandiloquence the highest emotional signification: the actor should feel it, but not necessarily demonstrate it.

Hieronimo's is not the only rhetorical mode employed in the play that can prove problematic to modern actors. Reviewing the Minneapolis production, Matthew Everett criticized 'Kyd's clunky rhyming couplets' – presumably referring either to Balthazar's see-sawing irresolution in assessing the likelihood of Bel-imperia's loving him (2.1.19–28), or to Horatio and Bel-imperia's stichomythic love dialogue (2.4.24–49). On the face of it, it seems difficult to imagine that Balthazar's rhetorical indecision is intended to be anything other than comic, but perhaps this simply reflects a modern inability to take a certain kind of linguistic playfulness seriously. Whether or not Kyd intended him as a comic character, it makes sense to portray Balthazar as an ineffective foil to Lorenzo's Machiavellian assurance – a performance tradition that has become well established in modern theatre practice. At Birkbeck in 1921 F. S. Boas approvingly noted the 'Osric-like affectations' of the unnamed actor playing Balthazar (Boas, *Lodestone*, 53). At Oxford in 1973, B. A. Young was uneasy that Afshin Khalatbary invested the role with 'an Afro hair-style, a high jokey voice and a penchant for easy anachronistic laughs',[51] but Don Chapman felt Khalatbary's 'neatly timed effeminacy' contrasted effectively with the 'steely fascism' of Adam Norton's Lorenzo.[52]

At the National in 1982, Michael Fenner's 'big, rather gauche Balthazar' was, in Richard Proudfoot's estimate, a 'likeable booby' (p. 74). At Oriel in 2009, Rebekah Owens characterized Emile Halpin's Balthazar as 'a hot-headed thug' who 'provided most of the comedy' in the play scene in his delight at being cast in the lead, his pre-show warm-up exercises and the way he 'hammed up his role to the admiration of his on-stage audience' (p. 138). And in the 2010 Rose Theatre production, Eoin Price described Nic Choulman's Balthazar as 'a wet, foppish sap pulled along by Richard Gee's Lorenzo'. However, though the character's 'ineptitude may have been funny to a degree, [...] it was difficult to picture him being involved in the bloody murder of Horatio'.[53] Such reservations regarding generic and psychological consistency do not seem to have troubled Kyd and his contemporaries.

Unexpectedly, at the Blue Elephant in 2013 Jamie Spindlove demonstrated that Balthazar's self-pitying love-rhetoric need not be played solely for its comic potential; instead, he deployed it to convey genuine emotional confusion.[54] This again suggested that conventional assumptions about how best to deliver Kyd's language may be misplaced.

'Endless tragedy': The 1997 RSC production

Every production of *The Spanish Tragedy* must chart its own course through the issues I have addressed in this chapter. The balance between historical reconstruction and contemporary relevance; the handling of the Revenge framework; the interpretation of the characters and delivery of their diverse rhetorical modes: all require careful and conscious decisions from directors and actors. Michael Boyd's RSC production, initially staged at Stratford's Swan Theatre in 1997, successfully negotiated the play's diverse challenges, though the speaking of the play's language was criticized. Alastair Macaulay disliked the inconsistency of the performance style, with the actors adopting 'a wide range of terrible verse-speaking methods' which he went on to enumerate.[55] The archive DVD of the production, however, shows the play's leading roles to have been strongly performed within Boyd's strikingly effective interpretation of the play.[56]

As Bel-imperia, Siobhan Redmond created a complex character whose motivation remained intriguingly ambiguous, placed as she was amid a constricting web of competing relationships. Her scenes with Tristan Sturrock's Horatio were touching and delicate, complicated by the constant presence of Patrice Naiambana's ghostly Andrea, haunting the fringes of the action and occasionally making physical contact with her. Robert Glenister's brutish Lorenzo clearly harboured incestuous desires for his sister, adding a disturbing frisson to his promotion of Darrell D'Silva's odious Balthazar as her wooer. The combination of emotional, patriarchal and misogynistic pressures working on Bel-imperia was developed in Redmond's performance into an urge towards self-mutilation, culminating in her cutting herself with a knife. This distinctly modern, tentatively feminist interpretation was supported by Redmond's sensitive articulation of the play's language, and reviewers were generally complimentary about her performance.

Peter Wight's Hieronimo, however, met with critical reservations similar to those directed at Michael Bryant. Commending his 'natural speaking', Macaulay problematized it as 'the naturalness of a desk sergeant or chartered surveyor', though Sarah Hemming was impressed that he 'manage[d] to speak some of the more laborious speeches as if he were coining them afresh'.[57] These comments expose underlying assumptions about the supposed incompatibility of rhetoric with both spontaneity and naturalism, along with the sense that the actor has, however modestly, prompted these critics to think afresh. The archive recording reveals, I think, an enormous critical undervaluing of Wight's performance, showing him to be fully in control of the role's emotional and rhetorical demands. His most moving scene was the interpolated adaptation of the 'Painter' addition, in which his dialogue with the conflated Bazulto/Bazardo, his counterpart as bereaved father, shifted the play into a different gear.

Boyd's staging of the play, despite the apparently conservative choice of period costume, lifted it conceptually way beyond Bogdanov's NT production. In a series of tableaux set in the Swan's rear stage area, characters were arranged, in Paul Taylor's words, 'like actors waiting in some purgatorial ante-room to be assigned a part, [highlighting] the sense of a world moving to a pre-ordained end'.[58] Charles Spencer evoked the 'brilliantly inventive final image' which raised 'the nightmarish possibility that the whole saga could be about to start all over again'.[59] This suggestion of characters at the mercy of an inescapable, cyclical destiny arose from Boyd's radical interpretation of Kyd's framing device.

Andrea's Ghost, played by Naiambana with none of the restraint previously noted as a prerequisite of the role, was released from the confines of his allotted scenes and prowled constantly round the play's action. He noted all references to his previous, living self; joined in the General's descriptions of the war's carnage; intervened in the dialogues of Horatio and Bel-imperia; and, most dramatically, disrupted the banquet in an outburst of physical violence, culminating in a paroxysm of screaming, floor-banging rage. Stabbed by an imaginary Balthazar at the start of 4.1, the Ghost lay prone through the subsequent action, rising on Isabella's invocation of Horatio's ghost (4.2.24–5). Following the bloody climax of 'Suleiman and Perseda' he lay weeping on Bel-imperia's body before joining her as she rose to take her place in the upstage tableau.

Influenced partly by Samuel Beckett's *Endgame*, Boyd's production explored a repetitive and mechanistic universe in which, as he said, 'the machinery of the state rolls on and over us, while we, as people, are worried for our souls and our identity, about what makes us – us'.[60] This was linked with the equally repetitive structures of the play's rhetorical figures and the mechanistic beat of its verse rhythms, in turn transmuted into the visual rhetoric of the suspended planks that represented the bower, 'dangling', as Taylor observed, 'like corpses from meat hooks' and set swinging at key dramatic moments like uncoordinated pendulums. Language, too, was seen and heard to be in a state of terminal disintegration, reduced in Kyd's text and Boyd's production to the babble of *'sundry languages'* in which the performance of 'Suleiman and Perseda' was enacted. In another manifestation of linguistic collapse, key phrases from Hieronimo's lamentation beginning 'Here lay my hope' (4.4.89–92) were projected on to the rear curtain. This textual fragmentation was echoed in the sound effect that enclosed the play, an unintelligible jumble of voices fading into a sense of eternal repetition: the play being rewound, perhaps.

At the beginning of the production, the play's language had to be kick-started, since Andrea was unable to deliver his opening speech without persistent prompting from Revenge. Crucial to Boyd's concept was the notion of Revenge not as a personalized character but, in Benedict Nightingale's words, 'sometimes a hooded grey figure, sometimes an offstage voice, sometimes a half-mad babble echoing from the distance'.[61] This disturbing entity was given physical embodiment by different actors, often with artificially amplified voices, and it was the removal of Revenge's individuality that allowed Boyd to achieve his closing *coup de théâtre*. Half way through his concluding speech, he removed his hood to reveal himself as Hieronimo; then, after his final line, 'I'll there begin their endless tragedy' (4.4.48), the play's opening was restaged, but with Horatio, not Andrea, being prompted through his lines by Revenge, his voice ultimately drowned by the babble of voices disappearing into ominous music. 'Endless tragedy' thus became the production's key motif, with the whole cycle destined to begin again, as Hemming noted, 'as if the story is on a hideous self-perpetuating loop'. Reviewers were mainly critical of Boyd's recrafting of the ending. Objecting to 'a crass piece of tinkering with the text', Macaulay condemned it as 'a Concept with all the dramatic subtlety of a cosh'. More to the point, perhaps, was the logical flaw in this 'rewrighting' of the conclusion. At the end, Horatio is not in a parallel position to Andrea at the start since his death has already been avenged. It would surely have been more appropriate to show Lorenzo or Balthazar in the concluding 'reveal', as their deaths have only just occurred. This would have emphasized, too, that not only the virtuous demand revenge.

The Spanish Tragedy's modern performance history is richly revealing. In addition to the productions mentioned in this chapter, it includes two BBC radio productions (1956 and 1996), an unfilmed screenplay preserved as a script reading on YouTube (recorded 2003),[62] and a one-hour distillation by Gameshow (2009) that presented it through text, music and movement, with a revival at a popup gallery incorporating 'performance installations' to begin and end the show.[63] Yet Kyd's masterpiece, despite its iconic status, lags far behind plays such as *Doctor Faustus*, *The Alchemist* or *The Duchess of Malfi* in the frequency of its revival. Perhaps there is something intimidating in its rhetorical architecture that distances us from its characters' emotional distress. Whatever the reason, the play still awaits a production that will earn it the wider appreciation it deserves.

Appendix: Post-1900 theatre productions of *The Spanish Tragedy*

Available information for each production is listed in the following order:

Year: Theatre or Venue; Producing Company; Director; Actors of Hieronimo and Bel-imperia.

1921: Birkbeck College, University of London; J. H. Lobban; Mr Nixon, Miss Cowie.

1926: Winchester College; John Firth; Richard Crossman, Kenneth Knowles.

1931: Birkbeck College, University of London; J. H. Lobban.

1932: Christ Church Library, Oxford; John Izon; Claude Burgess, Valerie Skardon.

1937: St Edmund Hall, Oxford; Nevill Coghill; Brian Cave-Brown-Cave, Daphne Levens.

1951: St John's College, Oxford; St John's Mummers.

1951: Old College, Edinburgh University; Edinburgh University Dramatic Society; Roy Smith; Alexander Grant, Moira Armstrong.

1968: Vandyck Theatre, Bristol; University of Bristol Department of Drama; Glynne Wickham and Graham Barlow; Paul Bettis, Eve Karpf.

1973: Mercury Theatre, Notting Hill Gate, London; Another Theatre; Philip Allen-Morgan; Mike Kellan, Jeffra Seberg.

1973: Oxford Playhouse; Oxford University Experimental Theatre Club; Francis Matthews [later known as Matthew Francis]; Crispian Cartwright, Jacinta Peel.

1976: College of William and Mary, Williamsburg, Virginia; J. H. Bledsoe.

1978: Citizens Theatre, Glasgow; Robert David MacDonald; John Sommerville, Celia Foxe.

1979: Wesley Memorial Church, Oxford; Worcester Buskins; Dave Skinner.

1982–4: Cottesloe Theatre, National Theatre, London (also Theatre Royal, Bath, 1983); Michael Bogdanov; Michael Bryant, Patti Love. Revived 1984, Lyttelton Theatre, NT; Michael Bryant, Miranda Foster.

1983: Globe Theatre, Los Angeles; Shakespeare Society of America; Lillian Wilds; Jeff Pomerantz, Michelle McElrath.

1986: Shakespeare Centre, New York; Classic Theatre / Riverside Shakespeare Company; Ron Daley; Paul Mentell, Jacqueline Chauvin.

1991: Old Red Lion Theatre, Islington, London; Welsh College of Music and Drama; Sarah Alexander; [unknown], Sarah Malin.

1994: Boston University; Willing Suspension Productions; Andrew J. Hartley; Colin Harris, Natasha Kruger.

1997–8: Swan Theatre, Stratford-upon-Avon (subsequently Newcastle Playhouse; Plymouth Pavilions; and The Pit, Barbican Centre, London); RSC; Michael Boyd; Peter Wight, Siobhan Redmond.

1997: Project (at) The Mint, Dublin; Loose Canon Theatre Company; Jason Byrne.

2005: Assembly Rooms, Durham; Captain Theatre.

2009: Oriel College, Oxford; Rabid Monkey / Oriel Lions; Will Maynard; Kate Lewin, Rob Hoare Nairne.

2009: Hoxton Hall, then Area 10 Peckham and CORPUS Gallery St John's Wood; Gameshow; Matthew Evans; Patrick Netherton, Sian Robins then Louis Brooke, Charlotte Bayley.

2009: Arcola Theatre, London; Doublethink; Mitchell Moreno; Dominic Rowan, Charlie Covell.

2010: Gremlin Theatre, Minneapolis; Theatre Pro Rata; Carin Bratlie; Keith Prusak, Amber Bjork.

2010: Rose Theatre, Bankside, London; Planet Theatre Productions; Adrian Brown; Hayward Morse, Rosy Langlands.

2010: New College Theatre, Harvard; Hyperion Shakespeare Company; Meryl H. Federman; Joshua O. Wilson, Harleen K. Gambhir.

2010: A1 Arts Theatre, University of New England, Armidale, New South Wales; Alex Robson; Joshua Osborne, Rebecca Coe.

2012: King's College Chapel, Cambridge; Perchance Theatre / Marlowe Society; Niall Wilson; James Parris, Stephanie Aspin.

2012: [staged reading]: Shakespeare's Globe, Read not Dead; James Wallace; Tim Treloar, Kate Sissons.

2013: Forest Meadows Amphitheatre, Dominican University, San Rafael, California; Marin Shakespeare Company; Lesley Schisgall Currier; Julian López-Morillas, Elena Wright.

2013: Blue Elephant Theatre, Camberwell, London; Lazarus Theatre Company; Ricky Dukes; Danny Solomon, Felicity Sparks.

2013: Curtain Theatre, Austin, Texas; The Baron's Men; Cherie Weed; Robert Stevens, Rachel Steed-Redig.

2014: [staged reading]: Shakespeare Institute, Stratford-upon-Avon, and University of Birmingham; Shakespeare Institute Players; Robert F. Ball; Peter Orford, Jenna Owen.

2014: St Mary's Great Hall, Baltimore; Mobtown Players; Joshua McKerrow; Frank Vince, Kat McKerrow.

2015: Little Nourse Theatre, Carleton College, Northfield, Minnesota; Experimental Theatre Board; Joss Olson; Matthew Pruyne, Emily Shack.

3

The Spanish Tragedy: State of the Art

Stevie Simkin

Overview and the advent of critical theory

The second half of the twentieth century saw a reassessment of Kyd's artistry, and a general shift from the standard judgement that it was a 'crude' play to seeing it as more complex and sophisticated. Geoffrey Aggeler cites Philip Edwards' introduction to a 1959 edition of *The Spanish Tragedy* as an early marker,[1] and notes the significance of the work of Charles and Elaine Hallett (1980)[2] and Peter Sacks (1982)[3] as pivotal in the shift in the play's fortunes. Tom McAlindon, in his study of *English Renaissance Tragedy* (1986), went so far as to describe the play as 'quite the most important single play in the history of English drama'.[4]

Around the same time, there was a new movement stirring in the academy, perhaps most starkly epitomized by Jonathan Dollimore's book *Radical Tragedy*; completed in 1982 and first published in 1984, it stands alongside *Political Shakespeare*

(1985) (edited by Dollimore and Alan Sinfield) as a key foundation text in the development of the movement known as cultural materialism. Both books can be read as responses to the political climate of their time. Deeply and vociferously committed to left wing politics at the height of Thatcherism, Dollimore, Sinfield and others challenged the essentialist principles of traditional criticism, laying bare the extent to which those principles, in their conservatism, were complicit with the political hegemony. This emergent, politically informed analysis of cultural texts would change the direction of literary studies from that point on, and early modern (and particularly Shakespearean) criticism was a key focus of the movement. As well as Dollimore and Sinfield, other key figures included Catherine Belsey,[5] Graham Holderness[6] and Terence Hawkes.[7] At the same time, the school of criticism that would be identified as new historicism was taking root on the other side of the Atlantic, via key works by Stephen Greenblatt,[8] Steven Mullaney[9] and others. Greenblatt opens *Shakespearean Negotiations* with the words, 'I began with the desire to speak with the dead' (p. 1) (an apt phrase when we consider the opening lines of *The Spanish Tragedy*), and this aim to engage with the past via the 'fragments of life' in the 'textual traces' of literature is what the two schools of criticism held in common, even if there have always been key differences in their approaches: new historicism gazes more intently at the past, while cultural materialists have always kept one eye on the political present (and future). This 'political turn' in criticism is evident in many of the essays and studies of Kyd's work from the late 1980s on.

Not that such work had come completely out of the blue. Several critics had anticipated elements of a politically engaged approach and a more nuanced understanding of the fundamental strangeness of the past, and its elusive qualities. C. L. Barber's chapter on *The Spanish Tragedy*, published eight years after his death in 1980, drew attention to the political radicalism of Kyd's play, speculating that it might have been the cause of his harsh treatment at the hands of the authorities following his arrest in 1593.[10] At a time when there was increased vigilance around Elizabeth on account of the assassination plots mounted against her, Barber writes, 'it is remarkable [...] that the public theater was able to take the liberty to represent, over and over again in a smash hit, an author-actor arranging, by a play, to butcher an entire royal line' (p. 160).

Both cultural materialism and new historicism are indebted to aspects of Foucauldian thought and Anthony B. Dawson's 1987 article, 'Madness and Meaning: *The Spanish Tragedy*', draws on Foucault directly to argue that Hieronimo's so-called insanity should be read as a familiar trope of the era, where 'Madness is represented as a kind of symbolic inversion, an escape from, or challenge to, hierarchical authority'.[11] 'The constant interruptions that madness has forced on the project of revenge', Dawson concludes, 'are finally circumvented by the semi-mad, semi-sane theatrical plot of the masque' (p. 62). Hieronimo's autoglossectomy becomes a political act: 'State power seeks explanation, fullness, disclosure, control over discourse (an ending), all of which Hieronimo refuses' (p. 64).

Catherine Belsey's *The Subject of Tragedy* casts Hieronimo as a kind of interstitial figure, reaching for liberal-humanist subjectivity on the one hand, but on the other 'haunted by the sovereignty which resides outside the self, uncertain whether he speaks in the name – the discourse – of heaven or hell, or neither': she interprets Hieronimo's self-inflicted violence as an act 'repudiating the right which defines the subject, the right of speech itself' (p. 75). Indebted to Belsey's work in terms of subjectivity, though disputing some key cultural materialist tenets, is Katharine Eisaman Maus's monograph *Inwardness and Theater in the English Renaissance* (1995) which studies works by Kyd, Shakespeare, Marlowe, Jonson and Milton alongside early modern pamphlets and medical and legal treatises and documents with a specific focus: the dialectic of exterior display and interior authenticity. Maus disputes the claims made by some cultural materialists and new historicists that the rhetoric of inwardness, of an essential self, is to be discounted, and that an early modern consciousness could only conceive of itself as a social being. For Maus, the stage 'machiavel' provides a powerful counter-argument, personifying as he does 'a radical, unprincipled estrangement of internal truth from external manifestation'.[12]

Frank Whigham follows in the postmodern tradition with his book *Seizures of the Will in Early Modern English Drama* (1996), a study which concentrates on moments of self-construction or identification: influenced by Pierre Bourdieu and Anthony Giddens in particular, Whigham considers how 'the struggle to gain or constitute or achieve personal identity was a central concern of early modern England' and explores how the binaries, conflicts and dialectics of the play's central concerns (such as eroticism, justice and state power) are played out, and how these binaries are 'funded, in a variety of ways, by fears of, and desires for, the seizure of identity'.[13] Another distinctively postmodern perspective is Richard Hillman's Lacanian take on subjectivity (1997) which examines the construction of the subject in Hieronimo's soliloquies (including the painter additions) and its subsequent breakdown, relating it to Lacan's notion of the psychotic state.[14]

Robert N. Watson's magisterial study *The Rest is Silence* (1999) is also preoccupied with subjectivity. Watson considers the fear of personal annihilation in early modern culture, asserting 'annihilationism' can be viewed as a 'transhistorical truth differently evaded in different periods'.[15] In this context, the body count of a play such as *The Spanish Tragedy* suggests that 'death is preventable as well as curable; it helps us regulate mortality-anxiety as well as mourning' (p. 58). 'Violence thus repeatedly –', Watson argues, 'perhaps in an odd way consolingly – appropriates the sovereignty of mortality' (p. 59). Watson goes on to examine the implications of the deaths of Andrea and Horatio, the bloody handkerchief, Pendringano's execution and the play's extraordinarily violent climax.

An early, important collection of essays featuring a number of early key proponents of cultural materialism, David Scott

Kastan and Peter Stallybrass's *Staging the Renaissance* (1987) included James Shapiro's study of *The Spanish Tragedy* which suggested that the play's staging of a hanging – the Elizabethan form of state execution – marked it out as politically radical. Kyd's play blurs the line separating official and theatrical violence, 'testing the boundaries between the prerogatives of the state and those of the theater'.[16] Jonathan Bate reached a similar conclusion, writing a couple of years later: 'by casting revenge in the form of an elaborate public spectacle, the drama reveals that the public performance known as the law is also a form of revenge action'.[17] Molly Smith also betrays a debt to Foucault's *Discipline and Punish* when she notes how the spectacle of public punishment is a crucial weapon deployed by the state, a manifest display of its power.[18] Like Maus, Smith sees the execution of Pedringano as an ironic reflection on the workings of state justice. She also suggests that the play's self-reflexivity (such as the play-within-the-play) offers the spectators the opportunity to critique the boundary that separates performer and audience. Sandra Clark works with a similar understanding when she suggests that scenes in revenge tragedies which depict condemned prisoners confidently awaiting pardons engineered by friends at court, only to find themselves disappointed, 'may well have chimed with English audiences' experiences of the consequences of unfounded trust in the law, with strong implications of the law's emptiness and inadequacy'.[19]

More recently, Timothy A. Turner has also chosen to explore the play's representations of execution and torture, suggesting that such representations 'can be seen to exploit questions raised by the sometimes wayward course of English justice'.[20] Turner draws on a number of contemporary references that problematized the state's use of torture in particular and concludes, as Barber had hinted, that the play's subversive challenge to the legitimacy of such practices may well have landed Kyd himself 'in the torture chamber at Bridewell' (p. 287).

The play has invited relatively few specifically feminist critiques. However, Maus's astute and authoritative introduction to the Oxford collection of *Four Revenge Tragedies* pays close attention to the character of Bel-imperia, noting her 'spirited refusal to comply with the dictates of a patriarchal system', her rejection of 'conventions of feminine reticence and pre-marital chastity' and her choice of lovers from the classes below her,[21] while Sandra Clark notes Bel-imperia's refusal to 'accept her allotted role as dynastic trophy' and political pawn (p. 135).

Finally, while there might seem something slightly forced conceptually about Andy Mousley's *Renaissance Drama and Contemporary Literary Theory* (2000) in its attempt to apply different schools of critical thinking to a selection of early modern plays, the discussion of *The Spanish Tragedy* through the lens of structuralism is enlightening, using Saussure's distinction between *langue* and *parole* to differentiate between the possibilities of shared language (the former) and the 'privatization' of meaning (the latter) that occurs in the play.[22] In this way, Mousley sheds further light on the play's tensions between the individual and the social.

Authorship, date, sources and influences

Despite the amount of scholarship pre-1980 devoted to analysis of Kyd's sources and in particular his influences, debates have continued to rage in the years since. The attempts to accurately date the play have not been a trivial sideshow; as I will explain, that particular discussion has a significant knock-on effect for a wider understanding of the play, particularly in terms of its topicality. Similarly, the differing opinions about Kyd's influences, in particular with regard to classical models of tragedy, ripple out to touch on more significant interpretative elements of the play, notably its cosmology.

Lukas Erne's major study (2002) attempts to provide an authoritative overview of the play's sources and likely influences, as well as the significance of the play for later Elizabethan dramatists.[23] Erne's book is possibly over-ambitious in its attempt to demand a reassessment of Kyd's *oeuvre*: he argues for the inclusion of *Soliman and Perseda*, *Cornelia*, *Don Horatio* and *The First Part of Hieronimo*, when the latter has generally been dismissed from the Kydian canon.[24] Furthermore, Erne's proposal that the play has a covert five-act structure is suppositional at best; solid evidence to back his claim is thin, as he himself concedes (p. 67). Similarly, his theory that the play may originally have had a Chorus fails to convince. In terms of dating the play, Erne considers 1587 the likeliest year of composition (p. 58), but this sets him at odds with a number of other critics, notably Frank Ardolino, who has devoted a large part of his career to understanding Kyd's play, and whose scholarship I will return to in due course.

There has been considerable discussion of the authorship of the 1602 additions to *The Spanish Tragedy*. Hugh Craig's 1992 essay took a quantitative approach, investigating the frequency of very common words to differentiate between Ben Jonson's authorial style and Shakespeare's; Craig's conclusion is that the evidence tends to confirm those suspicions (harboured by Charles Lamb and Coleridge amongst others) that Jonson was not the author of the additional scenes, thus strengthening the case for attributing them to Shakespeare.[25] In 2009, Craig published another study, based on two types of data – lexical words used more frequently by Shakespeare than other playwrights (and vice versa) and function words such as 'the', 'of' and 'and', with the results mapped on a scatter graph.[26] Brian Vickers is sceptical about some of Craig's working practices, but nevertheless concedes that Craig's conclusion matches his own convictions and proposes that the 320 lines added in the Quarto of 1602 'should in future be included in the Shakespeare canon'.[27] Douglas Bruster's 2013 article for *Notes & Queries* offered further evidence for Shakespeare's authorship of the additions via a study of Shakespeare's spelling habits (following John Dover Wilson's work) as well as his handwriting.[28]

The concept of authorship has also, perhaps unsurprisingly, proven a happy hunting ground for postmodernists. In 1999 Emma Smith, influenced by Foucauldian notions of the 'author function', proposed that the tension between 'writing author and speaking character' in many early modern plays destabilizes familiar notions of authorial attribution.[29] She cites a wealth of evidence that suggests *The Spanish Tragedy* was, for a considerable period of time, more readily identified with Hieronimo than with Thomas Kyd. A few years earlier, David Cutts had ruminated on early modern anxieties about the authorship of plays that he believes were emerging in the late sixteenth century, a time when plays were being published for the first time. Cutts argues that the play displays a preoccupation with the idea of writing: Hieronimo, after all, fashions his revenge out of a play he has written himself, although this is finally at the cost of his own life and some collateral damage: 'the author ultimately loses control of his creation', Cutts writes, 'and he is displaced by the text of his revenge'.[30]

Marguerite Tassi, in her book *The Scandal of Images* (2005), chooses to take the emphasis off the authorship issue and considers the painter addition dramaturgically: with Hieronimo commissioning a painting and then acting out the figures he wants to see represented in the painting, the fact that the painting itself 'as a tangible, visible form, is noticeably absent' from the scene 'allows the player greater freedom with *his* form [emphasis in the original]'.[31] Tassi connects Hieronimo's commission to a particular genre of painting in Tudor England, arguing that it can be read as a 'specific kind of memorial, a *memento vindictae,* whose purpose is to incite the viewer and the patron-commissioner to action' (p. 171). Carol Thomas Neely looks at the additions not as 'add-ons but significant textual revisions';[32] her discussion of the play traces the development of Hieronimo's madness and its cultural reception, arguing that it represents 'madness that is secular, disrupts body and mind, allows self-representation, and offer challenges to subjects' unity and to normative social order' (p. 45). Once again, a political subtext rises to the surface.

In terms of Kyd's classical borrowings, Barber's prescient essay had already conceptualized things neatly when he proposed that what Kyd creates is not a Senecan tragedy, but 'a Senecan mood and logic of violence breaking out in a world of positive social values of graciousness, loyalty, heroism, familial love, and romantic love' (p. 142). What he dramatizes, Barber suggests, is 'not a Senecan world but a good world becoming Senecan' (p. 143). Joost Daalder differs, arguing for a closer alignment of Kyd's play with Senecan thinking in an ingenious speculative reading of the character designated either 'Old Man' or 'Senex' in the play; he goes on to argue that Kyd is introducing his audience to a Senecan way of thinking, particularly in 3.13, following Hieronimo's famous declaration '*Vindicta mihi!*' which Daalder identifies as a Senecan phrase rather than, as it has more often been seen, a Biblical one.[33] In this context, the phrase would then be understood as 'revenge is mine' (Hieronimo's), and not read as a citation of the Biblical 'Vengeance is mine [saith the Lord]' (p. 255). Daalder challenges those critics who suggest audiences would have seen a revenger's actions as straightforwardly evil, contravening God's laws, suggesting that the revenger might have been viewed far more sympathetically (I return to the issue of 'justifying' revenge below). In the same year, Robert S. Miola identified another possible Senecan echo in the play, comparing Hieronimo's question to the king (4.4.179–80) with Creon's question to Oedipus in Seneca's eponymous play.[34]

Lukas Erne also provides a detailed rationale for understanding Kyd as working in Seneca's shadow (pp. 79–83), but others have been more circumspect: For Eugene Hill (1985), Kyd's play is a 'deeply self-conscious work' dealing with 'the problematic passage between Senecan and modern tragedy', and one that draws on Virgilian material to place 'the Senecan elements in an ironic light'; Hill focuses on the way that Andrea's voyage is portrayed as the 'inverse' of that of Aeneas.[35] Gordon Braden's study of *Renaissance Tragedy and the Senecan Tradition* argues that Hieronimo represents an 'unusually expansive version of Senecan selfhood' infiltrating the territory of revenge tragedy; this means the morality of revenge becomes a crucial consideration.[36] However, Braden argues that the play only briefly gives voice to those who would advocate Christian patience in the face of a great wrong; 'Otherwise, the moral rhetoric in this play [...] is overwhelmingly on the side of revenge, and directed against an inactivity for which no good name is forthcoming' (p. 203). Kerrigan's *Revenge Tragedy* places greater emphasis on the influence of Greek, as opposed to Roman, tragedy: 'Aeschylus shows the past inciting violence but notices how retrospection can offer its own satisfactions and draw an avenger back from his task'. He suggests that same ambiguity 'can operate to dramatic effect at high levels of structural and psychological detail' in Elizabethan drama, notably in *The Spanish Tragedy*.[37]

Finally, although it is mentioned briefly by Kerrigan (p. 175), Erne remarks that, at the time he was writing, he believed no one had paid close attention to the similarities and differences between Andrea's underworld and that depicted by Virgil in Book 6 of the *Aeneid* (pp. 52–3). Like others discussed by Tom Rutter in this collection, Erne points out that Kyd eschews Virgil's map, where one path leads to Tartarus (hell) and the other to Elysium (paradise) and offers a third path, which Andrea takes, and which leads to a world that seems to combine the two: 'Appropriately, the place which Andrea is taken to is not one of blessedness and rewarded virtue, but a purgatorial place' from which his soul returns to the earth (p. 53).[38] Erne concludes that Kyd's play 'appears to hide a Christian dimension underneath [its] pagan appearance' and connects the depiction of Andrea's journey with the Catholic doctrine of purgatory (p. 54), and while he stops short of concluding Kyd might have had Catholic sympathies as he explores a variety of additional evidence, he does concede that 'the possibility is certainly intriguing' (p. 55).

Protestantism, Catholicism and anti-Iberian prejudice

It is perhaps no surprise that, as new historicist and cultural materialist criticism flourished, locating the play in the context of the momentous upheaval of the Reformation became a preoccupation for some critics. Thomas Rist[39] provides a useful overview of the debate when he pinpoints Ronald Broude's 1973 article[40] as the foundation stone for a wing of scholarship insisting on the anti-Catholicism of revenge tragedy. Broude proposes that the narrative pattern of early modern revenge tragedy was 'shaped by and implied the providential interpretation of history in terms of which Protestants understood the Reformation', with the expectation of the end times and the downfall of the Antichrist (p. 490), and Rist identifies a series of scholars following in Broude's footsteps. They include Eugene D. Hill, mentioned above, and Frank Ardolino in two essays from 1990 and 1994.[41] Ardolino's first essay of the two notes that the Book of Revelation 'served as the primary theological source for Reformation attacks on the Pope as Antichrist and the Roman Catholic Church as the Whore of Babylon' (p. 49), and argues that the play can be interpreted as a mystery play in which Hieronimo is 'the Danielic figure, the judge [...], Anglophile representative of God's will at the court of Babylon-Spain' (p. 51).[42] J. R. Mulryne's 1996 essay follows Broude and Hill in arguing that the play engages with contemporary politics, especially tension and conflict between England and Spain. Mulryne focuses on the intended dynastic marriage of Balthazar to Bel-imperia as a 'bid for stability and political strength in an alliance between the states of Spain and Portugal' and notes how 'In the 1580s such an alliance would have particular meanings for an Elizabethan audience.'[43] Although there was no corresponding dynastic marriage between the two nations at the time, Mulryne believes that the play may well have taken advantage of English prejudice against the on-going diplomacy at the time between Spain and

Portugal, with Portugal largely compliant to the Spanish will (p. 104). Mulryne's scholarship also endorsed previous work that emphasized the idea of Spain as the 'whore of Babylon' and noted the familiar confounding of the terms Babylon and Babel (p. 97), the latter of course an appropriate reference for Hieronimo's climactic polyglot play.

Rist sifts through evidence gathered from the terrain of an England caught between Catholicism and Protestantism, and takes nothing for granted as he turns a quizzical eye on the Broudian line that assumes the revenge tragedy genre routinely demonized the 'Babylon of Catholicism' and critiqued its rituals and traditions. He also questions Andrew Hadfield's suggestion[44] that the handkerchief, stained with Horatio's blood, might recall the execution of Robert Southwell, the Jesuit priest hanged, drawn and quartered at Tyburn in 1595.[45] Rist questions Hadfield's conclusion that 'this act of veneration for the dead – which no English Reformer would have countenanced' is further evidence of the play's anti-Catholicism (Hadfield, 197).

Rist is adamant that 'antipathy to Imperial Spain is not to be equated simply with anti-Catholicism'. Irrespective of their faith, Elizabethans had enough cause to resent Spain on purely patriotic, rather than religious grounds, Rist suggests (pp. 27–8), and what we could call the anti-Iberian prejudice of the play has been another focus of considerable attention. In his article '*Corrida* of Blood in *The Spanish Tragedy*' (1984), Ardolino argues that Kyd's play is uncompromising in terms of its Reformation politics, and that it is nationalistic to boot, trumpeting 'little England"'s superiority over, and military success against, the Spanish empire.[46] Ardolino also argues that the assassination of the Duke of Castile, and the Spanish line of succession, effectively predicted the English conquest of Catholic Spain; it is a perspective that A. J. Hoenselaars endorses.[47] Hoenselaars identifies Hieronimo's masque in 1.4 as another piece of propaganda, where the English knights he names advertise 'the victories they have achieved for "Little England" (1.4.160) over both the Spaniards and the Portuguese' (p. 83).

Ardolino's 1995 monograph *Apocalypse and Armada in Kyd's Spanish Tragedy* posits that the 'central political subtext' of the play was the defeat of the Spanish Armada in 1588 (and for this reason, amongst others, Ardolino disagrees with the consensus that dates the play a few years later).[48] Crystallizing the argument of his article five years earlier that cast Hieronimo as a 'Danielic' figure,[49] he presents a conceptualization of the play as a Reformist Apocalypse and a celebration of England's history over Spain, the Whore of Babylon. Ardolino makes a series of connections with contemporaneous historical events, including the attempted assassination of Lorenzo and Giuliano de Medici, the St. Bartholomew's Day Massacre,[50] as well as individual details of the defeat of the Armada.

Although some critics have endorsed Ardolino – Steven Justice and Eugene Hill both insist on reading the play as a celebration of England's triumph over Spain[51] – his claims have also been challenged, notably by Erne, who finds them 'far-fetched' (p. 91). Erne is also unconvinced by the efforts of Ardolino and others to date the play to 1592, noting that 'It seems unlikely that Kyd would have brought forward half-invented stories about past English victories over Spain if he could have alluded to the real and recent glory' (p. 56). More recently, Eric Griffin, whose work features elsewhere in this collection, has also questioned the notion of anti-Iberian prejudice in two articles (2001 and 2009). In the former, he remarks that 'Kyd seems to go against his age by forgoing stereotypical Spanish Cruelty and granting most of his Dons a nobility they seldom attain in the religio-political discourse of the Protestant North';[52] the latter questions the significance of the Black Legend, noting that *The Spanish Tragedy* 'largely fails to register' it.[53]

Other critics have offered more developed perspectives on how the play might be situated in nationalist terms. Carla Mazzio's 1998 study begins with the acknowledgement that the sixteenth century saw the influx of thousands of new words from Latin, Greek, Spanish and Italian, leading to 'extensive debates about the presence of foreign and "barbaric" elements within the national vocabulary'.[54] She goes on to assert that if early modern theatre was 'imagined as a site for the articulation and transformation of linguistic "fashion", and hence for the re-negotiation of social and national modes of communication', then Kyd's play 'can be seen as seriously complicating the nationalistic sentiment that the play seems to celebrate' (p. 213). The crux of the argument is around the performance of Soliman and Perseda, with its 'polyglot structure', a 'kind of grotesque culmination of the alienating fusion and confusion of cultural differences that pervade the play' (p. 215). In more recent years, Barbara Fuchs has offered a different take on the play's so-called anti-Iberian prejudice, emphasizing how early modern representations often conflated Spain with the world of Islam, 'part of a sustained Orientalizing discourse that animates the Black Legend, figuring Spain's supposed cruelty and depravity in terms of the Mediterranean rather than the new World'.[55] The choice to represent Spain as 'Moorish' or 'Turkish', Fuchs points out, emphasizes the 'alterity of England's most powerful enemy' and coexists with the more familiar conceptualizations at that time that 'link Protestantism and Islam as iconoclastic religions aligned against the threat of Roman Catholicism' (p. 64). Like Hoenselaars, Fuchs notes the significance of the masque in Act 1 Scene 4 in terms of English humblings of Spain and Portugal (p. 66) and suggests that the climactic play within a play recalls 'Turkish' dramas of the time such as Marlowe's two-part *Tamburlaine* and Peele's *The Battle of Alcazar:* 'Kyd specifically associates Iberia with the world of the East, suggesting both the special vulnerability of Spain to Ottoman rapacity, and its enduring identification with Islam' (p. 68).

Class politics

Although a good deal of scholarly energy has been expended on discovering what the play might reveal about attitudes in

England towards Spain at the end of the sixteenth century, other writers have focused on domestic politics. It may well be that the popularity of the revenge tragedy genre can be explained at least in part by reading it as a response to the escalating tension between the aristocracy and the monarchy, tensions that would be exacerbated further by the arrival of King James VI of Scotland to take up the English throne in 1603. This is broadly the argument that J. W. Lever had proposed some years before in his *Tragedy of State* (1971).[56] C. L. Barber (writing in 1980, published in 1988) had emphasized in his essay the 'tensions between traditional, hierarchical society and the aspirations of the class from which Kyd himself derives' (p. 25). Hieronimo is effectively a 'middle class' professional in his capacity as a knight marshal; his son Horatio is 'a rising man, such as the old nobility often resented' (p. 137) and the younger man's love affair with Bel-imperia is likely to have been perceived as 'extremely dangerous' (pp. 137–8). Gordon Braden propounds a similar argument, suggesting, in an argument revisited in this collection, that the centralization of political power during the Tudor period was 'the overarching political event of the day' (p. 107).

Katharine Maus notes in her introduction to *Four Revenge Tragedies* that 'defectiveness of the status quo' (p. ix) is central to revenge tragedy ('virtually a precondition') (p. ix); the plays 'explore the particular stresses and incongruities produced by the highly stratified society of late sixteenth- and early seventeenth-century England' (p. xi). She suggests that the revenger is frequently 'caught in a double-bind' since on the one hand his revolt against an unjust ruler constitutes treason while on the other, 'in so far as the revenger aims not to overturn the social hierarchy but to restore its proper functioning, he is a conservative, not a revolutionary figure' (p. xiii). Sandra Clark concurs, suggesting that 'The conflict between the duty owed to family and kinsfolk and the allegiance claimed by the monarch and the forces of state control created dramatically exciting situations in plays like *The Spanish Tragedy* or *Hamlet*' (p. 129).

Out of this approach came proposals from a number of scholars that Kyd himself might be seen as a political radical: James R. Siemon's 1994 essay 'Sporting Kyd' draws on Bakhtinian theory and the Marxist cultural critic V. N. Voloshinov to analyse 'the conflict of specifically social valuations registered in the play'.[57] He explores social contention as thematized in narrative, character interaction (with a focus on the relative positions of Hieronimo and Lorenzo), and language, and also considers Kyd himself in terms of social stratification, speculating on how he might be seen in relation to Christopher Marlowe. Christopher Crosbie also sees the play pointing towards a more egalitarian politics in the way it draws on elements of early modern psychology, notably the Aristotelian notion of the vegetative soul.[58] He suggests Kyd had a particular interest in *oeconomia*, drawing attention to his 1588 translation of Torquato Tasso's *The Householder's Philosophy* (p. 6).

Linda Woodbridge notes the significance of social class in the play and acknowledges Siemon's work on Kyd's own social background when she draws attention to the way in which social status not only inflects the Spanish king's nepotism (favouring his own nephew over Horatio), and Bel-imperia's relationships,[59] but also determines the protagonist's vengeful course: 'Hieronimo turns to revenge because his low status blocks access to justice' (p. 239). Woodbridge speculates that part of the satisfaction for the 'ordinary folk' watching the performance might have come from seeing the mighty laid low: 'Hieronimo dies, but takes the upper echelons with him, leaving two royal families heirless – satisfying to the frustrated and powerless in the audience' (p. 240). James J. Condon's study also reads a political subtext into the play; building on others' work on its metatheatrical dimension (notably Kerrigan, Maus and Bate), Condon suggests that the original crimes that give rise to the revenge plots 'are products of the corrupt nobility's willful misapplication of the Crown's territorial privilege'.[60] While the noblemen cover their tracks and try to make themselves safe via exiles and imprisonments, 'the uniquely performative nature of the protagonist's final gambit allows him to momentarily fix his prey in place and appropriate his enemy's tyrannical control of space to seize the opportunity for vengeance' (p. 64).

For Brian Sheerin, one of the ways revenge tragedies connected with contemporary politics most directly was through an engagement with the idea of court patronage and sovereignty: 'revenge tragedy was able to call into question the very bonds of obligation defining sovereign/subject interaction in the royal court by creating a distorted mirror-image of the practices of donation, gift-bestowal, and patronage that comprised such bonds to begin with'.[61] Sheerin proceeds to explore these ideas in a number of key moments in Kyd's play, culminating in Hieronimo's biting off of his own tongue as an ironic offering to the Spanish King (p. 269).

Others have been more circumspect about, or at least not so closely wedded to, the emphasis on class struggle. Ian McAdam reaffirmed that notion that Kyd, and his play, contained radical potential, but qualified it by asserting that 'it is doubtful if we can regard the play as (in a political sense) a highly revolutionary work' in the way that cultural materialist critics might wish to claim.[62] McAdam actually chooses to turn the spotlight onto the play as a tragedy about 'the uncontrollable nature of *desire* [emphasis in the original], and more specifically about the conflation of the drives to sexual and religious self-justification' (p. 39). He provides a detailed reading of Bel-imperia and her lovers to justify his position. Retaining an historicizing approach, he perceives a confluence of psychological and political currents in the play, with the pressures applied by the 'self-idealizations of the Protestant Reformation' leading to 'expressions of narcissistic rage and disturbed sexual responses', including Bel-imperia's desire for 'virile, lower-class men', Lorenzo's 'homoerotic sadism' and Hieronimo's 'homicidal madness over the loss of the son on whom his own identity intensely depends' (p. 53).

Cosmology

The central pillars of Ardolino's monograph *Thomas Kyd's Mystery Play* (1985) include his proposal that Kyd 'combines the concern for the divine punishment of evil contained in the New Testament with the pagan notion of destiny being carried out by an act of just revenge to create a complex conception of universal justice'.[63] However, Ardolino presents a more nuanced and knotted picture of pagan retribution and Christian justice when he goes on to explore the ambivalent references to heaven (pagan or Christian?) and in particular Hieronimo's conflicted position in terms of personal vengeance or justice, and his eventual embrace of the former. For Ardolino, the induction scene establishes the idea of life as a journey through hell which ends in death, followed 'by a resurrection into eternal rewards or punishments' (p. 123); he also connects the death of Horatio to the pagan tradition of the hanged god (p. 145). He suggests that the play proper ends on a note of mourning (with the deaths of Lorenzo, Balthazar, Castile, Bel-imperia and Hieronimo) but that the epilogue 'presents the final ritual movement from grief to joy' as the good are rewarded and the villains sent to eternal punishment (p. 148).

Geoffrey Aggeler's 1987 essay exploring the 'eschatological crux' of the play was one of the first to question the apparent juxtaposition of 'a Christian world with a classical underworld' (p. 319). He argues that it is an essential part of its tragic design, pointing out that the depiction of the underworld seems to be modelled on the Hades described in Book VI of the *Aeneid* (p. 320). Aggeler's analysis reveals a work that is profoundly sceptical about the notion of divine vengeance on sinners. As he points out, it is 'anything but obvious that Andrea's dispensations are "the judgements of God."' He believes that the impression created by the Induction, that the gods 'are utterly indifferent to human suffering' is vividly confirmed by the denouement (pp. 329–30). *The*

Spanish Tragedy, in this formulation, is 'essentially a pagan humanistic Classical tragedy', closer to Homer or Euripides, depicting a world populated only by 'vengeance-possessed human beings, among whom Hieronimo towers morally by comparison' (pp. 330–1). Catherine Belsey, publishing two years earlier, discerns in the play 'two antithetical worlds, one authoritarian, divinely ordered and controlled, and the other disordered, unjust, incipiently secular and humanist' (p. 113).

Philip Edwards similarly finds a tragedy populated by a 'refurbished set of pagan deities' where 'For a mere whim of Proserpine [...] Hieronimo and his family are wiped out along with "the whole succeeding hope" of the royal households of Spain and Portugal.'[64] 'What seriousness is the theology of *The Spanish Tragedy* meant to have?' he wonders (p. 119). Edwards concludes that the play 'sets up a rather horrifying and totally un-Christian cosmic machinery in which metaphysical control is absolute and "justice" an irrelevance' (p. 131). Maus, in *Inwardness and Theater*, presents it as a work of dark pessimism, sceptical of orthodox beliefs about a providential God: the entire tragedy, she reminds us, is presided over by the ghost of the slaughtered Andrea, and the figure of Revenge (who sleeps through much of the performance). However, Lukas Erne takes a less despairing view: while Edwards sees the play as 'a denial of God's care for man',[65] Erne suggests that it is 'not so much a cosmic drama about a world deserted by God as the personal drama of Hieronimo deserting God' (p. 111). He believes it is 'surely significant that during the first stage [of his trajectory], Hieronimo appeals to Christian and/or heavenly powers, whereas in the second he turns to pagan deities' (p. 110).

William M. Hamlin adopts a similar approach, presenting the play as a revenge drama with 'an abundance of adjudications' and 'a scarcity of justice', one that repeatedly engages 'the sceptical paradigm of opposition' (refusing straightforward resolutions).[66] He believes that the play's 'abundant ironies invite ironic interpretation' even of the play's conclusion, where Revenge seems to deliver what she had promised

Andrea (the death of Balthazar at the hands of Bel-imperia); after all, why should Horatio have to die to grant Andrea justice? In this context, the death of Horatio remains 'brutally inexplicable – a just emblem of the prevailing injustice of human existence' (p. 165).

While there have been differing perspectives from a variety of critics on the cosmology of *The Spanish Tragedy*, one element of the play's frame of religious referents has proven to be an enduring preoccupation: memorializing rituals. C. L. Barber explored the concept, emphasizing Hieronimo and Isabella's grieving for their son Horatio; he remarks that 'memorializing by creating a sacred or accursed place is a common symbolic process in life, including the classical life and literature with which Kyd was familiar' – in other words, it is not necessarily a specifically Christian signifier (p. 153). Kerrigan, in his important study of revenge tragedy 'from Aeschylus to Armageddon', notes what he describes as 'a chain of remembrances' that are significant in the play, and which include the gory 'handkercher' Hieronimo dips in Horatio's blood and the scarf given to Bel-imperia by Andrea, and passed on by her to Horatio as a love token (p. 174). Andrew Sofer focuses on the bloody handkerchief but argues that the references are indeed specifically Christian. Drawing on Marvin Carlson's theory of 'ghosting' (spectators bringing memories of previous visits to the theatre with them which then colour their experience of the current performance), he suggests that the play is evoking memories of Catholic rites: 'Indeed, at the play's climax the ghost in the bloody handkerchief's folds is the Host itself, the "Real Presence" of Christ's body as it was embodied in the sacrament of the Eucharist'.[67] He draws on a variety of examples of 'holy cloths and sacred blood' (p. 129) in medieval dramatic texts to show the precedent Kyd echoes, and suggests that Hieronimo's fetishization of the cloth soaked with his son's blood is effectively a 'sacrilegious perversion of the Mass' which 'no doubt played into Kyd's spectators' fear and loathing of Catholic Spain' (p. 146).

Although Stephen Greenblatt is unfortunately rather dismissive of *The Spanish Tragedy* and its 'Senecan ghosts' (p. 248), his presentation in *Hamlet in Purgatory* (2001) of a culture in transition in terms of religious belief is instructive. He argues that the Protestant abolition of the doctrine of purgatory in the mid-sixteenth century failed to rid the people of the structures of belief that had persisted for so long, 'the longings and fears that Catholic doctrine had focused and exploited' (pp. 256–7), and claims that 'the space of Purgatory becomes the space of the stage where old Hamlet's Ghost is doomed for a certain term to walk the night' (p. 257): in other words, the ghosts that haunted plays such as Shakespeare's *Hamlet* and Kyd's *Spanish Tragedy* fulfilled that need to commune with the dead. The central thesis of Rist's *Revenge Tragedy and the Drama of Commemoration in Reforming England* (2008) is not dissimilar, arguing that revenge tragedy is not an anti-Catholic genre, but one in *dialogue* with Catholic tradition, particularly in terms of its rituals of memorialization. Rist also notes that Horatio's funeral rites have a distinct Latinate flavor. For Rist, *The Spanish Tragedy* (as well as *Titus Andronicus* and *Hamlet*) represent such melodramatic remembrance of the dead that they might even be considered as 'denoting and championing popish "excesses" in Protestant England' (p. 75).

Alexander Leggatt offers a fascinating parallel reading of the play with Tony Kushner's *Angels in America* (1993), considering how they both represent border crossings, including journeys across the line between life and death (Andrea), between actor and spectator (when Hieronimo breaks the fourth wall and kills the Duke of Castile), and both simultaneously: 'As a stage ghost, [Andrea] is also an actor making an entrance, crossing from one space to another, from the tiring-house to the stage'.[68] Finally, William Engel's *Death and Drama in Renaissance England* (2002) proposes that the century from around 1570–1670 marked a revival of interest in the classical Memory Arts, and that one manifestation of this revival was a preoccupation with certain 'framing mechanisms' in tragic drama of the period, 'cunning, initially mute, staged spectacles that evoked images of fatal destiny'.[69] According to Engel, the dumb show of 3.15 is a 'mnemonic placeholder' (p. 57) which, as interpreted by Revenge, predicts the doom of those within Andrea's vengeful crosshairs. When Andrea metes out punishment to the newly released souls crowding the stage at the end of *The Spanish Tragedy*, the audience is invited to participate vicariously: 'We become the co-authors of Andrea's proposed script when we stage, and can imagine that we hear, the torment of his victims in the theatres of our minds' (p. 63).

Revenge

In offering an overview of recent criticism of a seminal, foundational revenge tragedy, it seems fitting to start to draw the chapter to a close with a look at how perspectives have shifted on the play's exploration of justice and revenge, and the revenger figure himself. Once again, we find critics attempting to reassess these themes in the wake of a demand for a more nuanced approach to the idea of historical context. Jordi Coral Escola summarizes the critical orthodoxy on Elizabethan attitudes towards private revenge by citing Maus's 1997 edition of *Titus Andronicus*: 'Spectators could experience a vicarious thrill of sympathy with the avenger, even while, at the end of the play, acknowledging the moral unacceptability of revenge and the necessity of the avenger's death.'[70] Escola challenges this rigid view by focusing instead on the 'subjective crisis of the avenger and what it reveals about his identity'.[71] From this perspective, Hieronimo's challenge to the court is not primarily a political act but a plea for his suffering to be recognized and acknowledged: 'it is a restoration of the severed or violated bond between himself and his fellow beings' (p. 71).

In considering the state justice context for Kyd's audiences, Ronald Broude's essay had complicated the understanding of the legal system at the end of the sixteenth century by pointing out how public and private blurred in a legal system which placed a burden of responsibility on victims and witnesses to pursue perpetrators. Hutson's thesis (2007) suggests that plays such as *Hamlet* and *The Spanish Tragedy* 'lay [...] bare, by the political denial of due process, the painful, ethical question of what it means, in a Protestant world, to pursue justice, to risk being mistaken in one's own judgement that someone else's guilt was deserving of death'.[72] Sandra Clark, publishing in the same year, considers the tension between orthodox Elizabethan belief, which prohibited private revenge, and the Senecan doctrine of avenging the death of a family member (p. 136). Simon Barker and Hilary Hinds's introduction in their *Routledge Anthology of Renaissance Drama* (2003) takes a similar line, noting how the play places Hieronimo in a position where he is 'caught between the strictures of Christian teaching [forbidding revenge] and the seductive reasoning of Seneca' (p. 35).[73]

In his outstanding meditation on the meanings and implications of acts of revenge Gregory M. Colon Semenza identifies two schools of thought, the first led by Lily B. Campbell who espouses the view that Hieronimo would have been perceived as a villain because there are so many early modern documents condemning revenge; on the other side of the divide, Fredson Bowers argues that there was a strong tradition of secular defences of revenge and that consequently audiences would have found Hieronimo a sympathetic figure.[74] Semenza says to argue one or the other is missing the point: it is the tension between the two that Kyd maintains that is important. Kyd wants his audience to suffer the same feelings of anguish and uncertainty that Hieronimo experiences (p. 56). He also suggests that the play 'loudly declares that there is no such thing as a clean act of revenge' and that it demonstrates this nowhere more clearly than in the denouement, which moves from the satisfaction of Hieronimo's acts of vengeance, to his grotesque acts of self-harm and self-annihilation (p. 51). Semenza considers the Elizabethan context in some detail, noting the historical evolution from the wergild system of Anglo-Saxon society, via the medieval 'appeals' system, to the 'indictment' system of the Renaissance (p. 51). However, the sucker-punch of his essay is in the parallels he is able to draw between our own time and Kyd's: 'Whereas the specific laws and customs of Renaissance society differed from our own, revenge remains a topic that binds us because the impulse toward self-government emerges precisely out of those moments in which specific laws and customs break down or fail to achieve their intended purposes' (p. 55). I will return to Semenza's essay in my concluding section.

Steven Justice's article acknowledges that debates about the ethics of revenge were no doubt on-going at the time Kyd was writing, but also reminds us that the moral question needs to be subject to the understanding that 'a dramatic character can make only those choices that the dramatic society around him offers'. He believes that 'the judgement of the play falls less on Hieronimo than on a kind of society, that the tragedy results from a way of life' (p. 272). In this respect, Hieronimo's tragedy is 'not so much that of a man who makes the wrong choice as that of a man to whom the right choice is unavailable' (p. 278). Katharine Maus, in her *Four Revenge Tragedies* introduction, suggests that the play presents a series of moral conundrums – 'How are we to evaluate the actions of the revenger? Does the protagonist's victimization exonerate him, partially or fully? Do we condone crimes that retaliate for previous crimes?' (p. x) – and Rist believes that these questions prompt an even more urgent one – 'How just is Hieronimo's final vengeance in view of the wrong he suffers?' – in other words, how appropriate is his revenge? Rist suggests that the answers are conflicted and paradoxical, and imply a tension between the drama's aesthetics (extravagance and excess in both grief and thirst for revenge) and the religio-political impetus of the Reformation: 'To the contemporary audience, the implication is therefore this: the artistry before you is against the Reform; to enjoy it, even to partake in it, endorses a resistance to Reform' (p. 43).

Other voices have nominated Hieronimo as a more straightforward, justified avenger. Although Ardolino's 1994 contribution to *Spanish Tragedy* scholarship is intended as an addition to his long-running thesis about the play as a commentary on the history of Anglo-Iberian conflict, he also draws a parallel between Kyd's tragic hero and the Samson of Milton's poem *Samson Agonistes*, claiming that both writers 'use similar conceptions of the sanctified revenger' (p. 161).[75] Duncan Salkeld points out how the suicides of Isabella and Hieronimo 'conform to contemporary expectations of insanity' but also notes that it is madness that 'constitutes a moral justification for the act of revenge'.[76] For Linda Woodbridge, confronting the question of whether or not Hieronimo's famous cry, '*Vindicta mihi*' is an allusion to the Pauline injunction to leave revenge to God, the solution is very straightforward: 'I don't think Hieronimo rejects *vindicta mihi*', she writes; 'he simply nominates himself as God's agent' (p. 125).

Legacy

In concluding, I would like to offer two more perspectives: first of all on the legacy of Kyd's play as it has been perceived over the past thirty years or so, and secondly on the enduring appeal of the revenge theme in contemporary culture. A number of critics have explored the influence of *The Spanish Tragedy* on some of his near contemporaries, notably Philip Edwards,[77] Jonathan Bate in the connections he traces between *Titus* and *The Spanish Tragedy*[78] and Stanley Wells (2006) who gives diverse examples of plays bearing Kyd's imprint including *Hamlet*, *King Lear* and *Henry VI Part 2* and, as one would expect, *Titus Andronicus*, which Wells believes Shakespeare wrote 'in direct emulation' of Kyd's play.[79] More generally, Martin Wiggins's study of the assassin in early modern theatre (1991), notes its significance in terms of its development of the Machiavellian villain (Lorenzo).[80] Wiggins also notes how 'Lorenzo uses his economic power to buy villainy, and Pedringano is the first hired assassin in English drama' (p. 103); he describes a form of the assassin plot that would become familiar in subsequent plays: the assassin becomes a 'victim of dramatic irony: he goes about his business, while we see his employer plotting to double-cross him' (pp. 132–3). Rebekah Owens's 2007 essay on 'Parody and *The Spanish Tragedy*' aims to offer a fresh perspective on the play by looking at the parodies and homages to the play that have been mentioned frequently in Kyd scholarship, but not necessarily given close attention. 'Though by no means hard facts', Owens concedes, 'parody and allusion can supply elusive glimpses as to the staging techniques and acting styles of the play.'[81] She notes how references to Kyd evolve as a kind of 'parodic short-hand for overly-emotive rhetoric' (p. 30) and, often, such references imply 'a sense of detachment' (p. 30); 'There is an accompanying awareness of this use of tropes and figures from the play to *represent* love or grief' [emphasis in the original] (p. 31).

Gregory M. Colon Semenza's previously mentioned essay begins in startling fashion, collapsing the historical distance between our time and Thomas Kyd's when he cites the story of the suicide of Carla Hochhalter, the mother of one of the survivors of the 1999 Columbine Massacre. Semenza notes how the media largely downplayed the story, coming as it did on the six-month anniversary of the shootings, at a time when the dominant narrative was one of hope and rebirth; he suggests that the human tendency is to 'impose comedic resolutions onto our news coverage, our philosophies and religions, and most of our art because we find too terrifying the idea that the cosmos may be indifferent to our suffering' (p. 50).

Revenge narratives bring their own consolations. Two years after Columbine, the US was shaken to its core by the destruction of the World Trade Centre. Allowing for an intervening period of gestation, then, it is perhaps no surprise to find that a few years later, at the beginning of May

2004, three of the top four slots at the US box office were occupied by revenge movies: *Man on Fire*, *Kill Bill Vol. 2* and *The Punisher*. President George Bush's rhetoric (such as his insistence to all other nations that 'you are either with us or with the terrorists') served to polarize debate and allow nothing but supposedly clear-cut morality, and a Hollywood-esque world of good guys and bad guys.[82] It is not difficult to see a connection between an apparent revival of interest in the revenger figure and the devastating national psychic trauma of 9/11. The revenger is someone prepared to go to any lengths in pursuit of 'natural' justice once the legal system breaks down, and the appeal of the man of action on the cinema screen (and, in this genre, he is almost invariably male), unencumbered by the obstacles, inconveniences and moral shackles of reality, is unmistakable.

Almost 450 years on from *The Spanish Tragedy*, the revenge narrative remains a familiar one in Western film culture (and beyond – notably in Korean cinema).[83] Most often, it still remains centred on the family – fathers avenging their sons in *Death Sentence* (2007) and *In the Bedroom* (2001); a mother her daughter in *Eye for an Eye* (1996); a husband his wife in *Memento* (2000); a woman her fiancé in *The Brave One* (2007); men their entire families in *Death Wish* (1974), *The Punisher* (2004) and *Law Abiding Citizen* (2009). Occasionally, though far less often, there are political overtones analogous to Kyd's explorations (*V for Vendetta*, 2005). Almost all of them have as a mainspring the protagonist's frustration at the state's failure to administer swift and effective justice (in *Law Abiding Citizen*, the protagonist aims to bring down the entire justice system, promising the District Attorney pitted against him, 'It's gonna be Biblical'). Amongst the easy comforts of some of these movies, however, one can trace a vein of more interesting film texts including Clint Eastwood's revisionist Western *Unforgiven* (1992), his contemporary revenge story *Mystic River* (2003), and the independent thriller *Blue Ruin* (2013), all of which are markedly more ambivalent about the spur to revenge as well as its aftermath. Crowning them all, perhaps, is the lamb-dressed-as-mutton cop procedural movie *Se7en* (1995): on the surface a tale of two police officers trying to catch a serial killer engaged on a spree fashioned around the seven deadly sins, it touches on a number of Kyd's themes. Just as Semenza admires the ability of *The Spanish Tragedy* to 'demonstrate at once the visceral appeal of revenge and the devastating repercussions of enacting it' (p. 50), so *Se7en* offers not only a profound meditation on the hollow echo of revenge, but on the meaning of damnation in a world without God. Some of Kyd's questions remain stubbornly unanswerable, 400 years on.

4

New Directions: Seneca and *The Spanish Tragedy*

Gordon Braden

A line in the first chorus of Seneca's *Agamemnon* foresees the killing of the king of Argos: 'placet in uulnus maxima ceruix' (line 100; the greatest neck invites wounding). In the original this is one item in a brisk catalogue illustrating something like a law of nature: 'sidunt ipso pondere magna' (line 88; great things fall of their own weight). In John Studley's Elizabethan translation (1566) the line stands out in its vindictive physicality: 'Whose neck is larded best his throat shall first be cut.'[1] The Latin is in comparison abstract, almost legalistic. Studley fleshes out *maxima* with the sarcastic grossness of 'larded', and with 'first' intensifies the sensation of finding oneself in a slaughterhouse (Seneca's *armenta uilia*, the plebeian cattle, roam free to live another day). The English fits twice as many words as the Latin into almost the same number of syllables, and does not feel wordy; a Latinate syntax with some of the musculature of Seneca's own prose tightens the impact. The moment catches the Elizabethan encounter with Senecan tragedy at its most intense: a savage premise acquiring newly forceful, even brutal embodiment in the vernacular. Studley's is one of a flurry of translations from the first decade of Elizabeth's reign, a kind of common enterprise centred on the Inns of Court. They are eventually gathered in a collected volume in 1581 including all the Senecan plays; the translators are not steadily up to the challenge, but they meet it often enough to anticipate some of the poetry flourishing in the playhouses of London before the 80s are done.

They join a taste of English Seneca incongruously available in Tottel's *Miscellany* (1557), the popular anthology that introduced Petrarchan love poetry to the reading public, where Thomas Wyatt's translation of the kingship chorus from *Thyestes* (lines 391–403) – 'Stand whoso list upon the slipper wheel | Of high estate ...' – is nested among the sonnets.[2] Wyatt's more personalized version of the same message, 'Who list his wealth and ease retain', stayed in manuscript; its first stanzas paraphrase Seneca's *Phaedra*, lines 1123–40, with a Latin tag from that passage – *circa regna tonat* (there is thunder throughout the kingdom) – as a refrain. That poem draws directly on Wyatt's own experience in prison under Henry VIII; its most harrowing lines – 'The bell tower showed me such sight | That in my head sticks day and night' – probably recall witnessing Anne Boleyn's decapitation.[3] They also recall the traumatized Messenger in Seneca's *Thyestes*: 'haeret in uultu trucis | imago facti' (lines 635–6; the image of the savage act clings to my sight), a Virgilian locution for erotic obsession ('haerent infixi pectore uultus | uerbaque', *Aeneid* 4.4–5; his face and words cling fast to her heart – Dido thinking of Aeneas) registering now the experience of indelible horror. Words for such experience are the central legacy of Senecan tragedy to Elizabethan literature.

Something like that has long been the common wisdom, and I think rightly, but getting it into focus has been a slow business. Objective but localized evidence that Elizabethan dramatists were aware of Senecan tragedy, or at least some of its *disiecta membra*, was offered by John W. Cunliffe at the end of the nineteenth century as proof 'that the influence of Seneca was paramount in the origin and development of Elizabethan tragedy'.⁴ That conclusion was sometimes accepted at face value, but the hastiness of the case became clear once examined closely. The arguments eventually mounted against it by Howard Baker and especially G. K. Hunter are strong and much better articulated.⁵ They are better informed (Seneca was not in fact a common presence on school curricula), and they draw on a fuller sense of what was going on in English culture at the time, not only of 'the other competing influences that were raining down' but also of the sheer messiness of literary history within which individual filiations can be impossible and pointless to trace: 'it is only in the compost-heap of history that new literatures breed' (Hunter, 162, 164). It does not help that Cunliffe's summary judgements are mainly aesthetic, and not very searchingly so: 'That Seneca misled English dramatists into violence and exaggeration cannot be denied; but these are faults which have their favourable side' (p. 125). An intuition that more is at stake than just that, that the case against which Baker and Hunter were arguing had never really been made, prompted two book-length affirmations of Seneca's relevance: my own, concerning European drama generally, but with attention to the special situation of England, and Robert Miola's, concerning Shakespeare.⁶ Neither of these is interested in rehabilitating the 'chronological view of the development of a separate genre "tragedy", at the head of which ... stood the tragedies of Seneca' (Hunter, 174); neither indeed is primarily polemical in intent, and they seem to have been sufficiently successful to have neutralized any controversial charge to the topic.

This opens up the welcome possibility of looking at the whole landscape afresh, with unprejudiced eyes, though in the way of these things it also seems to have drained some of the energy from the drive to do so. Colin Burrow, in a well-considered recent survey of Shakespeare's classicism, writes of 'an overwhelmingly *prima facie* case that Shakespeare read and was influenced by Seneca', based in great part on the fact that 'playwrights who influenced Shakespeare at the start of his career – Kyd, Marlowe, Peele – not only read but showed their audiences that they had read Senecan tragedy' – while also noting the virtual disappearance of this awareness from the critical mainstream: 'editors of Shakespeare's plays ... have been astonishingly reluctant to discuss Seneca in their introductions, or to record even evident and well-established parallels in their notes'.[7] Burrow attributes this lack to their being 'pushed by fashion into attaching more weight to the performance history of Shakespearian drama than to its origins' (p. 163), though the cause is not necessarily so specific. Engaged new work on the topic has certainly been done – Burrow's own chapter is not a perfunctory overview – but it has seemed more a matter of individual interest than part of an agenda for the profession at large.[8]

What attention there has been has concentrated, naturally enough, on Shakespeare, but Kyd (as Burrow signals) occupies an important place on the map of Seneca's fortunes on the Elizabethan public stage. He is for one thing the only major playwright to contribute to England's experiment in the neoclassical dramaturgy that was the influential French response to Seneca and his Greek predecessors, forecasting the theatre of Corneille and Racine. Kyd's *Cornelia* (1594), his translation of Robert Garnier's *Cornélie*, joins similar works by the Countess of Pembroke and others attempting to establish an English dramatic form of self-consciously stately speeches separated by choral odes, with minimal dialogue, action mostly off-stage, and some observance of Aristotelian unities.[9] The ambitions behind such efforts are serious ones, those of a 'literary *avant-garde*'.[10] This is the kind of drama which Philip Sidney was hoping for in his *Defense of Poetry*; the enterprise will eventually bear distinguished fruit in Milton's *Samson Agonistes*, though as an episode in English theatrical history it leads down a cul-de-sac. We do not know why Kyd took this turn in the last year of his life; Lukas Erne, in a well-informed recent assessment, unglamorously favours 'pecuniary need after getting into trouble with the authorities' (p. 215). As a translation *Cornelia* commands respect ('From the point of view of the language ... Kyd's maturest work';

Erne, 210), and as a companion piece to *The Spanish Tragedy* it completes a uniquely full address to the possibilities of dramatic form in its time and place.

Still, *The Spanish Tragedy* is the work that counts. It disputes with Marlowe's *Tamburlaine* a never-to-be-settled claim to be the first mature drama on the Elizabethan public stage. Its opening scene, in which the spirit of Revenge greets Andrea to join him in witnessing the eventual avenging of his own death (the two of them will, as he puts it in an overt invocation of classical dramatic form, 'serve for chorus in this tragedy' [1.1.91]), is an unmistakable homage to the first scene of Seneca's *Thyestes*, where Furia summons the father of Atreus and Thyestes to set things in motion; the important differences from classical precedent which Baker (pp. 113–18) and Hunter (pp. 195–6) note are only made visible by the allusion.[11] Before the first act is out, Kyd's ghost will have quoted Senecan tragedy quite specifically ('Come we for this ... ?' [1.5.1 = *Phaedra*, line 1213, 'In hoc redimus?']).[12] Other quotations, some of them in Latin, are sprinkled conspicuously throughout the play. Some of these would have been available in the numerous *florilegia* circulating at the time (Hieronimo may bring one on stage in 3.13), but not all of them; when Hieronimo asks 'What lesser liberty can kings afford | Than harmless silence?' (4.4.177–8), he is quoting lines that seem not to have been anthologized, from one of Seneca's signature exchanges on tyrannous *imperium* (*Oedipus*, lines 523–4: 'Tacere liceat. ulla libertas minor | a rege petitur?').[13] Some of these quotations are inexact. The deviations, which have been closely scrutinized by critics, may or may not be intentional; we may or may not be meant to notice them.

In more general terms, there is repeated imitation of the declamatory style of the speeches in Senecan tragedy: not just a matter of indebtedness to classical rhetoric, an indebtedness which has much wider roots and characterizes a much wider range of Renaissance literature, but specifically of the agenda of some of Seneca's most aggressive characters. His Medea, as

A. J. Boyle puts it, 'purloins the universe for the construction of herself':[14]

> quae Scylla, quae Carybdis Ausonium mare
> Siculumque sorbens quaeue anhelantem premens
> Titana tantis Aetna feruebit minis?
> non rapidus amnis, non procellosum mare
> pontusue coro saeuus aut uis ignium
> adiuta flatu possit inhibere impetum
> irasque nostras: sternam et euertam omnia.
>
> (*Medea*, lines 408–14)

> What Scylla, what Carybdis sucking in the Italian, the Sicilian sea, what Etna crushing the breathless Titan will seethe with such threats? No swift river, no stormy sea, or ocean enraged by the north wind or force of fire inflamed by the wind could restrain our power and rage: I will flatten and overturn everything.

What begins as a grandiose rhetorical question becomes a propulsive metaphor for the speaker's emotional state, and in the end self-incitement to comparably hyperbolic action. Seneca's characters are at times capable of making good on that incitement with harrowing literalness; by the time his Medea is through, Corinth is ablaze with a supernatural fire that water cannot quench. The Elizabethan theatre never goes that far, but Kyd made Hieronimo one of the most famous characters in its history with verbal performance that heads in that direction:

> The blustering winds, conspiring with my words,
> At my lament have moved the leafless trees,
> Disrobed the meadows of their flowered green,
> Made mountains marsh with spring-tides of my tears
> And broken through the brazen gates of hell. (3.7.5–9)

Marlowe's Tamburlaine talks like this too, with more confident belligerence: 'with our sun-bright armor as we march | We'll chase the stars from heaven' (*1 Tamburlaine* 2.3.22–3). The fustian extravagance associated with both roles became a common object of fun, but the mockery was testimony less to its obsolescence than to its ongoing popularity and influence; four different companies performed *The Spanish Tragedy* between 1592 and 1604. The tumultuous but carefully articulated *Schreirede* is present at what now seems like the real beginning of Elizabethan tragedy, a galvanizing revelation of what could be done on an almost bare stage with the right actor and the right words (in the right metre). Providing a model for those words, Roman tragedy passes on not just an isolated feature but 'the Senecan paradigm of the linguistic base of the Renaissance self, its foundation on the ability to construct and fix itself through and in language' (Boyle, 175). Local borrowings take place within the context of a momentous underlying affinity.

Appreciation has grown of another, not unrelated affinity. The two samples of Seneca from Wyatt's pen register it quite specifically: poetry from the court of a murderous autocrat. Key to recent interest in Senecan tragedy in its own right has been an understanding of its rootedness in the dangerous experience of the Roman privileged classes in Julio-Claudian Rome: evident occasionally in what look like specific allusions to current events, but on a deeper lever in the plays' deviations in form and story from Greek precedent. Those deviations were long seen as artistic blunders, but many of them now make sense as manifestations of the immense political and cultural change from contentiously pluralistic (and partly democratic) Greece to the unitary authority of imperial Rome – an authority that by Seneca's own time in the circles of power had become with seeming inevitability a matter of homicidal derangement at the top.[15] Renaissance interest in Seneca shows signs of being conditioned, consciously or intuitively, by a feeling that modern times and Seneca's had significant common ground in this regard. The first Renaissance work in the self-conscious category of 'tragedy', Albertino Mussato's Latin *Ecerinis* (1315), treats of Ezzelino da Romano, the murderous *signore* whom Jacob Burckhardt places at the head of his story of Renaissance Italy as the first of 'a crowd of tyrants' who announce a new phase in European political history.[16] It is a story that continues into the rest of Western Europe in the sixteenth century on an increasingly large scale with the imperial ambitions of the new absolutist states. Historians will come to describe what happens in more impersonal and long-range terms, but the states in question are almost all monarchical, and to the eyes of the time it is the age of princes and their intensifying power.

The dire abuse of that power is repeatedly cited as the prime substance of tragedy as a genre. Sidney affirms in his *Apology of Poetry* (sometime from the early 1580s) that it is 'high and excellent tragedy ... that maketh kings fear to be tyrants, and tyrants manifest their tyrannical humors'.[17] He illustrates the point with a quotation from Seneca's *Oedipus* (lines 705–6). His friend Fulke Greville claims the same purpose for his own efforts in the genre: 'to trace out the highways of ambitious governors, and to show in the practice of life that the more audacity, advantage and good success such sovereignties have, the more they hasten to their own desolation and ruin'.[18] Their slightly hopeful tone may owe something to the (relative) security of Elizabethan England (rightly or not, historians have tended to avoid referring to Elizabeth's 'judicial murders' as they do to her father's), but any sense of the ameliorative potential of art is missing from Justus Lipsius's *De Constantia* (1583/4), written in the terrorized Netherlands. The unrestrainable savagery of despots is the climactic topic in the torrential catalogue of contemporary miseries with which that work ends. Lipsius's influential book puts Senecan Neo-stoicism prominently on the intellectual map of late-sixteenth-century Europe; such a severe philosophy is what this age of tyrants calls for, though tyranny itself is no more than you should expect. Lipsius lifts a comedian's quip from the late classical *Historia Augusta* – 'All the good Princes can be inscribed on one small ring' (*Aurelian* 42.5–6) – and justifies it with a darkly total vision of human possibility:

It is, doubtless, ingrained in the human race to wield government insolently, and it is not easy to make measured use of that power that surpasses all measure. Those of us who complain about tyranny cherish the seeds of tyranny ourselves, enclosed within our hearts; and in many of us it is not the will to make these seeds sprout that is lacking, but the capacity.[19]

What Augustine calls *libido dominandi*, the lust for dominance, is the great tragic truth about our species.

The king on view in *The Spanish Tragedy* is not in any obvious way a tyrant, but as Katharine Maus has pointed out the lethal motor of Kyd's plot is still the arrogance of royal power, distributed among the presumptive heirs Lorenzo and Balthazar and displayed in their casually ruthless dealings with the family of Hieronimo.[20] Those dealings begin in disrespect and by the end of the second act have escalated to murder. Hieronimo has significant standing as Knight Marshall of Spain, though we hear of no title of nobility; Maus describes him as 'a civil servant who holds his position by virtue of expertise and hard work', one of those who 'seem to have realized a dream of upward mobility shared by many able men of undistinguished origins, including Kyd himself' (pp. xiv–xv). But that standing counts for nothing when it's most needed, and Hieronimo resigns his office when he realizes its uselessness and vows to 'go marshal up the fiends in hell' (3.12.76). He finds himself making unexpected common cause with Bel-imperia, who has royal rank but is similarly rendered helpless by her gender. Hieronimo's intolerable powerlessness both deranges him and motivates him to engineer a bloodbath that claims almost everyone concerned, including himself. At the end there are six dead bodies on stage, an apocalyptic killing floor for both masters and slaves.

A recent line of criticism has explored a more specific sense of the political import of the play. For most of the first half of the sixteenth century Spain had been ruled by Emperor Charles V, claimant to the title of successor to the emperors of classical Rome, and the reach of this authority from the Netherlands in the northwest to Nueva España across the Atlantic exceeded at least in theory (*plus ultra*) that of his ancient predecessors. Even with the fractioning of that authority in the latter half of the century Spain remained the dominant imperial power in a highly competitive field; the competition with England reached its spectacular flash point in 1588 with the launching of the Armada. Even if the play pre-dates the Armada (I agree with the fuzzy consensus for 1587), it seems perplexing that (aside from the English names given in connection with Hieronimo's dumb-show in 1.4) the historical context should be so vague; the King is never named, all the characters and events appear to be fictional, and with small changes we might as well be anywhere in more or less contemporary Europe.

It may not be as vague as it looks; in their recent Arden edition of the play Clara Calvo and Jesús Tronch demonstrate at length (pp. 30–40) how Kyd's apparently made-up plot reconfigures things that did indeed happen in recent Iberian history, and builds to something momentous that might have happened but didn't. The slaughter in the last act spares the somewhat clueless King but leaves both Spain and Portugal without clear dynastic succession. This, Calvo and Tronch suggest, is the reason for the last-minute, seemingly gratuitous killing of Castile, the King's brother. Elizabethan eyes would be quick to spot the dynastic rupture: a dangerous situation for a state to be in, especially an imperial one. Spain was never in fact without an heir apparent during the sixteenth century, but four of Philip II's sons died between 1568 and 1582, leaving only an unhealthy four-year-old. In 1584 Richard Hakluyt celebrates the prospect: 'surely the more I think of the Spanish monarchy, the more me thinketh it is like the empire of Alexander the Great, which grew up suddenly and suddenly upon his death was rent and dissolved for fault of lawful issue. In like manner the King of Spain ...'[21] Kyd contrives a plot bringing Spain to just that pass.

The thesis that Kyd's play is not just a tragedy that takes

place in Spain but the tragedy specifically of, as it happens, Seneca's homeland has been explored by a number of critics, beginning with Eugene D. Hill in 1985: 'identifying Seneca's nightmarish realm of political tragedy with the Spain of the Black Legend, Kyd has made the *energies* and the *implications* of Senecan tragedy available to the English popular stage' (pp. 159–60). At the centre of the destructive passions in play is the sexually active young heroine with the strange name, 'the beautiful, war-inspiring Idol of Empire'.[22] *The Spanish Tragedy* is a national tragedy of imperial desire: potentially a celebration of England's better fate, guided by 'another and truer imperial virgin' (Hill, 161), but also potentially a warning to avoid the same consequences. England is here in effect thinking through its own future. This theme has been explored aggressively by Frank Ardolino in *Apocalypse and Armada in Kyd's Spanish Tragedy* (1995), and with greater patience and nuance by Eric Griffin in two substantial articles (2001, 2009), and now in his contribution to this volume.

Pursuit of this topic, however, moves discussion away from Senecan tragedy – Griffin takes it for granted that *The Spanish Tragedy* is in 'the high Senecan style' ('Nationalism, the Black Legend', 359), but says so only in passing – and also from what has long been recognized as the documentable impact of Kyd's play itself.[23] Without that play, the history of English imperialism, even the history of England's relations with Spain, would scarcely look different; English theatrical history would be conspicuously altered. *The Spanish Tragedy* sets the distinctive pattern for the revenge tragedy, a uniquely English genre that remains dominant in English tragedy until the closing of the theatres. The general terrain of that history has been well mapped since Fredson Bowers's *Elizabethan Revenge Tragedy* (1940), but any sense that the books on it could be closed, and specifically on the question of what Senecan tragedy had to do with it, was dissipated by John Kerrigan's *Revenge Tragedy* (1996), which places the narrowly defined English Renaissance genre within a wide historical context (*Aeschylus to Armageddon* is his subtitle) but also raises provocative questions about Seneca and Christianity and the morality of revenge.

The Senecan dramatic corpus contains no revenge plays in the English mode. Revenge is one of the main motivations at work in them – for Atreus, Medea, Clytemnestra – but none of the plays in which they appear show the pattern that Emrys Jones argues influences Shakespeare at an early stage, in *Titus Andronicus*: 'intensification of tragic grief until it is converted into the ferociously gleeful pleasure of wrath spending itself in a hated victim'.[24] For that Jones goes to Greek tragedy, specifically Euripides's *Hecuba*, which (against the common wisdom) he thinks it likely Shakespeare knew. Seneca skips the first phase of the pattern, the hapless suffering that has nowhere to go. His avengers are fully empowered in their lethal mission by the time we meet them; his Medea, unlike her Attic predecessor, has already received her sentence of exile before the play begins, and her famous declaration of implacable aggression – 'Medea superest' (I still have Medea) – comes early, at line 166 of a 1027-line script. And, despite some forecasts, Seneca's avengers are triumphant and alive at the end of their plays, whereas Kyd's Hieronimo, after a very Senecan moment of self-affirmation – 'princes, now behold Hieronimo, | Author and actor in this tragedy' (4.4.145–6) – ends the bloody proceedings he has engineered by killing himself as well. He sets a very important precedent. In continental dramas on similar themes the aggrieved protagonist may or may not die in completing his mission, but the avenger in an English Renaissance revenge tragedy is firmly expected to. The audience certainly expects it; some avengers seem to expect it, and don't necessarily mind; 'my heart is satisfied', says Hieronimo as he faces his end (4.4.128). In those few instances when the avenger doesn't die, there is a reason the case is special, a point that is being made. Revenge on the English stage can be a passion of Senecan intensity ('drown the stage with tears | And cleave the general air with horrid speech, | Make mad the guilty and appal the free ...' [*Hamlet* 2.2.497–9]), but it is contained in an un-Senecan way.

The death sentence on the English avenger is a theatrical convention that proves extremely fruitful of compelling drama; it has seemed reasonable to many critics to infer from it a stern moral stand against private vengeance as a crime equivalent to murder, one that must not go unpunished, even (or perhaps especially) in a play. Such a stand would not have been an easy sell in a society in which, as Edward Muir memorably puts it, 'feuding constituted the principal framework for all social relationships'.[25] Behind the conflicts driving revenge tragedy we can sense legal and social dimensions having to do with the monarchy's centralization of justice and residual claims of aristocratic privilege, but the most frequently cited strictures against vengeance are religious: Christianity forbids it as a mortal sin. In a much-studied soliloquy near the centre of *The Spanish Tragedy* (3.13.1–44) Hieronimo seems to confront the conflict of traditions that bear down on his situation. He begins with what sounds like a vow to take justice into his own hands – '*Vindicta mihi*' – and might even be aligning himself with Nero (*Octavia* 849: 'haec uindicta debetur mihi', this is the vengeance owed to me); but he is actually quoting ('Mihi uindicta' in the Vulgate) St. Paul to exactly contrary effect: 'Dearly beloved, avenge not yourselves, but give place unto wrath. For it is written, Vengeance is mine, I will repay, sayeth the Lord' (Rom. 12.19; Geneva Bible). This is indeed the classic prooftext for an uncompromising Christian line on private revenge, and Hieronimo's next words make it clear that this is what is on his mind:

> Ay, heaven will be revenged of every ill,
> Nor will they suffer murder unrepaid.
> Then stay, Hieronimo, attend their will,
> For mortal men may not appoint their time. (2–5)

He apparently has talked himself out of it. Yet in his next line he is (perhaps because of the book in his hand) quoting Senecan tragedy, this time Clytemnestra: '*Per scelus semper tutum est sceleribus iter*' (*Agamemnon*, line 115, inconsequentially rephrased: The safe route for crimes is always through crimes). His application of this text is uncompromisingly retaliatory: 'Strike, and strike home, where wrong is offered thee' (7). As the speech proceeds he quotes Senecan tragedy three more times, twice in Latin and once in English, and at the finish he is set on his vindictive path, his only restraint being tactical:

> thou must enjoin
> Thine eyes to observation and thy tongue
> To milder speeches than thy spirit affords ...
> Till to revenge thou know when, where, and how.
> (39–41, 44)

A Christian soul is fatally seduced by 'un-Christian sophistry'.[26]

There have been numerous readings of the speech in more or less these terms – by me, among others – but this is the contrast of Christian and pagan values that Kerrigan wishes to upset: 'the value-systems which now dominate the West do not include anything so simple as a conflict between "pagan" anger and Christian love. ... There are varieties and traditions of anger, and in this ... we are products of that great confluence of classical and Christian ideas which gathered during the Renaissance.'[27] Romans 12.19 can be read differently depending on how you relate it to the Old Testament verse where 'it is written': 'Vengeance and recompense are mine ... for the day of ... destruction is at hand' (Deut. 32.35). What Kerrigan sees in Romans is not a contrast between the New and the Old, but an elision of forbidden 'wrath' into divinely sanctioned 'vengeance', 'bringing Paul's God closer to the wrath-dealing Jehovah of the Pentateuch'; with that, 'retributing wrong becomes consistent with a divine promise ... and an avenger can regard himself as God's agent' (p. 120). Kerrigan's immediate destinations here are *Paradise Lost* and *King Lear*; when he later discusses Hieronimo's soliloquy in 3.13 he doesn't dispute that Romans 12.19

is deployed there as a restraint on his vindictive passions (pp. 177–8). But he clearly thinks the initial associations of '*Vindicta mihi*' are not irrelevant, dramatically or theologically; the Pauline passage is enough of an endorsement of revenge that it indeed 'encouraged the efflorescence of English revenge tragedy' (p. 120). It was, Kerrigan suggests, Christian influence that led Jasper Heywood to add a fiery new speech at the end of his translation of *Thyestes* in which Thyestes prays for a highly detailed vengeance to be visited on Atreus. The speech expands on a curt prediction (a line and a half in the Latin) which Seneca doesn't even allow to be the play's final word; that goes to the still triumphant Atreus. The deities named in the new speech are pagan, but Kerrigan argues that the speech's dynamics are those of a committed Christian (Heywood was about to take the dangerous step of joining the Society of Jesus) who believes in the efficacy of prayers to a just God capable of vindictive anger. Heywood's *Schreirede* is Senecan in its rhetorical scope, but it's a speech Seneca didn't write. The classical writer, Heywood seems to have thought, didn't go far enough; not doing so, Seneca left his universe without hope.

The notion that the Christian/pagan contrast is a contrast between love and anger is also complicated by the extreme position – even by classical standards – that Seneca takes in his prose works against anger. For the wise man (*sapiens*), anger (*ira*) is absolutely forbidden, and vengeance is never contemplated. It is precisely from a Senecan perspective that the sound and fury of Senecan tragedy is, insofar as it signifies anything, a wholly negative *exemplum*, the spectacle of what happens if you give an inch. But for just that reason, the pacificism of the philosophy is a doctrine that offers no comfort. The reason the wise man cannot be angry at anything is that if he allowed it he would be angry at everything: 'A wise man will not stop being angry if once he starts. ... If you want the wise man to be as angry as the indignity of crimes demands, he would have to become not angry but insane [*insaniendum*]' (*De Ira* 2.9.1, 4). The wise man is an explosion waiting to happen. As for vengeance: 'That great soul, one with true self-knowledge, does not revenge injury because it does not perceive it' (*De Ira* 3.5.7–8; cited by Kerrigan, 115). A world in which the strict alternatives are demented rage and inhuman coldness is a bleak one, not in any ordinary sense of the term liveable. For relief from this bleakness, Kerrigan gives innovative attention to *De Beneficiis*, the longest but possibly least consulted of Seneca's moral essays.[28] Its seven books testify to a faith only briefly signalled in *De Ira*: 'Human life rests on benefaction and concord, and is bound in allegiance and communal support, not by terror but by mutual love' (1.5.3). Yet to come to *De Beneficiis* from the tragedies is to see that 'the psychology of Senecan beneficence resembles that of *furor* to the extent that excess is integral to both' (Kerrigan, 134), since the generosity involved is not just obligatory but competitive: 'who owes a debt of gratitude never catches up except by outdoing' (*De Beneficiis* 1.4.3), exactly the principle Atreus applies to vengeance ('scelera non ulcisceris, | nisi uincis' [*Thyestes*, lines 195–6], you do not avenge crime unless you surpass it). Failure to prevail in the game of gift giving is perceived as ingratitude, not a social misstep but *facinus*, another word for crime, the worst crime in a nasty list (1.10.4), and a strong incitement to retaliation. 'The law of benefits is a difficult channel.'[29] *De Beneficiis* radiates not the warmth of communal belonging but the edgy contentiousness of Rome's endangered upper class. Kerrigan thinks the treatise has a lot to do with *Timon of Athens* and *King Lear*; for the latter play, so does Burrow (pp. 195–9).

In other words, the contrast 'between "pagan" anger and Christian love' may be an oversimplification, but there is still something significantly harsher about the pagan heritage, at least as mediated by Seneca. I think part of what we want to know about Seneca's 'influence' is how much of it involves an active appetite for a harshness beyond Christian recuperation. The pattern for English revenge tragedy is a particularly cruel one: the avenger will destroy himself achieving justice. That role is provided for in Christian terms by the concept of *flagellum*

Dei, the scourge of God, who will be the instrument of God's will, only to be in the end rightly destroyed by the God whose ends he has served. The theory has Old Testament roots (Isa. 10.5–16); it is invoked in the sixteenth century to reassure victims of contemporary tyrants that the outrages visited upon them serve some higher end and will themselves eventually be avenged.[30] The term is used repeatedly in *Tamburlaine*, and shows up on the title-page of the first printed text. It occurs only occasionally in revenge tragedy, though there is a famous instance in *Hamlet* (3.4.173).[31] It applies conceptually to the whole genre as it develops in England, but with a different focus: not on the experience of the victims but on that of the scourge who does God's will but is beyond the reach of His mercy. 'For necessary is it that example of it happen', writes one theorist of the violence of the likes of Tamburlaine, 'but woe be unto him by whom it happens.'[32] In revenge tragedy, that woe is at the centre, the main point of view.

Extensive critical debates about the redemptive sympathy we do or do not feel for the avenger take place within the cruel terrain mandated by the genre: terrain where there may be a kind of satisfaction perhaps, but no redemption. The last word we have on Hieronimo's fate isn't actually all that bad – 'I'll lead Hieronimo where Orpheus plays, | Adding sweet pleasure to eternal days' (4.5.23–4) – but this is the pagan underworld, a circumstance that can be interpreted in different ways; no matter how you interpret it, it gets little purchase dramatically on the spectacle of Hieronimo's woe. The most careful reading of his soliloquy in 3.13, by Scott McMillin, yields one of the most despairing accounts of that woe as a 'lively form of death' (3.2.2): 'from the moment he discovers his dead son's corpse ... he knows that his son's death is the figure of his own death. ... His heart is dead, his life is his dead son.' His only purpose is to 'preserve himself until he can arrange for suicide and revenge to coincide. ... He intends to die in the achievement of revenge, and his "safety" is a matter of playing for time until the right combination of action and self-loss can be found.'[33] 'Safety' translates a word in one of Hieronimo's

Latin quotations from Seneca, *salus* (*Troades*, line 511). It is also the word for salvation in the Christian sense, but that sense no longer has any relevance to his state. McMillin argues that Hieronimo systematically misconstrues the texts he quotes, but in doing so actually absorbs a desperate message from their context in Senecan tragedy: each of the speakers 'is caught on the verge of an extremity in which one's act of saving becomes self-destructive'; 'preservation and loss, at moments of extremity, are figures of each other' (p. 205). Beyond that suicidal calculus there is nothing of importance.

There are less hopeless subtexts to Hieronimo's suffering; elsewhere in this volume Tom Rutter discusses the ways in which Virgilian references (also invoked by Hill) work with Christian ones to locate the action not in hell but purgatory. But the texts in 3.13 are explicitly Senecan, and I suggest that part of what is at stake in the question of Senecan influence on English Renaissance drama is the degree to which we are willing to accept a starkly nihilistic message. Hunter gathers many of his arguments about Seneca and the Elizabethans under the general claim that the latter were Christian and the former was not: 'this distinction has not always been allowed the central importance it undoubtedly has to explain both the attraction of Seneca for the Elizabethans and the inevitability of their failure to be like him' (p. 179). Telling instances of that failure abound. Perhaps the single most disturbing passage in Seneca for Renaissance Christian readers is the chorus on death from the *Troades*: 'Post mortem nihil est ipsaque mors nihil' (line 397; after death there is nothing, and death itself is nothing).[34] Heywood, bringing the play into English for the first time (1559), makes this notorious line almost unrecognizable: 'nothing tarry'th after dying day' (*Elizabethan Seneca*, 100) – less mistranslation than a seemingly instinctual inability to accept or even perceive what's being said. Hunter treats such deflections as evidence of the sturdiness of Christian faith in the period (e.g. p. 166), but that is not the only way to see them. We need not assume that the evaded possibility isn't capable of having its impact; the evasion itself suggests the impact. One of the supreme achievements of English Renaissance drama I think draws its power from both the Christianization of the Senecan legacy and the recovery of its bleakness.

Shakespeare's Lear, awaking at long last from his madness – 'Where have I been? Where am I? Fair daylight?' (*King Lear* 4.7.52) – remembers the famous movement of Seneca's Hercules as he similarly regains consciousness: 'Quis hic locus, quae regio, quae mundi plaga? | ubi sum?' (*Hercules Furens*, lines 1137–8; what place is this, what country, what part of the world? where am I?). Neither character knows what he will be seeing, but the similarity of language dramatizes a momentous difference of context.[35] Hercules will discover the bodies of the wife and children whom he has murdered; Lear will discover the living child whom he had every reason to believe he had lost forever. Cordelia, there in front of him, offers him an enduring love which he has not earned but has failed to destroy: in the setting of prehistoric pagan Britain, she embodies a Christian experience of divine grace more luminously than any other character in Shakespeare. But it is a cruel set up. Lear finds her again only to lose her irrevocably – 'thou'lt come no more, | Never, never, never, never, never' (5.3.306–7) – and to assault the gods in what he knows is impotent rage: 'Howl, howl, howl, howl! O, you are men of stones! | Had I your tongues and eyes, I'd use them so | That heaven's vault should crack' (2.3.225–7). Appalled onlookers can only ask, 'Is this the promised end? | Or image of that horror?' (5.3.261–2). The play containing Shakespeare's most blessed moment comes to this. Commentators from Edward Capell on have found the language of those final questions Biblical, invoking the last judgement prophesied by Jesus in the Gospels and John in Revelations, but the second of them points in another direction. Its slightly odd phrasing mimics the Senecan passage that stuck in Wyatt's head – 'trucis | imago facti', the image of the savage act – and the very Senecan 'horror' is not a word of Biblical resonance.[36] The translators of the Geneva and King James Bibles use that word nowhere in the New Testament, not even in Revelations, and rarely in the Old. It is the idiom of an un-Christian apocalypse, one that is all darkness.

5

New Directions: Geopolitics and *The Spanish Tragedy*

Eric Griffin

The most consequential geopolitical development of the last quarter of the sixteenth century was Philip II's consolidation of Portugal and its overseas possessions within the Spanish Empire. Brought on by his nephew Sebastian I's presumed death in the Battle of the Three Kings, as the culminating engagement of Portugal's ill-starred Moroccan expedition soon became known, the loss so traumatized the Portuguese nation-state that it rendered union with Iberia's Spanish kingdoms a virtual necessity.[1] The ensuing dynastic realignment precipitated a structural shift. Philip II's decisiveness in the wake of the Portuguese disaster had given birth to history's first truly global power, a 'Universal Monarchy' upon which the sun never set.[2] This is the historical moment that inspired Thomas Kyd's *Spanish Tragedy*.

The play Kyd composed during the 1580s is a tragedy of 'the Spains', as the peninsular kingdoms styled themselves during the sixty years of their political union, 1580–1640;[3] among *The Spanish Tragedy*'s 'firsts' is thus its attempt to grapple dramatically with the meaning of the Iberian incorporation.[4] Indeed, this foundational drama, which commanded audiences in England and abroad during nearly the entire epoch, construes the joining of the Iberian crowns as the historical basis upon which a tragedy exploring the religio-political implications of these period geopolitics could be raised.

This chapter attempts to demonstrate how and why the historical circumstances in which *The Spanish Tragedy* was written, performed, published and revised matter. After establishing the play's late-sixteenth century grounding – as suggested by both the argument of its earliest print edition and contemporary constructions of England's Iberian rivals – it will explore several of the ways in which emendation by later playwrights, one of whom is now believed to have been William Shakespeare, re-tuned Kyd's 'original' for audiences receiving the play amid the shifting geopolitical currents of the seventeenth century.

I

That Kyd imagines a unified Iberia is observable in the *dramatis personae* pages accompanying modern editions.[5] The highest-ranking figure in *The Spanish Tragedy* is the apparently childless King of Spain. Below him in status comes his brother, the Duke of Castile, whose son Lorenzo and daughter Bel-imperia represent Spain's 'whole succeeding hope' (4.4.203). Ranking above Castile and his offspring, but below the Spanish king, is the Viceroy of Portugal, whose son and heir, Balthazar, will be betrothed to Bel-imperia, with the Viceroy's brother Don Pedro one step down among the Portuguese nobility. Beneath all of these are the play's other nobles and courtiers, including the deceased Don Andrea and his friend Horatio, son of the play's vengeful agent of justice, Hieronimo, Knight-Marshall of Spain. That Portugal is ruled in the play by a viceroy rather than by a king indicates that a joining of the Spanish and Portuguese crowns is a precondition of the drama. Although Kyd's casting does not represent actual historical figures, he stages a viceregal arrangement rooted in history. Following the brief period of Philip II's personal rule, during which time the Spanish king resided in Lisbon as Philip I of Portugal, that kingdom was administered until 1640 either by a viceroy or a council comprised of native governors.[6]

The military action that sets the play's argument in motion does not attempt to portray accurately the Battle of Alcantara, the Spanish victory that sealed the Iberian union. But Kyd includes enough detail reminiscent of the event to evoke the geopolitical circumstances of the 1580s as noted in period sources.[7] Like the Alcantara engagement, the battle has taken place 'Where Spain and Portingale do jointly knit / Their frontiers, leaning on each other's bound' (1.2.22–3), even as the rhetorical structure Kyd's Castilian general voices in these lines establishes Hispano-Lusitanian proximity and interconnection.

Still, the outcome of *The Spanish Tragedy*'s opening conflict differs significantly from the consequences of the actual campaign. In the aftermath of Kyd's battle, no surviving pretender awaits an opportunity to reclaim the Portuguese throne, as was the case with the historical Dom Antonio of Avis, nor has the border-clash been associated with a struggle for Portuguese independence. Instead, the strife has been occasioned by Portugal's withholding of taxes due the Castilian crown. Kyd does not portray this confrontation as an act of national rebellion; rather, the Portuguese Viceroy's refusal to pay 'Tribute and wonted homage' (1.2.9) is figured as an indication of bad faith and personal hubris. In the words of Kyd's Viceroy, who, at this moment in the play, believes his son Prince Balthazar to have been killed in the engagement, '[m]y late ambition' occasioned the 'bloody wars' and death of 'my sweet and only son' (1.3.33–8). The Viceroy soon intensifies the hubris topos:

> Thou false, unkind, unthankful, traitorous beast,
> Wherein had Balthazar offended thee
> That thou shouldst thus betray him to our foes?
> Was't Spanish gold that bleared so thine eyes
> That thou couldst see no part of our deserts?
> Perchance, because thou art Terceira's lord,
> Thou hadst some hope to wear this diadem,
> If first my son and then myself were slain;
> But thy ambitious thought shall break thy neck.
> Ay, this was it that made thee spill his blood;
> But I'll now wear it till thy blood be spilt. (1.3.77–87)

Even as he deploys the period commonplace that identified desire for 'Spanish gold' as a source of Europe's geopolitical ills, the very flaw Kyd's Portuguese Viceroy recognizes in himself – the 'ambitious thought' that had divided him from his lord, the King of Castile – gives him cause to suspect like ambition and duplicity in the apparently guiltless Alexandro of Terceira.

Although in *The Spanish Tragedy* 'Terceira's lord' is not the Portuguese claimant, it does appear at this moment that Kyd alludes to contemporary geopolitics. Following Spain's victory at Alcantara, it was at Terceira in the Azores that a Portuguese garrison – backed by a French and English naval operation – held out against a Spanish force led by the Marques of Santa Cruz, whose brilliant victory would earn him the command of Philip II's Enterprise of England.[8] Among Portugal's provinces, only this island colony had demonstrated the will to back native son, Dom Antonio, the Prior of Crato, who at the time of *The Spanish Tragedy*'s production was frequenting the courts of both England and France in an effort to challenge the Spanish succession.[9]

More telling than this opening act topicality, though, is the way in which Kyd's scene mobilizes the one attribution that, in a Europe envious of its dynastic manoeuvring and geopolitical attainments, often appeared to characterize the ethos of Hapsburg Spain, that of boundless Ambition. Whereas a theme so commonplace as 'aspiring pride', which inheres in all tragedy, Classical and Renaissance alike, may initially appear reductive, it bears recalling that in the political discourse of the sixteenth century an incalculable number of polemics attribute many of Europe's geopolitical problems to Spanish Ambition.[10] Indeed, the contemporary source that might be expected to shed significant light on *The Spanish Tragedy*, *The Explanation of the True and Lawfull Right and Tytle, of the Moste Excellent Prince Anthonie* (1585), is among those that build most insistently upon this topos. Reporting the outcome of the Terceira engagement, the treatise circulated in Dom Antonio's name also blasts the 'excessive and unmeasurable ambition' of 'the King of Castile', who 'would else in tract of tyme, invade not only all Christiandom, but also the rest of the world, & that under the faire colour of maintaining the Catholicke Romish religion ... might easily and freely spred his armies over England, Germany, France & other nations'.[11]

The topic of naked Spanish Ambition – which would earn Philip II the appellation 'Spanish Nimrod'[12] – predates the confessional conflict that gave rise to the Armada crisis. So do *The Explanation*'s allegations linking Spanish Machiavellian designs to dominate 'all Christiandom' and 'the rest of the world as well' by advancing 'under the colour of maintaining the Catholick Romish religion'. Propagandist arguments along these lines evidence lines of descent that can be traced through Philip's father, the Holy Roman Emperor Charles V, at least as far back as his great-grandfather, Ferdinand II 'the Catholic', who, it may be recalled, was Machiavelli's exemplary 'New Prince'.[13] These three Spanish kings – Ferdinand of Aragon, Charles V, and Philip II – if not 'better' at geopolitical manoeuvring than their European neighbours, summoned more ideological drive: an impulse commemorated in the Spanish Hapsburgs' *Plus Ultre* iconography, to which Philip added *Non Sufficit Orbis* in celebration of his peninsular union.[14] This insatiable imperial desire – the ethos of Empire: 'yet still further', 'the world is not enough' – also drives the argument of *The Spanish Tragedy*.

II

That Kyd's argument turns on the topos of Empire is signalled the moment Don Andrea introduces himself to begin act one:

> When this eternal substance of my soul
> Did live imprison'd in my wanton flesh,
> Each in their function serving other's need,
> I was a courtier in the Spanish court.
> My name was Don Andrea, my descent,
> Thought not ignoble, yet inferior far
> To gracious fortunes of my tender youth:
> For there in prime and pride of all my years,
> By duteous service and deserving love,
> In secret I possess'd a worthy dame,
> Which hight sweet Bel-imperia by name. (1.1.1–10)

Although criticism has tended to read 'sweet Bel-imperia' as a princess in the literal sense, it has less often been noted that there is something terrible about her beauty. Don Andrea may boast, 'In secret I possess'd a worthy dame' (1.1.9), but his remark is the first instantiation of a pattern: rather than possessing her, one by one, each of the play's Dons, first Andrea, then Horatio, next Balthasar, and finally, even Hieronimo, are possessed by Bel-imperia. As indicated by Don Andrea, 'who for his love tried fortune of the wars, / and by war's fortune sought both love and life' (1.1.39–40), and emphasized again when Horatio and Bel-imperia commence their revenge plot and their love-making with 'Then thus begin our wars' (2.4.35) – even as Horatio is about to be brutally slain – the argument of Kyd's tragedy suggests that there is something perilously seductive about his imperial mistress's charms. As her name indicates, 'Bel-imperia' is a double, related both to *bellum*, or war, and to *belle*, or beauty. An allegorical figure as much as a princess in a 'real' or literal sense, the attention drawn to her name in the opening speech announces a web of significance associating the play's argument with Empire as the concept governing its action, as in fact it governed contemporary geopolitics.[15]

The Spanish Tragedy also represents an empire jealous of its possessions. Kyd's Spanish king states this bluntly in act one: 'Now, lordings, fall to. Spain is Portugal, / And Portugal is Spain' (1.4.132–3). Still, as his greeting to his counterparts at Bel-imperia's betrothal in act three shows, the King of Spain's command does recognize Portugal's key role in the attainment of a monarchy that, knitted together with his own kingdoms, has attained global dominion:

> And now to meet these Portuguese,
> For as we now are, so sometimes were these,
> Kings and commanders of the western Indies.
> Welcome, brave viceroy, to the court of Spain,
> And welcome all his honourable train. (3.14.5-9)

If *The Spanish Tragedy* explores Empire's beautiful and warlike compulsions, its representation of the imperial ethos does not suggest that the Spanish nation alone is drawn to her incorporative attractions. Nor does it necessarily follow, as is sometimes suggested, that the desire for imperial expansion represented in the play replicates period Hispanophobia.[16] Although its acquisitive accomplishments in the early stages of the colonial era outstripped those of its neighbours, Spain was far from singular in its embrace of the age's twin, and somewhat contradictory geopolitical inclinations: national self-definition and imperial incorporation.[17] As the play recognizes, the first phase of European overseas expansion had seen the Portuguese take the lead. Nor were the Spanish singular in drawing lessons from the most exemplary expansionist model history had yet revealed. As Anthony Pagden observes,

> It was, above all, Rome, which provided the ideologues of the colonial systems of Spain, Britain and France with the language, and political models they required, for the *Imperium romanum* has always had a unique place in the

political imagination of Western Europe. Not only was it believed to have been the largest and most powerful community on earth, it had also been endowed by a succession of writers with a distinct, sometimes divinely inspired purpose.'[18]

Nonetheless, of Europe's imperial aspirants only Spain could claim to have equalled, even to have surpassed, the ancient Roman precedent. With the son and heir to Charles V ruling history's first truly global empire, a culture-wide emulation of the 'Spanish fashion' came to dominate many fields of late-sixteenth and early-seventeenth century European life.[19] *The Spanish Tragedy* reflects this contemporary Hispanophilia as much as it does the Hispanophobia criticism has strained to hear in the play's argument.

III

Among the sixteenth century's most ardent Hispanophiles, Kyd's elder English contemporary, the important Tudor humanist, historiographer, astronomer, geographer and mathematician Thomas Blundeville (c. 1522–c. 1606) assessed Spain's geopolitical dominance.[20] A member of the elite circle associated with the famous Elizabethan magus John Dee, Blundeville first invoked 'Tarraconensis, Lusitania and Betica', the tripartite division of Roman Hispania following the imperial conquests of Augustus, and then delineated the familiar, modern Iberian subdivisions: 'Castilia, Aragon, Portugall, Gallicea, Lyon, Navarra, Toledo, Valentia, Murcia, Granado, Cordoba, and Algarbia [the Algarve]'.[21] Had these territories been sooner 'reduced to one bodie of a Realme' as the Spanish provinces 'be at this houre', Blundeville argued, Spain would much earlier have been what it had lately become, 'without doubt one of the most mightie and puissant kingdomes of *Europe*' (p. 251). Listing the achievements of the Iberian peoples, who were 'renowned in the art militare, and in feates of warre', Blundeville observed how, in the present age, the 'provinces of Spaine are become very rich and mightie, by reason of their nauigatio~ into *America, Africa, Arabia, Persia, India*, the Iles *Moluecas* and *China*, in which Prouinces (*China* excepted) the king of *Spaine* possesseth manie countries that be rich and of great power, and many townes and fortresses ... round about the earth' (p. 251).

Modern scholarship has often constructed early modern Iberia much in the way Blundeville does, explaining its global attainments in terms of the region's emergence from its medieval re-conquest as a society organized for war. Less commonly recalled is Iberia's intellectual heritage, which the Englishman was also keen to invoke. In Blundeville's geography, Spain's militarists and mariners walk hand-in-hand with its 'great Clearkes'. Alongside influential sixteenth-century humanists such as Juan Luís Vives of Valencia, Benito Arías Montano of Extremadura, and Johannes Osorio of Portugal, a trio that may or may not indicate Roman Catholic sympathies on his part, Blundeville traces a 'Spanish' intellectual tradition reaching back to the important Roman authorities who were also Iberian: Seneca, Quintilian, Lucian and Martial (p. 251).

That Blundeville gives Seneca pride of place among these Roman Spaniards suggests a need to re-situate the problem of *The Spanish Tragedy*'s Senecan influence, explored by Gordon Braden and Edel Semple in these pages, within the geopolitical context. Working back from this literary lineage to the geographical perspective Blundeville advances, an unremarked Senecan association comes into view, one that ought to be weighed in relation to *The Spanish Tragedy*'s geopolitical calculus.

From the earliest moments of Spain's New World primacy, all available precedents – whether historical, legal, philosophical, or theological – had been marshalled in order to justify expanding imperial dominion. However much contemporary rivals objected to Spanish methods and protectionist policies, they understood that the appeal to 'heavenly favour', based on the reward of the discoveries themselves, constituted perhaps Spain's most persuasive argument. Among the ancient authorities seized upon as prophetic of Iberia's rise to international prominence was none other than the 'Spanish' philosopher-playwright Seneca. As the early historian of the New World Peter Martyr d' Anghiera (1457–1626) argued in *De Orbe Novo* (Alcalá, 1530), Seneca appeared to have predicted the Spanish discoveries in a prophetic passage from the act two chorus of his *Medea*. As Englished by Richard Eden in 1555, Martyr made this claim:

> All this I speake consyderynge the sayinge of the poet Seneca in his tragedie of Medea, where his woordes seeme in all poyntes to agree with the discoverynge of the Indies founde of late by Chrystofer Colon & the Spanyardes, The woordes of Seneca, are these,
> Venient annis
> Saecula feris, quibus Oceanus
> Vincula rerum laxet, et ingens
> Pateat tellus, Tiphisq[ue] novos
> Detegat orbes,
> Nec sit terries ultima Thyle.
> That is to saye: There shall come worldes in late yeares, in the which the Ocean shall unlose the bondes of thynges, and a great lande shall appeare. Also Typhis (that is navigation) shall discover newe worldes: And Thyle shall not be the furthest lande.[22]

Maintaining the legitimacy of Spain's extension of the boundaries of civilization beyond 'the furthest land', 'Thyle' (or Thule), arguments by geographer-theologians such as the Jesuit José de Acosta (1539–1600) and the Dominican Tomasso de Campanella (1568–1639) would muster Senecan prophecy in support of a Universal Monarchy well into the seventeenth century.[23] Not surprisingly, Spain's English opponents, Sir Francis Bacon (1561–1626) among them, countered that the Senecan 'prophesy of the discovery of America' was no 'divination', but among the sort of 'impostures' hatched by 'idle and crafty brains, merely contrived and feigned, after the event passed'.[24] That Bacon sought to discover the Senecan precedent as a falsehood suggests the degree to which the age had given it purchase. When *The Spanish Tragedy*'s Castilian king calls together the play's Iberian nobles as 'Kings and commanders of the western Indies' (3.14.7), it would appear that Kyd enacts the geopolitical prophecy contemporaries accorded Seneca's *Medea*.

While the importance of this expanded Senecan intertext bears significant implications for *The Spanish Tragedy*'s relation to contemporary geopolitics, it is also likely that Kyd, following the Spanish fashion, wrote about contemporary Spain in a Senecan mode because Senecanism, *El Senequismo*, was a recognizable hallmark of the Iberian literary and philosophical landscape. From the fifteenth century onward, no European culture bore the influence of Seneca more thoroughly than did Renaissance Iberia, where exemplary Senecan stoicism was enfolded within a widely observed habitus of 'honour'. Within this complex, slights against honour demanded acts of retribution, and although Seneca himself proscribed the sort of vengeance enacted by his Renaissance imitators, the Senecan focus on the demands of justice led to his association with its dictates, an obvious feature of the developing revenge genre.[25] While *The Spanish Tragedy* has often been interpreted in relation to excessive devotion to this 'virtue' – which in Spain, as elsewhere in Mediterranean feudal society, coalesced as a positive cultural value[26] – criticism has failed to observe that Kyd's choice to write a tragedy about Spain in the Senecan mode constitutes a significant Hispanophilic gesture. By embodying in a richly ambivalent way a society that could be construed as bearing simultaneously the marks of Senecan greatness and the failings of hubristic blindness, Kyd was able to write against the reductively Hispanophobic currents that increasingly dominated the era's geopolitical discourse. Indeed, when *The Spanish Tragedy* is set against the backdrop of the geopolitical invective that has come to be known as the Black Legend of Spanish Cruelty, the utterly different quality of Kyd's representation of Spain becomes patent.[27]

IV

Nevertheless, as *The Spanish Tragedy* moved through time its reception was tempered by the Hispanophobic attitudes typical of the age in which it flourished on stage and in print. It was clear to numerous contemporary observers that the consolidation of the Iberian kingdoms under one crown had raised the hegemonic potential of the burgeoning Spanish Empire beyond that of even imperial Rome.

As directly descended from the Romans, the Spanish viewed themselves as having been accorded the grace of extending Rome's *imperium*, their global navigations and conquests completing the process their ancestors had begun. Long-cherished interpretations of St. Augustine's theory of the Four World Monarchies added Judeo-Christian authority to their claims, interpreting the Old Testament Book of Daniel so as to mark the progress of History in relation to a hallowed succession of four global empires: Babylon, Persia, Greece, and Rome.[28] Together, these precedents elevated the Iberian consolidation to the apocalyptic plane upon which contemporaries often placed its significance.

Despite predicting different outcomes, Catholic and Protestant theorists drew similarly upon ancient authorities in their efforts to read the workings of Providence; for both, the marriage of Biblical and Roman precedents made historical divination possible.[29] If Christian exegetes traditionally identified Rome as the terminating world kingdom, late-Renaissance panegyrists could claim that it was the Spanish, as heirs to the empire of Caesar Augustus, who had been chosen 'to be the agents of the final unification of the world'.[30] The possibility of a global 'British Impire',[31] to borrow John

Dee's coinage, may have existed in potentia, but Spain's was the exemplary *translatio imperii* of the early modern period: from Troy to Rome via the line of Aeneas, from Rome to the Spanish Hapsburgs by way of Augustus.[32]

An apocalyptic vision countering England's Spanish contemporaries has come to be associated with Thomas Kyd. Following the line of critical thought initiated by S. F. Johnson, numerous critics, myself included, have read the play in light of the Protestant providentialism Kyd arguably encodes.[33] Although Eugene Hill's often cited 'Senecan and Virgilian Perspectives in *The Spanish Tragedy*' (1985) neglects to link Seneca's Medean prophecy to the play, the essay suggests several ways that Kyd links 'Senecan and Vergilian forms and themes' in order to enact 'an historical rearticulation of privileged cultural models', or *translatio studii*, which works to represent 'the impending decline of Spain and rise of England on the next cycle of history'.[34] Set within this prophetic context, *The Spanish Tragedy*'s weave of Senecan and Virgilian intertexts offers a provocative interpretative network against which its geopolitical significance may be traced.

To read *The Spanish Tragedy* in relation to an English imperial translation is to align Kyd politically and doctrinally with contemporaries like Dee and Richard Hakluyt. Indeed, the latter's unpublished *Discourse of Western Planting* – which likened 'the spanishe monarchie' to 'the Empire of Alexander the greate, w[hich] grewe upp soodenley and soodenly upon his deathe was rent and dissolved for faulte of lawfull yssue'[35] – offers a reading of ancient history associating the decline of the ancient Greeks with a dynastic crisis much like the one represented in *The Spanish Tragedy*. Such a reading also places Kyd alongside his fellow Merchant Taylor's school alumnus Edmund Spenser, who, during the same historical conjuncture, similarly codes Roman Catholicism in relation to classical (or 'pagan') archetypes in *The Faerie Queene* (1590), and thereby interprets the dramatist as a literary and ideological descendant of England's Geneva reformers John Bale and John Foxe.[36]

Although the play provides ample indices to support such 'reformed' readings, it is important to recognize the inherently ambiguous nature of these providentialist thematics. If they have registered ambivalently in criticism, no doubt this is so because *The Spanish Tragedy*'s various intertexts draw upon a common textual inheritance. The play's Virgilian interpolations certainly recall the origins of Rome and the age of imperial expansion associated with Augustus, with the Senecan counterpoint evoking simultaneously the extension of the empire beyond the seas associated with *Medea*. But these Roman associations also conjure the imperial corruption and decadence experienced by the 'Spanish' dramatist-philosopher during his own lifetime under the reigns of Caligula and Nero, an ambivalence that, in turn, may be associated with the Spain of Kyd's drama.

The ambivalent potential of these intertexts, especially in relation to period apocalypticism, is made evident by the idiosyncratic form the two most important plays treating the matter of the Portuguese incorporation hold in common – a phenomenon hitherto unobserved by criticism. With their four-act structures both Kyd's *Spanish Tragedy* and Cervantes's *El cerco de Numancia* – which praises 'un Carlos, y un Filipo y un Fernando' (4.1999) as the lineage that had made the Iberian consolidation possible[37] – may be linked symbolically, allegorically, and formally to the geopolitics of imperial translation.

From the Spanish perspective, Cervantes's four acts imply a realization – the re-unification of Hispania under Philip II consummates Rome's imperial mission by encircling the globe and thereby fulfilling the prophecies of Seneca's *Medea* and the Book of Daniel. In opposition, Kyd's four-act structure suggests that the unification of the Iberian crowns represents a step toward the emergence of a succeeding imperial power. In contradistinction to *El cerco de Numancia*, *The Spanish Tragedy* thus implies that the extension of the Roman imperium enabled by Iberian unification may fulfil the meaning of empire four, but the phenomenon becomes in this adjusted providential scheme a necessary step on the way toward the realization of empire five, a future, millenarian 'Fifth Monarchy' that could be associated with English Protestantism.[38] Whatever Kyd's own confessional identification, in line with the geopolitical vision that was unfolding in the minds of early English imperialists like Dee, Hakluyt, Spenser and others, his four-act staging of 'the fall of Babylon / wrought by the heavens' (4.1.195–6) chimes the apocalyptic clock by which contemporary anti-Spanish visionaries were attempting to time England's emergence as a global power.

V

The edition of *The Spanish Tragedy* published in 1602 made available a set of emendations that had accrued to Kyd's play in performance during the decade since its earliest printing.[39] Although long thought to have been written by 'bengemy Johnsone',[40] recent analyses by three different authorities, including one employing computational stylistics, suggest that the authorship of at least some of *The Spanish Tragedy*'s added material should now be attributed to William Shakespeare.[41] Together, these additions, which together serve to intensify Hieronimo's grief, also draw Kyd's play toward *Hamlet* and *Othello*, tragedies the playwright was himself composing and revising, c. 1600–3.[42] At the same time they intensify the thematics of remembrance Thomas Rist and others have associated with the developing revenge genre, and religious coordinates other than those of England's Genevan reformers.[43]

Whereas recent scholarship has preferred the 'original' as printed ten years earlier, as Emma Smith has reminded us, 'all editions after 1602 carried the additional passages'.[44] By this date, the long rule of Philip II had finally passed into history, and the reign of Elizabeth Tudor was about to do so. Showing an early determination to assert his father's imperial aims, Philip III (1578–1621) had supported the Kinsale invasion the previous year, an attempt to redress England's post-Armada attacks on the Spanish homeland via a backdoor invasion of Ireland.[45] Within England itself, Elizabeth I's imminent departure was unloosing numerous religio-political factions. Some Catholic sympathizers and even the occasional Protestant were going so far as to consider a Spanish succession preferable to the Scottish claim of James VI, which remained unconfirmed until Elizabeth Tudor's death on 24 March 1603.[46]

While Janette Dillon's admonition that *The Spanish Tragedy* 'cannot be reduced to a piece of Protestant propaganda' provides a reasonable counterweight to what will follow,[47] it is also evident that the Jacobean years would see *The Spanish Tragedy* appropriated to propagandistic effects. Although Robert Cecil sealed a Spanish Peace at the Somerset House Conference of May 1604, plays performing English patriotism in opposition to Spanish tyranny continued to appear on stage and in print.[48] Even as James proscribed anti-Spanish polemic and countenanced greater toleration for England's Roman Catholics, the play written by Kyd amidst very different historical circumstances, and updated with some degree of sympathy by Shakespeare as the Tudor era came to a close, would be appropriated and re-appropriated in support of his Protestant nationalist opposition.

The first such adaptation was apparently the *First Part of Hieronimo* (1605), sometimes known as the 'Spanish Comedy'. In spite of the fact that, two decades on, Iberian union was largely working to the advantage of Philip III's kingdoms, the 'miraculous' turn-of-the-century appearance of an individual claiming to be Sebastian I engendered a flurry of Portuguese nationalist sentiment.[49] In this context, *1 Hieronimo*, thought by some critics to have been fashioned from the lost opening play of a diptych composed by Kyd himself, borrowed material from *The Spanish Tragedy* in order to memorialize 'the Warres of Portugall, and the life and death of Don Andrea' as an anti-Spanish celebration of

Portuguese nationality.⁵⁰ In a similar vein, the anonymous *Famous History of Captain Thomas Stukeley* (also printed in 1605) questioned the legitimacy of Hapsburg rule by treating Dom Antonio as a sympathetic figure.⁵¹ Having based its own plan for the unification of Britain on the precedent set by Philip II, the Jacobean regime was far from sympathetic to this resurgent Portuguese nationalism because these geopolitics bore implicitly on the legitimacy of British Union. As James's counsellor Henry Savile pointed out, the dynastic linkage of Portugal with Spain is 'the likest to ours'.⁵²

The Jacobean years would see *The Spanish Tragedy* reprinted in 1603, 1610, 1611, 1615, 1618 and 1623, the latter three editions bearing the illustrated title page thereafter associated with the play and Hieronimo's vengeful madness.⁵³ Throughout this era James sought to seal his *Pax Hispanica* by attaining a 'Spanish Match' – first, for his eldest son Prince Henry, and later, following Henry's death in 1612, for the future Charles I.⁵⁴ James's desire to return to the 'most antient Confederacy' that historically had linked England and Spain ushered in a period of Hispanophilic aesthetic tastes unmatched since Katherine of Aragon had been England's queen.⁵⁵ And yet the years associated with the attempt to marry Charles with the *Infanta* María, daughter of Philip III and sister to Philip IV, would reveal how thoroughly implicated in period Hispanophobia *The Spanish Tragedy* had become.

During the years 1617–24 especially, England's most militant Protestants obsessed over suspicions that Spain was once again harbouring designs on the nation's throne. If the Elizabethan regime had worried that a significant number of native Roman Catholics might rise in support of a Spanish invasion, now Protestant factions in the House of Commons feared the British king's un-English policies and the crypto-Catholic 'Hispaniolization' they perceived to be rampant among Britain's hereditary nobility.⁵⁶ With Hapsburg ambitions toward 'Universal Monarchy' continuing to haunt contemporary geopolitics, the period experienced an explosion of anti-Hispanic propaganda that may have surpassed that of the 1590s.[57] So intense was the Hispanophobic onslaught that James I would be pressured to appease Parliament by breaking off the marriage negotiations he had pursued for two decades, a failure of policy that led directly to the resumption of Anglo-Spanish hostilities in March 1624.

But it was not the reification of late-sixteenth-century print propaganda alone that contributed to this geopolitical breakdown; the theatre played a significant role in turning the English away from Jacobean openness and toward Protestant nationalist recalcitrance. The elder statesmen of Jacobean drama, playwrights who had in their youth experienced the Hispanophobic flush of the Armada crisis busily produced a new spate of Spanish plays.[58] Their work from the era demonstrates a thorough acquaintance with the rhetorical and representational strategies of Elizabethan anti-Hispanism.

William Rowley's *All's Lost By Lust* (c. 1618–19) – which recounted the widely disseminated legend of Rodrigo I, Spain's last Visigothic king, in order to discover the font of Spanish decadence in the Moorish conquest of CE 711 – may serve as a token of the type. Racializing Spain in the manner of his Elizabethan predecessors, Rowley represented 'typical' Iberian sexual intemperance by staging the act of miscegenation from which the Spanish nation was alleged to have been born. Together with Thomas Middleton, Rowley would soon produce *The Changeling* (1622), the most rabidly Hispanophobic play of the era, excepting perhaps Middleton's own anti-Spanish tour de force, *A Game at Chess*, which lampooned Hapsburg Machiavellianism and Stuart Hispanophilia with equal force. Thickening this theatrical context were dramas written by a cadre of playwrights including John Webster, Thomas Dekker, John Fletcher, Francis Beaumont, Philip Massinger and John Ford, who often drew upon the Spanish literary titles that had become available during this period of Anglo-Iberian openness in order to frame from Spanish sources the antithesis of all things English.[59] Important though these new dramas were, as significant was the republication and theatrical revival of the

Elizabethan era's 'Spanish plays'. Foremost among them was *The Spanish Tragedy*.

It has been well documented that the drama of James I's later reign bears the marks of period Hispanophobia as expressed in the writings of England's most vehement and prolific anti-Hispanist, the Puritan preacher and propagandist Thomas Scott. This is especially evident in the case of Middleton's *A Game at Chess* (1624), wherein Scott's influence is demonstrably strong. Therefore, rather than rehearsing the relationship of this inflammatory religio-political discourse to the drama, this chapter will close by considering a phenomenon less often observed, the reciprocal interrelation of the two. For the discursive circuit of period Hispanophobia did not flow unidirectionally – the propaganda influenced the plays even as the plays influenced the propaganda. Because his writing discloses the way material from one genre could be projected into another within the sphere of print culture, Scott's polemic is particularly revealing in relation to *The Spanish Tragedy*'s reception within this later geopolitical context.

Forced to flee to the Netherlands after issuing *Vox Populi, or Newes from Spayne* (1620), a scurrilous denunciation of the amity between King James and Philip IV's ambassador, the Count of Gondomar, Scott issued *Vox Regis*, the 'Voice of the King' (1624), in an effort to enter a public defence of his actions. In response to government allegations that his attack on James's pro-Spanish policies had been 'too full of conjectures', and that he had written in a manner not appropriate for a churchman, but rather 'like a fabulous poet or an Historian', Reverend Scott blurred the distinctions between divinity, poetry, and history even further than in his original polemic.[60] Referring with some generic accuracy to the marriage suit of Charles and the Spanish *Infanta*, Scott asked,

> And might I not borrow a Spanish name or two, as well as French or Italian, to grace this comedy with stately actors? Or must they be reserved for kingly tragedies? Why not Gondomar as well as *Hieronymo* or Duke d' Alva? And

why not Philip as well as *Peter*, or *Alfonso*, or Caesar? Or might I not make as bold as them, as they with our Black Prince, or Henry the Eighth, or Edward the Sixth, or King James, or the King and Queen of Bohemia? If this be censurable being a fiction, it is surely lack of a fool, which, they say, comedies should not be without, and for need, this witty objector may supply the place. (p. 10)

Drawing a comparison between his own arguments and the 'plays and masks' in which 'Kings are content ... to be admonished', Scott countered that if rebuke were permissible in tragedy, then why could he not 'supply' the 'fool' in 'this comedy'? In other words, if it were admissible to instruct the crown by drawing from history in the 'kingly tragedies' James so favoured, why then could he not do likewise in his own satirical writing?

The litany of names Scott marshals in *Vox Regis* places on the same historical plane figures from the past (among which 'Peter' may conjure one of England's most popular Spaniards, the captured Spanish Armada commander Pedro de Valdés),[61] and figures from the present (including Count Gondomar, Philip IV, if not also his predecessors, Philips II and III, King James himself, and the royal son-in-law and daughter, the King and Queen of Bohemia). While all of the figures Scott mentions had been personated in recent dramatic performance,[62] his most notable innovation is this: defensively begging the question – 'might I not borrow a Spanish name or two, as well as French or Italian'[?] – Scott does not distinguish between actual Spaniards and fictional ones. Although 'Hieronymo', 'Peter' [or Pedro] and 'Alfonso' could no doubt be attached to alternative referents, they can quite surely be linked to a theatrical tradition, some thirty-five years running, of representing Spain on stage. The key index, of course, is 'Hieronymo', the widely known revenger of *The Spanish Tragedy*: the most influential play of the English Renaissance, referred to in stage shorthand as simply 'Hieronymo'.

As *Vox Regis* demonstrates, by the decade of the 1620s the figures Scott names have through their repeated representation become *mythical*[63] – so much so that in crossing multiple times between the historical and the fictional, the fictional and the historical, the significance of these Spanish dramatic characters, most especially, *The Spanish Tragedy*'s Hieronimo, had become fixed in English popular imagination.[64] If, as Clara Calvo and Jesús Tronch suggest, 'Madness and Hieronimo' had become 'inseparable on the early modern stage' (p. 25), so had the madness associated with Kyd's fictional Spaniard come to signify the 'madness' of entertaining geopolitical relations with Spain.

* * *

The Hispanophilic qualities observable in *The Spanish Tragedy* were very much of their age. Although during the years between the composition of Thomas Kyd's most famous play and his too-early death, virulent Hispanophobia became an increasingly palpable presence in English public culture – a phenomenon which could possibly have inspired the playwright to fashion something like the prequel Henslowe may refer to as 'the comodey of Jeronymo'[65] – the epoch's taste for Spanish fashions in dress, art, and especially literature, is also obvious. To view *The Spanish Tragedy* within a geopolitical context spatially and temporally thicker than scholarship has imagined is to glimpse how Kyd's original argument may have been appropriated amidst the shifting currents of historical circumstance. Continuing analyses of the production, emendation, and reproduction of his play will no doubt reveal how literary revision and reinterpretation contributed substantially to processes of dramatic representation and national self-definition during the highly unsettled geopolitical conjuncture that saw *The Spanish Tragedy* flourish.

6

New Directions: *The Spanish Tragedy* and Virgil

Tom Rutter

Although Hieronimo's grief for his son Horatio, and his struggle to achieve justice for him, are the emotional and thematic focus of *The Spanish Tragedy*, Kyd also supplies the play with a framing device of unusual prominence and detail: the story of Don Andrea, whose words introduce and conclude the action and who watches it unfold, providing occasional comment and thus serving along with Revenge as 'chorus in this tragedy' (1.1.91). In the opening scene, Andrea's Ghost briefly summarizes his birth, life at court, love for Bel-imperia, and death in the war against Portugal. He then offers a more detailed account of his soul's descent to the Underworld, the disagreement between Minos, Aeacus and Rhadamanth over where he should spend eternity, and the decision of Proserpine that he should return to the upper world where, in the words of Revenge, he is to see

> the author of thy death,
> Don Balthazar, the Prince of Portugal,
> Deprived of life by Bel-imperia. (1.1.87–9)

At this point the tragedy proper begins with the entry of the Spanish King and the other characters.

Kyd's decision to open *The Spanish Tragedy* with speeches from a Ghost accompanied by Revenge was probably suggested by the practice of the first-century dramatist Seneca (see Gordon Braden's chapter in this collection), whose *Thyestes* begins with an exchange between the Ghost of Tantalus and a Fury in which the bloody events of the play are anticipated and whose *Agamemnon*, in turn, opens with a speech from the Ghost of Thyestes. However, the details of Andrea's posthumous journey show the clear influence of an earlier Latin poet, namely Publius Vergilius Maro or Virgil (70 BC–19 BC), whose twelve-book epic the *Aeneid* includes a description of the hero's descent to the Underworld. The current chapter surveys some of the ways in which Kyd's use of Virgil has been understood by critics, before considering his play in the light of two texts from his own era that seem to address the broader question of how popular drama should position itself in relation to the classical tradition of which Virgil was a part: Thomas Nashe's Preface to *Menaphon* and Christopher Marlowe's *Doctor Faustus*.

*

In book 6 of Virgil's poem, the hero, Aeneas, whose wanderings by sea after fleeing the destruction of Troy have finally brought him to Italy, is led by the prophetic Sybil into the land of the dead. Here he encounters former comrades, is told of the punishments suffered by evildoers, speaks with his dead father Anchises, and sees a vision of the future foundation and history of Rome before returning to the world of the living. This sequence provides considerable material that finds its way into Andrea's narrative. The ferryman Charon's insistence that with Andrea's 'rites of burial not performed, | I might not sit amongst his passengers' (1.1.21–2) recalls the fate of Aeneas's friend Palinurus, unable to cross the river Styx while his body remains unburied. The Sybil helps Aeneas past the three-headed guard-dog Cerberus with the help of drugged honey, while Andrea talks of 'pleasing Cerberus with honeyed speech' (1.1.30). The judges Minos and Rhadamanth appear in the *Aeneid*, although there they are allotted different portions of the Underworld. The idea that lovers and 'bloody martialists' (1.1.61) are kept separate in the afterlife is Virgilian, as is the description of the punishments suffered in 'deepest hell' (1.1.64) or Tartarus; so, too, are the 'gates of horn' (1.1.82) leading out of the Underworld, although Aeneas, unlike Andrea, departs through separate gates of ivory. And Aeneas, of course, is a living man rather than a ghost – only one of several major points of divergence between the two texts.

Kyd was not doing anything particularly out-of-the-way in alluding to Virgil. In a culture that prized classical literature both as a moral and as a stylistic exemplar, the *Aeneid* had pride of place among the high points of ancient poetry: anyone who went to an Elizabethan grammar school would have been familiar with it, and in Latin.[1] For those who could not read Latin, or preferred not to, there were translations such as that of Thomas Phayer (books 1–7, 1558; 8–9, 1562; completed by Thomas Twyne, 1573) or, more controversially, Richard Stanyhurst's version of books 1–4 in unrhymed English hexameters (1582). On a basic level, then, Kyd can be seen as claiming authority for his drama by associating it with prestigious literature of the past: perhaps hoping, as Michael Neill puts it, 'to exhibit his own learning and thereby elevate himself above the status of mere popular entertainer'.[2] A more complex, and political, rationale for Kyd's use of Virgil has been suggested by Eugene D. Hill, who reads Kyd's allusion to the book of the *Aeneid* that prophesies the future glories of Rome as an attempt to stake a claim for England as an imperial power that would supplant Spain. While this providential vision 'can be stated ... only indirectly and in passing in the Spanish setting', it is hinted at in Hieronimo's staging of a sequence of English defeats of Spain and Portugal as a court entertainment in 1.4, the inclusion of a character called

Bel-imperia over whom various males compete, and the utter collapse of the Spanish royal dynasty at the drama's climax.[3]

The inherently covert nature of Kyd's alleged imperial theme makes Hill's argument, while suggestive, unverifiable. However, critics of *The Spanish Tragedy* have identified other ways in which Kyd's use of the *Aeneid* modifies our experience of the play. For one thing, as Katharine Eisaman Maus notes, it provides him with a model of the afterlife that is at odds with the 'vaguely Christian otherworld presided over by a just, all-knowing God' imagined by the drama's more sympathetic living characters, such as Hieronimo when he describes how his sighs and passions 'Beat at the windows of the brightest heavens, | Soliciting for justice and revenge' (3.7.13–14).[4] This disparity raises questions both about the validity of the characters' religious assumptions and about the workings of a supernaturally administered justice; it is also a means by which Kyd figures Hieronimo's psychological disintegration. As Hieronimo loses his sanity, his vision of the afterlife also seems to change: in Philip Edwards's words, 'the rhetoric of his crazed imagination veers toward what the play's induction showed as the real location of cosmic power, Pluto's infernal court', as exemplified by his descriptions of the Underworld at 3.12.7–16 and 3.13.107–22.[5]

A further effect of the play's Virgilian frame is to ironize the actions of the characters considerably. As we have already seen, Andrea is told at the outset that Bel-imperia is going to take revenge upon Balthazar, and his repeated complaints later on that this is not happening are met with the assurance that it is inevitable. Indeed, Proserpine's verdict on his case – 'Forthwith, Revenge, she rounded thee in th'ear, | And bade thee lead me through the gates of horn' (1.1.81–2) – only makes sense if she knows what he is going to see over the following scenes. Although there is nothing remotely Virgilian about Andrea's return to earth as a ghost, the centrality of revenge as a theme in *The Spanish Tragedy*, or the presence of a character called Revenge, one could draw a parallel between this sense of inevitability and the way Virgil manipulates time in *Aeneid* 6. There, Aeneas is given a vision of a future that, for the reader, has largely already happened: the founding of Alba Longa and, centuries later, of Rome; the history of Rome up to the ascendancy of the Caesars. Although Aeneas must still undergo the hardships involved in bringing this about, it is, from a divine perspective, already ordained: 'te tua fata docebo', says Anchises, 'I shall reveal to you your own destiny'.[6] Andrea is allowed a much scantier knowledge of future events, but it is no less clear that they are bound to happen: 'imagine thou', Revenge tells him, 'What 'tis to be subject to destiny' (3.15.26–7).

If the events of *The Spanish Tragedy* have indeed been predestined, this has certain implications for the way we view its characters. At one extreme, it can be seen as reducing them to mere cogs, albeit terribly suffering cogs, in a system of divine justice; not the 'independent and self-willed individuals they suppose themselves to be', in G. K. Hunter's words, but 'puppets of a predetermined and omnicompetent justice that they (the characters) cannot see and never really understand'.[7] Alternatively, it can be argued that just because Proserpine knows what is going to happen, it does not mean that she (or anyone) is shaping events: as Donna B. Hamilton puts it, 'She names what the future will be because she knows how men turn circumstances into chaos'.[8] Several recent commentators have noted that the questions of free will raised by the frame narrative of *The Spanish Tragedy*, like those raised by the witches' prophecies in Shakespeare's *Macbeth*, may reflect sixteenth-century controversies about salvation. Elizabethan Protestants were taught that due to the Fall of Adam, 'we haue no power to do good workes pleasaunt and acceptable to GOD, without the grace of God by Christe preuentyng [i.e. anticipating] vs, that we may haue a good wyll, & workyng with vs, when we haue that good wyll'. Salvation was entirely dependent on God's grace, and had been predestined by God 'before the foundations of the worlde were layde'.[9] The Church of England was in this respect influenced by the teachings of the French theologian Jean Calvin, who stated in his *Institutes* (translated 1561) that 'man hathe not free will to do good workes, vnlesse he be holpen ... by speciall grace whiche is geuen to the onely elect'.[10] Catholic theology as codified in the Council of Trent (1545–63), on the other hand, rejected the idea 'That mans Free-will is lost and extinct by *Adams* Fall'. Although it was heretical to say 'That a man by his Works ... may be justified before God', it was also heretical to say that man's free will 'Works nothing together with God assenting, exciting and calling, whereby he may dispose and prepare himself to obtain the Grace of Justification' but is merely passive.[11] The tension Lucas Erne locates in *The Spanish Tragedy* 'between the determinist frame, showing the characters entirely at the mercy of supernatural powers, and the intrigue plot in the play within, where the characters shape their own destiny by histrionic means', can be understood in relation to this doctrinal crux (although the attitude Erne opposes to Calvinist determinism is not that of the Catholic Church but Neo-Platonist stress on self-fashioning).[12] It would have been unsafe for Kyd to have addressed such a controversial topic directly, particularly if *The Spanish Tragedy* was written after 12 November 1589, when it was explicitly forbidden for players 'to handle matters of Divinity and State' in their plays.[13] However, the non-Christian religious context offered by Kyd's appropriation of a Virgilian Underworld allows a more oblique allusion to it.

Another aspect of Kyd's religious environment that may inform his use of Virgil relates to the problem of remembrance. In their discussions of early modern drama, critics such as Michael Neill, Stephen Greenblatt and Thomas Rist have emphasized the impact of Protestantism's rejection of the doctrine of Purgatory: the idea that before ascending to heaven, those who die having committed venial or lesser sins must endure a period of punishment and purification in the afterlife. In dismissing this doctrine as unbiblical, the argument goes, Protestant theologians changed the relationship between the living and the dead, to traumatic effect: the dead were now to be considered as immutably located either in heaven or in hell, not in any third place where the prayers of the living might diminish their sufferings.[14] As Rist shows, *The Spanish Tragedy*, with its multiple grieving parents, its emphasis on the rites of burial, and its tokens of remembrance from Andrea's scarf, which Horatio 'plucked from off his lifeless arm' (1.4.42), to Horatio's actual body, left unburied by Hieronimo until he reveals it after the climactic massacre, is a play in which contemporary anxieties over appropriate forms of mourning are insistently and obtrusively thematized.[15] More specifically, though, Kyd's use of Virgil can be seen as another way in which his play engages with these debates. For one thing, the description by Anchises of the dead having 'the stain of evil washed out of them under a vast tide of water or scorched out by fire' (6.741–2; 156) was quoted by writers and theologians from Saint Augustine onwards when discussing Purgatory: as David Scott Wilson-Okamura demonstrates, even hostile Protestant writers recognized the affinity, making Virgil's account of the afterlife (in Rist's words) 'a motif freighted with Catholic significance'.[16] For another, there are specific aspects of Andrea's account that seem to bear sectarian implications. His inability to cross the Styx until 'By Don Horatio, our Knight Marshal's son, | My funerals and obsequies were done' (1.1.25–6), with its implication that 'post-mortem remembrance benefits the dead', can be seen as chiming with the Catholic practice of praying for the departed that Protestantism had rejected.[17] And various critics have noted Kyd's difference from Virgil in the matter of Underworld geography: while the path taken by Aeneas divides in two, one way leading to Tartarus and the other to Elysium, Andrea explains that 'Three ways there were' (1.1.59), adding a third way that leads to the fields 'Where lovers live and bloody martialists' (1.1.61) through which Virgil's Aeneas has already passed. Lorna Hutson, like Erne and Rist, sees Kyd's practice here in doctrinal terms: 'This third *way* … corresponds to the notion of Purgatory as a third *place*, the locus of torment not as damnation but as trial and purification'.[18]

The broad argument that (in Neill's words) plays like *The Spanish Tragedy* 'catered for a culture that was in the throes of a peculiar crisis in the accommodation of death' resulting from factors including the Reformation, plague, the growth of cities, and the rediscovery of classical authors is hard to dispute, and the significance of Virgil in debates about Purgatory is undeniable.[19] However, if Kyd's Virgilian Underworld does indeed 'evoke Purgatory', it does not do so in any straightforward way.[20] For one thing, the 'Elysian green' to which Andrea's 'middle path' brings him contains the 'stately tower' of Pluto and Proserpine (1.1.72–4), but no one else of whom we are told, neither souls in bliss nor souls being purged. There is thus no neat correspondence between the three ways and the three dwelling-places of Heaven, Hell and Purgatory. For another, Andrea's experience over the course of the play is not exactly one of purgation. In the final scene his Ghost lists the killings he has observed, of friends and foes alike, and comments, 'these were spectacles to please my soul' (4.5.12), expressing a sense of gratification that does not sound very beatific, before going on to describe the punishment he anticipates for his enemies in the afterlife. Souls in purgatory are supposed to be 'assisted and helpt by the Suffrages of the Faithful, but in a more especial manner by the acceptable Sacrifice of the Altar', that is, by prayers and by the Mass – not by acts of vengeance.[21] And indeed, once Horatio has arranged Andrea's funeral Andrea is largely forgotten by the other characters: Bel-imperia does claim that she loves Horatio in order to 'further [her] revenge' (1.4.66) on Andrea's behalf, but by the time of her bloody letter from prison she is urging Hieronimo to 'revenge Horatio's death' (3.2.30), not Andrea's. The figure whose posthumous narrative supplies one of the main arguments for the play's thematic concern with Purgatory is denied the kind of remembrance from which purging souls were supposed to benefit.

Furthermore, while Hieronimo's response to the death of a loved one may, as suggested above, relate to an English context in which Catholic mourning ritual was no longer prevalent, the form it takes is very different to that sanctioned by Catholic doctrine. If due burial (as in the case of Andrea) is supposed to stand for the ways in which the prayers of the living could benefit the dead, then this is a benefit that Hieronimo denies Horatio for the majority of the play, instead preserving Horatio's body as a prop for his final act of revenge and then killing himself before he can ensure that appropriate rites are done over it. Far from wanting to remember Horatio, which would mean acknowledging his death, Hieronimo at times simply wants to be with him, as when he meditates suicide at the start of 3.12, when he digs at the earth in order to 'ferry over to th'Elysian plains, | And bring my son to show his deadly wounds' later in the scene (3.12.71–2), or when he mistakes Bazulto for his son at 3.13.130.

Hieronimo's emphasis on the Underworld as a place in which to encounter his dead son is another aspect of *The Spanish Tragedy* that makes the *Aeneid* an appropriate source. In Virgil, it is a vision of his dead father Anchises that tells Aeneas he must 'come to the home of Dis in the underworld and go through the depths of hell to seek a meeting with me' (5.731–3; 127). When the two are finally reunited, the emotional focus is as much on the father's desire to see his son as on the son's to see his father:

> When he saw Aeneas coming towards him over the grass, he stretched out both hands in eager welcome, with the tears streaming down his cheeks, and these were the words that broke from his mouth: 'You have come at last,' he cried. 'I knew your devotion would prevail over all the rigour of the journey and bring you to your father.' (6.684–8; 154)

At the same time, Virgil wrings pathos from the incomplete nature of the encounter, as when Aeneas asks for Anchises's embrace: 'As he spoke these words his cheeks were washed with tears and three times he tried to put his arms around his father's neck. Three times the phantom melted in his hands, as weightless as the wind, as light as the flight of sleep'

(6.699–702; 154). The episode may be a source for Isabella's vision of a dead son whom she is unable to touch:

> Ay, here he died, and here I him embrace.
> See where his ghost solicits, with his wounds,
> Revenge on her that should revenge his death. (4.2.23–5)

She sees Horatio tempting her to suicide, which she imagines as a journey 'To hear Horatio plead with Rhadamanth' (4.2.28). Thus, recognition of the *Aeneid*'s significance in sixteenth-century debates about Purgatory should not obscure the less doctrinally specific fact that book 6 supplies Kyd with a narrative about a parent and a child being reunited in the Underworld.

*

In the first part of this chapter, I have surveyed some modern responses to Kyd's use of Virgil in *The Spanish Tragedy*, noting the way Virgil's Underworld offers the playwright a non-Christian model of the afterlife that ironizes the actions and beliefs of the living characters. If Andrea's narrative is taken as providing an accurate account of the nature of things, then perhaps this makes *The Spanish Tragedy* (in Edwards's words) 'an un-Christian play' in which any characters who assume a beneficent heavenly deity are simply deluded.[22] Alternatively, the conflict between the frame narrative's implication that everything has been arranged in advance and the lived struggles of the characters may be seen as a way of figuring contemporary debates over predestination and free will. Furthermore, Kyd's alterations to Virgil may be read as indirect allusions to the Catholic doctrine of Purgatory – or, less specifically, the play's interest in remembrance can be interpreted as a response to the questions that the Reformation had raised over the relationship between the living and the dead. And as I have suggested, the importance of parent/child relations in the *Aeneid* makes it an apt intertext for *The Spanish Tragedy*. In the latter half of this chapter, however, I want to return to a topic that was briefly mentioned at the beginning, and that concerns the relationship between living and dead not as individuals, but in a broader cultural sense: Virgil's status as a representative of the classical tradition whose recuperation was the defining project of the Renaissance. I will begin by making reference to another text that seems to have some sort of significance for Kyd's play, although precisely what significance has been debated: Thomas Nashe's preface to *Menaphon*.

Robert Greene's 'pastorall historie' *Menaphon: Camillas Alarum to Slumbering Euphues, in His Melancholie Cell at Silexdra* was first printed in 1589, prefaced by a dedicatory epistle from his fellow Cambridge graduate Thomas Nashe 'To the Gentlemen Students of both Vniuersities'.[23] The presumption of a shared educational background informs the tone of Nashe's epistle, a survey of the English literary landscape that directs its invective against the unlettered and uninspired: critics who 'feed on nought but the crummes that fal from the translators trencher'; orators who are not able 'in anie English vaine to be eloquent of their owne' but must borrow from Ariosto or Cicero; undiscerning readers whose judgement 'makes drosse as valuable as gold'; controversialists who do not understand logic. However, it is Nashe's discussion of 'triuiall translators' that has sometimes caught the attention of commentators on Kyd:

> It is a common practise now a daies amongst a sort of shifting companions, that runne through euery arte and thriue by none, to leaue the trade of *Nouerint* whereto they were borne, and busie themselues with the indeuors of Art, that could scarcelie latinize their necke-verse if they should haue neede; yet English *Seneca* read by candle light yeeldes manie good sentences, as *Bloud is a begger,* and so foorth: and if you intreate him faire in a frostie morning, he will affoord you whole *Hamlets*, I should say handfulls of tragical speaches. But ô griefe! *tempus edax rerum,* what's

that will last alwaies? The sea exhaled by droppes will in
continuance be drie, and *Seneca* let bloud line by line and
page by page, at length must needes die to our stage: which
makes his famisht followers to imitate the Kidde in *Aesop*,
who enamored with the Foxes newfangles, forsooke all
hopes of life to leape into a new occupation; and these men
renowncing all possibilities of credit or estimation, to inter-
meddle with Italian translations: wherein how poorelie they
haue plodded, (as those that are neither prouenzall men,
nor are able to distinguish of Articles,) let all indifferent
Gentlemen that haue trauailed in that tongue, discerne
by their twopenie pamphlets: & no meruaile though their
home-born mediocritie be such in this matter; for what can
be hoped of those, that thrust *Elisium* into hell, and haue
not learned so long as they haue liued in the spheares, the
iust measure of the Horizon without an hexameter.[24]

This is an intriguing but mystifying passage. The references
to the 'trade of *Nouerint*', to imitation of Seneca, to the kid
in Aesop, to Italian translation, and to thrusting Elysium into
Hell all seem relevant to Kyd, whose father was a legal clerk
('the trade of *Nouerint*'), whose drama has Senecan qualities,
who translated Torquato Tasso's *Il padre di famiglia*, and
whose Don Andrea refers to the 'Elysian green' in *The Spanish
Tragedy*. (The allusion to 'whole *Hamlets*' has also led to
speculation that Kyd wrote the version of *Hamlet* known to
have existed before Shakespeare's.)[25] Yet as Nashe's editor
R. B. McKerrow points out, the phrase 'Blood is a beggar' has
not been found in Kyd or anywhere else; the section about
the kid in Aesop (really Spenser's *Shepheardes Calendar*) need
not be a reference to Thomas Kyd, and nor need the allusion
to the trade of Noverint; Kyd was 'by no means the only
translator from Italian'; and Andrea's description does not
actually thrust Elysium into hell.[26] Not all subsequent critics
have been as conservative as McKerrow, however: Erne, for
example, argues that in placing an Elysian green alongside
a tower suggestive of the hellish Tartarus Kyd 'consciously

mixed Elysium and Tartarus or, in Nashe's words, "thrust Elysium into hell"'.[27] Erne uses this view of Kyd's infernal landscape as neither one thing nor the other to support his reading of the play as alluding to Purgatory.

I would argue, however, that Nashe's remarks make better sense when considered in the context where they appear: a dedicatory epistle about the current state of English literature, albeit one perhaps delivered with an eye on potential future patrons.[28] The preceding paragraphs attack uneducated writers and readers; those that follow praise 'those men of import, that haue laboured with credit in this laudable kinde of Translation'. These include Erasmus, for his translations from Greek into Latin; Sir Thomas Elyot; George Gascoigne; George Turberville; Arthur Golding for his translation of Ovid; and 'Master *Phaer* ... in regard of his famous *Virgil*'. Indeed, Virgil is used by Nashe as a kind of touchstone for successful translation: Phayer's version is compared favourably with that of Stanyhurst, who 'recalled to life, what euer hissed barbarisme, hath bin buried this hundred yeare; and reuiued by his ragged quill, such carterlie varietie, as no hodge plowman in a countrie, but would haue held as the extremitie of clownerie'.[29] Here, Nashe reverses and degrades a familiar Renaissance metaphor for the recovery of the classical tradition. As Thomas M. Greene argues in *The Light in Troy*, 'imagery of resurrection and rebirth' was pervasive in the Renaissance, reflecting the period's consciousness of antiquity as a lost culture that needed to be retrieved: he refers to the 'necromantic metaphors of disinterment, rebirth, and resuscitation' that can be found in French and (to some extent) English literature of the time.[30] Nashe uses the image of resurrection in a similar way later in the epistle when he writes that 'there are extant about *London*, many most able men, to reuiue Poetrie, though it were executed ten thousand times' (although there it is the Puritans who are imagined as executioners). Stanyhurst, however, who ought to be bringing Virgil back to life, has only succeeded in reanimating a literary barbarism that would have been better left buried. Nashe's discussion reveals what was at stake in the early modern work of translation: a translator might enrich the language like Arthur Golding, praised for 'his industrious toile in Englishing *Ouids Metamorphosis*, besides manie other exquisite editions of Diuinitie, turned by him out of the French tongue into our own'. Or he might reproduce the 'strange language' and 'terrible ... stile' of Stanyhurst.[31]

Nashe's emphasis on the cultural value of translation, and his related anxieties about the barbarism of bad translation, offer one way of relating his remarks about thrusting Elysium into hell to what we see in Kyd's play: in placing a Christian character in a classical Underworld derived from Virgil (one which contains the blissful Elysian fields as well as the more conventionally hell-like Tartarus), Kyd can be seen as committing an artistic solecism comparable to Stanyhurst's use of 'rounce robble hobble' to convey the sound of Jove's thunderbolt.[32] An appropriate point of contrast may be Nashe's own dramatic adaptation of Virgil in the 1580s play *Dido, Queen of Carthage*, attributed to Marlowe and Nashe on its 1594 title page.[33] Like *The Spanish Tragedy*, *Dido* includes a supernatural frame narrative, set on Olympus rather than in Hades, in which capricious deities interfere in the lives of mortals.[34] However, while Kyd's play juxtaposes modern Spain and a Virgilian Underworld, Nashe and Marlowe keep the cosmology of the frame consistent with that of the main plot, where gods such as Mercury, Venus and Cupid turn up in Carthage. Far from thrusting Elysium into hell, they leave Olympus and heaven decorously apart.

A document that may support this reading of Nashe is one that McKerrow refers to in his sceptical analysis of the 'triuiall translators' passage. In rejecting *The Spanish Tragedy* as the referent of the lines about thrusting Elysium into hell, McKerrow adduces the third scene of Marlowe's *Doctor Faustus*, where the protagonist tells the devil he has just raised:

This word 'damnation' terrifies not him,
For he confounds hell in Elysium.
His ghost be with the old philosophers![35]

The verbal similarity is, indeed, suggestive. I would disagree, however with McKerrow's interpretation, that 'Faustus regards the ancient Elysium, the abode of the old philosophers ... as part of the Christian hell': the word 'confounds', as Marlowe would have known, comes from the Latin *confundere*, 'to pour or mingle together, mix up, confuse, confound' (OED 'confound', *v.*), and this sense of mingling and confusion is very different from the topographically neater view of Elysium as part of hell (like the first circle of Dante's Inferno) that McKerrow finds.[36] Faustus's words are defiant: he insists that he can, as if by an act of will, make the Christian hell one with the more congenial Underworld imagined by the pagans. But given that he is speaking to a creature that has actually come from hell, they also seem deluded, the product of the same category error as that described by Nashe: the confusion of classical and Christian understandings of the afterlife.

In support of this argument for reading *The Spanish Tragedy* in relation to *Faustus*, it may be pointed out that the confounding of hell in Elysium is not the only piece of thematic, linguistic or scenic territory that the two plays share. Both bring members of the *dramatis personae* up from the Underworld: Mephistopheles and the other devils in *Doctor Faustus*, Andrea's Ghost and Revenge in Kyd's play. Indeed, both plays make the Underworld more convincingly present and responsive than the Christian heavens: Hieronimo's sighs and passions may beat at their windows, but their walls 'Resist my woes and give my words no way' (3.7.18), and when Faustus calls upon 'Christ, my Saviour, | Seek to save distressèd Faustus' soul' (2.3.82–3), it is Lucifer, Beelzebub and Mephistopheles who materialize. Both include protagonists who contemplate suicide while holding 'a poniard in one hand and a rope in the other' in the case of *The Spanish Tragedy* (3.12.0.1–2) and 'a dagger' in *Faustus* (5.1.51.0). Both include the motif of writing in blood, whether the 'bloody writ' of Bel-imperia's letter (3.2.27) or the 'deed of gift' written 'with thine own blood' (2.1.35) in which Faustus conveys his soul. And both make scenes of reading, or misreading, from the Latin Bible crucial to their plots. Faustus constructs a syllogism from passages in 'Jerome's Bible' (1.1.38) that proves he is damned already. Hieronimo, whose name is a variant of 'Jerome', quotes the words 'Vindicta mihi' (3.13.1), 'vengeance is mine', from Romans 12.19, again in the Latin of Saint Jerome; at the outset it is unclear whether he is proposing that revenge should be left to God as the Bible enjoins, or whether he is claiming for himself the right to avenge ('vengeance is *mine*').[37] These overlaps between the two plays are particularly suggestive in light of Kyd's recollection in 1593 of his and Marlowe's 'wrytinge in one chamber twoe yeares synce'.[38] It is unknown for how long the two dramatists used the same room as their study, and it is uncertain how close together in date *Doctor Faustus* and *The Spanish Tragedy* might have been; but this period of personal contact between Kyd and Marlowe may be connected to the points of contact between their most famous plays.

Saint Jerome is not the only Latin author in whom *Doctor Faustus* and *The Spanish Tragedy* share an interest, however: Virgil is a tangible presence in Marlowe's play, as in Kyd's. When Faustus describes the cities he has seen with Mephistopheles, he includes Naples:

> There saw we learnèd Maro's golden tomb,
> The way he cut an English mile in length
> Thorough a rock of stone in one night's space. (3.1.13–15)

As Margaret Tudeau-Clayton notes, this allusion to the medieval myth that Virgil was a magician as well as a poet is appropriate to a play about a latter-day would-be magus.[39] At other moments, however, it is clearly Virgil's poem that Marlowe has in mind. In Faustus's dialogue with Valdes and Cornelius, he boasts that he has:

> made the flow'ring pride of Wittenberg
> Swarm to my problems as the infernal spirits
> On sweet Musaeus when he came to hell … . (1.1.116–18)

The allusion is to the poet Musaeus whom Virgil gives pre-eminence among the spirits in Elysium: 'the whole great throng looked up to him as he stood there in the middle, head and shoulders above them all' (6.667–8; p. 153). And when Faustus says to Lucifer, 'O, might I see hell and return again, how happy were I then!' (2.3.168–9), he unwittingly echoes the Sybil's discouraging words to Aeneas: 'it is easy to go down to the underworld. The door of black Dis stands open night and day. But to retrace your steps and escape to the upper air, that is the task, that is the labour' ('hoc opus, hic labor est') (6.126–9; 136).

The Sybil's words provide an ironic undertone to Faustus's proposed journey to hell and back, and should perhaps make us question what Don Andrea is doing in the world of *The Spanish Tragedy*: in terms of Virgilian cosmology, he should not really be there at all. But the reference to Musaeus is striking because it typifies the way in which hell serves as the location of a classical tradition with which Faustus desires to engage. As he says when rejecting thoughts of suicide:

Have not I made blind Homer sing to me
Of Alexander's love and Oenone's death?
And hath not he that built the walls of Thebes
With ravishing sound of his melodious harp
Made music with my Mephistopheles?
Why should I die, then, or basely despair? (2.3.26–31)

Faustus's pact with the devil gives him direct access to Homer and the mythical harpist Amphion, as if to literalize the 'necromantic metaphors' that Greene finds in Renaissance discussions of antiquity: as Francis Bacon would later put it (in Greene's translation), through imitation 'the Literary Spirit of each age may be charmed as it were from the dead'.[40] This emphasis on the Underworld as the dwelling-place of great poets of the past is also identifiable in *The Spanish Tragedy*, in whose final scene Andrea's Ghost anticipates how 'I'll lead Hieronimo where Orpheus plays, | Adding sweet pleasure to eternal days' (4.5.23–4). Indeed, in his earlier account of 'pleasing Cerberus with honeyed speech' Andrea may be alluding to Orpheus as well as to Aeneas. In his *Georgics*, Virgil writes of Orpheus descending to hell in search of his dead bride Eurydice, and describes how 'Cerberus held agape his triple mouths' at his song: Orpheus thus supplies Andrea with a precedent for a return journey to hell that is achieved through verbal (and in Orpheus's case musical) artistry.[41] He also, by implication, offers the same precedent to Kyd. After all, there is something inherently strange about the idea of Andrea pleasing Cerberus with his speech: why should a dead man need to talk his way into Hades? The image works better as a comment on the dramatist's own situation, using his verbal facility to gain access to a literary tradition imaginatively located in the Underworld.

Whether popular drama was an appropriate vehicle for this sort of cultural project seems to have been a moot point, however. At the beginning of his preface to *Menaphon*, Nashe bemoans the pretentious diction of the uneducated – 'euerie moechanicall mate' – and attributes it to their imitation of what they have heard in the theatres. He goes on to attack 'idiote art-masters, that intrude themselues to our eares as the alcumists of eloquence; who (mounted on the stage of arrogance) think to outbraue better pens with the swelling bumbast of a bragging blanke verse': 'this kinde of men that repose eternitie in the mouth of a player'. Once again, it is not entirely clear who Nashe is criticizing here, but broadly speaking he seems to mean playwrights with ideas above their station, who think their grandiloquent lines more impressive than the work of better writers. When he later refers ironically to 'deepe read Grammarians' among their number, the phrase seems socially coded, implying those (like Shakespeare and Kyd) with only a grammar school rather than a university education; and in dismissing those who 'repose eternitie in the mouth of a player' he seems to express anxiety about the whole notion of using the disreputable public stage as the arena in which to seek literary immortality. *Dido, Queen of*

Carthage, by contrast, was staged in one of the more socially exclusive indoor theatres, as was the only English drama Nashe praises in the preface, George Peele's *The Arraignment of Paris*.[42]

Once again, I would argue, the play *Doctor Faustus* seems to engage with these problems in ways that shed light both on Nashe and on Kyd's practice in *The Spanish Tragedy*. There, Faustus is asked by the Emperor of Germany to 'raise ... from hollow vaults below' (4.1.36) Alexander the Great, whom the Emperor is grieved never to have seen, along with his paramour. Faustus agrees, but has to offer a caveat:

> ... it is not in my ability to present before your eyes the true substantial bodies of those two deceased princes, which long since are consumed to dust. ... But such spirits as can lively resemble Alexander and his paramour shall appear before your Grace in that manner that they best lived in, in their most flourishing estate ... . (4.1.47–50, 53–6)

The Emperor, then, is not going to see Alexander and his paramour, but spirits made to look like them – although neither Faustus nor the Emperor is really in any position to judge. This episode – in a scene, incidentally, often attributed to Marlowe's collaborator, who may have been Nashe himself – has important repercussions for our understanding of the rest of the play.[43] It implies that Faustus has not really heard Homer sing, or Amphion play: like Alexander and his paramour, they can only have been spirits, demonic actors offering a plausible likeness of what Faustus wants to see and hear. Faustus is happy to put to one side his awareness of this – as he is in the climactic scene where he asks Mephistopheles to bring him Helen of Troy, the most beautiful woman who ever lived. As well as wanting to distract himself with her 'sweet embracings' (5.1.86), Faustus sees in Helen the incarnation of the classical tradition with which he desires to commune, the opportunity to participate in the story of Troy of which Homer and Virgil wrote:

I will be Paris, and for love of thee
Instead of Troy shall Wittenberg be sacked,
And I will combat with weak Menelaus,
And wear thy colours on my plumèd crest.
Yea, I will wound Achilles in the heel
And then return to Helen for a kiss. (5.1.98–103)

This desire allows Faustus to ignore the reality that Helen is an infernal spirit in disguise, in a theatrical moment that seems to express a deep cynicism about the possibility of reviving the spirit of antiquity: Helen is dead, and all Faustus can do is summon up a likeness of her, and a corrupting likeness at that. His willingness to accept a simulacrum of the classical tradition for the real thing also serves as a comment on the seductive power of theatre itself, where men and boys might enact the roles of Alexander or Helen for paying audiences. And when Faustus observes, after asking Helen to 'make me immortal with a kiss', 'Her lips sucks forth my soul. See where it flies!' (5.1.93–4), Nashe's words about reposing eternity in the mouth of a player are literalized. Faustus reposes his eternity in the mouth of Helen, who is really a devil playing the part of Helen, who (at another level of representation) is really a boy actor playing the role.

It would, of course, be rather too neat to read *Doctor Faustus* and the preface to *Menaphon* as engaged in literary and theoretical comment on *The Spanish Tragedy*, and on each other, in any systematic way, even if the plays' dates were not so notoriously mobile.[44] All three texts have so much more going on in them than self-conscious discussion of the relationship between classical literature and the popular stage that such an interpretation would rely on a distortion of their artistic priorities. However, the biographical proximity of their authors – linked by Marlowe, who cohabited with Kyd and collaborated with Nashe on a play based on, of all things, the *Aeneid* – does invite speculation about the significance of their shared interest in the relationship between Christian hell and the classical Underworld, Elysium and all. In this chapter,

I have suggested that all three, in their different ways, use the Underworld as a way of exploring the relationship between modern literature and its classical inheritance. Kyd selects Virgil's description of Hades as his source text for an extended piece of literary allusion; Nashe takes Virgil as his touchstone for effective translation, while also using the notion of thrusting Elysium into hell (I would argue) as an example of failure to maintain decorum on the translator's part. Marlowe, by contrast, makes the confounding of hell in Elysium a symptom of his protagonist's spiritual as well as intellectual error; but he also resembles Kyd in treating the Underworld as the symbolic location of a classical tradition associated with Orphic poets (and for which Virgil's description of Hades, in *Aeneid* 6, serves as a kind of synecdoche). Both dramatists' practice in this respect accords with the Renaissance trope of reviving the dead that figures in Nashe's preface. However, Marlowe's play literalizes this trope not as necromancy but as demonic illusion, evoking pessimism about the recovery of tradition that finds its epitome in Faustus's encounter with Helen of Troy. By contrast, Kyd's treatment of the theme, for all his play's apparent scepticism in other respects, seems much less self-disabling. In implying a parallel between the descents of Andrea, Orpheus and the dramatist himself, he offers a more assertive statement of the modern poet's ability to engage with classical literature on the popular stage.

And Kyd, of course, turned out to be right. In 1607, Thomas Dekker would conclude his vision of hell in *A Knights Coniuring* by describing a '*Groue of Bay Trees*' inhabited by Chaucer, Spenser, 'learned *Watson*, industrious *Kyd*, ingenious *Atchlow*', and Bentley the player; '*Marlow*, *Greene*, and *Peele* had got vnder the shades of a large *vyne*, laughing to see *Nash* (that was but newly come to their Colledge,) still haunted with the sharpe and *Satyricall spirit* that followd him heere vpon *earth*'.[45] Dekker thrusts into the Christian hell an Elysium modelled on Virgil, but where the place of Musaeus is taken by English poets and dramatists – Kyd, Marlowe and Nashe included. All three, in death, can be assimilated to the classical tradition towards which their works express mingled attraction and anxiety. Not only that: a generation after *The Spanish Tragedy*, Dekker intimates that the English stage has a classical tradition of its own.

7

New Directions: Female Mourning, Revenge and Hieronimo's Doomsday Play

Katharine Goodland

Missing from studies of *The Spanish Tragedy* is a consideration of perhaps the most evocative influence upon a drama in which a bloodied corpse becomes the focus of incessant, agonized lamentation, cries for vengeance and concludes with a 'Judgement' play in which the indifferent, the devious, and the tyrannical get their comeuppance: the Corpus Christi plays. They were still being performed during Kyd's formative years. He was twenty-two and already a working playwright in 1580 when they had ceased production under the pressure of Elizabethan Ecclesiastical legislation.[1] Two professional playhouses had risen phoenix-like from the ashes of the former civic religious drama and were already in operation: the Theatre constructed in 1576 and London's Red Lion, built in 1567. As Andrew Sofer puts it, 'the commercial

Elizabethan playhouses filled a theatrical and spiritual void left by the suppression of the devotional Corpus Christi drama on the one hand and the rituals of the Catholic church on the other' (129).

Thomas Rist argues that the funeral rituals disrupted by this suppression shape the genre of Revenge tragedy, which is 'pervasively' determined by an 'aesthetics of mourning' and that we are invited to judge the genre 'on the terms of this aesthetic'.[2] I agree, but propose that this 'aesthetics of mourning' is itself shaped by the ethos of mourning and vengeance embodied in the genre of female lament, which drives the plots of the Corpus Christi 'Slaughter' and 'Passion' plays. Beyond the plays, Jesus' 'Passion' and his mother's grief over his suffering and death was the organizing narrative of English medieval religious culture. From popular piety to theological and meditative treatises, from private devotion to public theatre, the Virgin Mary's Compassion, the technical name for her mourning under the cross, bestowed emotional legitimacy upon the Christian narrative of sacrificial death. Every church in England had a figure of the pietà, otherwise known as 'Our Lady of Sorrows'.[3] Every medieval cycle included the Virgin's lament, a lyric interlude so dramatically compelling that E. K. Chambers listed it as an independent episode in his study of the medieval English stage.

The figure of the Virgin embracing her son's dead body is generally understood as an icon meant to elicit compassion and religious piety in those who meditate upon it. Yet, as the Corpus Christi plays vividly demonstrate, the image also encompasses an ethos of justice. For the mother's sorrow also expresses the monstrous injustice of her innocent son's death and implies God's vengeance. This implication is made explicit in the Doomsday Christ 'showing his wounds all fresh, new and bleeding', an image that was '[d]epicted above every Rood-loft and dramatized as the climax of all the cycles of Corpus Christi plays' (Duffy, 309). In the theological mystery of the Trinity God has three aspects: the Father, the Son and the Holy Spirit. Because father and son partake of one being, the one who is wrongly judged thereby returns on the Day of Doom to judge and punish those who wronged him: 'The whole machinery of late medieval piety was designed to shield the soul from Christ's doomsday anger' (Duffy, 309).

This cultural edifice of mourning and vengeance, compassion and justice haunts Kyd's dramaturgy. It informs the portrayals of Hieronimo, Isabella, Bel-imperia, and Proserpine, and the unfolding action. As in Kyd's play, with its repeated scenes of lamentation and emphasis on Horatio's wounds and bloody corpse, the medieval English Passion sequences are driven by the outrageously disproportionate suffering of their central character, Jesus, and repeated scenes of lamentation over his suffering and wounds. They are preoccupied with the same themes: the pitting of the disenfranchised against the powerful, the failure of justice, brutality, cruelty, indifference, suffering and loss. These problems are passionately articulated in the vengeful laments of the mothers of the slaughtered innocents in the Herod plays, and the Virgin Mary and her sisters in sorrow of the Passion. Shakespeare did not forget the 'mad mothers' whose 'howls confused' did 'break the clouds' when 'Herod's bloody-hunting slaughtermen ... pitted upon pikes' their 'naked infants' (*Henry V*, 3.3.38–41). They rise again in *Richard III* in the portraits of his grieving queens.[4] Kyd did not forget them either. In creating his impassioned revenger, crazed by grief, injustice, and an unquenchable need for reparation against the greed of underlings and the indifference of kings, Kyd need look no further than the mourning women of the Corpus Christi plays.

Of course Kyd did look elsewhere, and like Shakespeare after him, he was an adept synthesizer of sources: he found analogues for his own troubled age in the classical literature he studied in school and was especially inspired by the works of Seneca and Robert Garnier.[5] Scholars have identified significant ways in which these sources inform *The Spanish Tragedy*, while C. L. Barber, Lisa Hopkins, Lucas Erne, and Andrew Sofer among others trace moments in the play that point to the influence of medieval English drama. I follow these traces further, arguing that the ethos of mourning and vengeance embodied in the Corpus Christi cycles shapes the dramaturgy of *The Spanish Tragedy*. As with Shakespeare, so with Kyd: the plays themselves provide the most convincing evidence of this influence.[6]

'This signe schall vengeaunce calle / On yowe holly in feere': The Crucifixion of Horatio

C. L. Barber may have been the first to note that Horatio's murder evokes the crucifixion: 'Horatio, like Christ, is hung "on a tree" and Isabella, like the Virgin Mary, embraces the wounded body beneath it (4.2.23)'.[7] Hieronimo's '"From forth these wounds came breath that gave me life" (4.4.95) reinforces these parallels' (Erne, 94). Barber, as Lucas Erne puts it, interpreted this 'Christian shaping' as being 'used to express family feeling in extremis' (Erne, 94). Lisa Hopkins notes the Christ-figure allusion, commenting that when 'Horatio is hanged in the arbor, he becomes ... an analogue of the crucified Christ in a Gethsemane-like garden (with the handkerchief as a Veronica's veil?) ...'[8] Sofer finds that this moment specifically resonates with the Passion plays of the Corpus Christi cycles.[9] His analysis focuses on the semiotic journey of *The Spanish Tragedy*'s central prop – the bloody handkerchief – from the *Quem Queritas* trope of the eleventh century through its transformation into the Veronica cloth and grave clothes of Christ in the Corpus Christi drama and then into Kyd's play where it further changes hands, bodies, and meanings from Andrea to Horatio to Bel-imperia, back to Horatio, and finally to Hieronimo. He vividly imagines the resonant cultural memory it embodies, 'ghosted' as it is by its prior Catholic meanings as a salvific totem for a theatre-going public during 'the most turbulent stage in English religious history' (138). Sofer observes that when Hieronimo finds the handkerchief soaked in blood on his son's corpse it becomes the embodiment of Horatio: 'If the Corpus Christi cloth [in the Resurrection] suggests the "felt absence" of Christ's body in the tomb, Kyd's handkerchief is now literally imbued with the substance of Hieronimo's dead son' (143). Hieronimo holds the bloody handkerchief aloft for the audience to behold, promising vengeance: 'Seest thou this handkerchief besmeared with blood? / It shall not from me till I take revenge. / Seest thou those wounds that yet are bleeding fresh? / I'll not entomb them till I have revenged' (2.5.51–4). For Sofer this gesture expresses contradictory impulses: 'On the one hand, Hieronimo's virtual canonization of his son invites us to see Horatio as a Christ figure: Hieronimo describes the "harmless blood" dishonoured within "this sacred bower" (2.5.20–7). On the other hand, we witness the Knight Marshal of Spain preparing to embark on a very un-Christian vendetta against those whom God should punish' (143).

This analysis overlooks what is possibly Kyd's most potent evocation of female lament. Hieronimo's canonization of Horatio and his attendant vow of revenge conjures a nearly identical moment in the Corpus Christi plays. In the York *Road to Calvary* the Third Maria compassionately wipes Jesus' face with her headcloth. Upon discovering the miracle that the fabric is imprinted with his image, she raises the vernicle aloft, and curses the soldiers tormenting Jesus: 'This signe schall vengeaunce calle / On yowe holly in feere' (196–7).[10] Three of the four extant cycles – the Towneley, York and Chester – dramatize this precursor to Hieronimo's vow of revenge.[11] Here the miracle and the call to vengeance are not contradictory but instead symbiotic impulses: the vengeance emerges from the 'signe', and Maria's voice carries the binding promise of retribution. Kyd's allusion suggests that Hieronimo's oath might not be a declaration of private vengeance as Sofer argues, but can also be understood in the communal semiotics of the theatre as a call to a collective public witnessing and reckoning. If by virtue of the Corpus

Christi plays' civic nature, the audience is already established as a collective witness to the action, this moment similarly transforms Kyd's audience into an important character. No longer a random gathering of people attending a play, the audience, willingly or not, is implicated in the play's moral dilemma, for it has become a collective witness to a hideous crime and its aftermath.[12] The framing narrative in which Andrea is doomed by Proserpine to sit with Revenge and act as Chorus for the audience illuminates this phenomenon. As a resonant figure of mourning responsible for souls in the underworld, Proserpine also conjures associations with the Virgin Mary, who as 'Empress of Hell', had juridic power over the souls in purgatory.[13]

Like Sofer's analysis, much of the scholarship on *The Spanish Tragedy* wrestles with the distinction between 'private revenge' and 'God's vengeance'. Yet Kyd's hero does not seek the simple satisfaction of killing his son's murderers. Above all Hieronimo wants a public reckoning, one akin to that in the Corpus Christi plays where the vengeful laments of mothers elicit God's retribution.

'Veniance, I cry and call … Veniance Lord, Upon them Fall':[14] The Mad Mothers and Their Cloud-Breaking Cries

Henry V's description of naked infants pitted upon pikes alludes to one of the most brutal scenes in medieval drama, second only to the buffeting, torture, and crucifixion of Christ. It is based upon the Slaughter plays, which depict Herod's henchmen gleefully boasting that they will make infants hop on their spears.[15] In the N-Town the second soldier revels in his 'swerdys sharpe' as it stabs the livers and lungs of 'barnys ȝonge', making the mothers 'sing' for sorrow: 'as An

Harpe / quenys xul karpe / and of sorwe synge' (66–8). The soldiers' bragging ironically redounds upon them. For the simile indicates that the mothers' cries, like Angels harps, as figured in the Book of Revelation, are the language of heaven. Heaven will hear and exact retribution. In the Chester, the second soldier delights in telling a mother that her infant will learn a new game: hopping on the end of his spear: 'Dame, thy sonne, in good faye, / hee must of me learne a playe: / he must hopp, or I goe awaye, / upon my speare ende' (321–4). Even as the women wail in anguish, they struggle fiercely against the soldiers, calling down vengeance upon them.

Scholars have long recognized that concepts of divine retribution shape the dramaturgy of the Slaughter and Passion plays, a moral and aesthetic structure embodied in female lamentation.[16] These plays contrast secular, human law with divine justice, dramatizing the belief that there is a higher justice articulated in the mothers' laments that will, in the fullness of time, overthrow tyrants. The Corpus Christi and Digby Slaughter plays invoke this ethical matrix.[17] In the N-Town, Digby, and Chester plays, Herod dies at the end in a manner that emerges from the women's laments.[18] The N-Town is unique in that, while the women do not call for vengeance explicitly, the manner of Herod's death emerges from the poetry of their pain. Believing he has destroyed his rival, Herod celebrates, ordering his minstrel to play a merry tune: 'Amonges all that grett rowthte / he is ded I have no dowte / Þerfore menstrell rownde a-bowte / blowe up a mery fytt' (229–32). The word 'fytt', here, as in Kyd's play, is pointedly ironic: in the medieval dialect it denotes a tune or song, but it also means punishment. When the minstrel starts playing, he 'blows up' a different kind of 'mery fytt', for it summons Herod's punishment: Diabolus enters, slays Herod, and turns to the audience, declaring: 'I xal hem brynge on to my celle / ... / and show such myrthe as in helle' (234–6). Mors enters next and warns the audience 'his lordchep is *al lorn* / ... / his sowle in helle ful peynfully / of develis is *al to-torn* (254–8)' echoing the first mother's exclaim: 'Longe lullynge have *I lorn*' as she looks upon her child that was '*al to torn*' by the soldiers' swords (89, 93; my emphasis). Kyd's complex tragedy follows this deceptively simple blueprint: an upper class tyrant murders a lower class rival, the mother mourns, and during the festivities to celebrate his success, the tyrant is killed in retribution for his crime. Just as Andrea finds 'spectacles to please his soul' in Hieronimo's revenge play, so the medieval audience no doubt had some merriment upon witnessing the blow-hard Herod's demise.

The Digby and Chester blend tragedy and comedy in a different way. They show the women bravely assaulting the cowardly soldiers with rocks and distaffs. In the Digby *Killing of the Children* the women say they will use these 'weapons' to make them knyghtes (310). When the soldiers murder their children, each woman invokes revenge: The first woman declares, 'A vengeaunce I aske on them alle for this grett wrong' (318); the second cries, 'a very myscheff mut come them amonge, / ... / For thei haue kylled my yong sone John!' (319–21). The third demands, 'a shamefulle deth I aske upon Herowde oure kyng, / That thus rygorously oure children hath slayn!' (322–3), and finally the fourth prays 'God bryng hym to an ille endyng / And in helle pytte to dwell euer in peyn!' (324–5). When the knights and their clownish leader Watkyn report back to Herod, they tell him of the women's curses: 'Ther be but women, and thei crie in every stede: / "A vengeaunce take Kyng Herode, for he hath our children sloon!"' (360–1). Upon hearing this, madness sweeps over Herod. He bellows that he grows 'madde!' and his 'wyttes be ner goon!' (365), before having a premonition of death: 'I wene I shalle dey þis day! / My hert tremelith and quakith for feere!' (381–2). He then desperately prays to 'Mahound' before his 'legges faltere' (388), and he falls down dead.[19] The Chester, like the Digby, stages a fierce struggle between mothers and soldiers, an engagement that overlays brutal slaughter and lament with an energetic, comic battle of the sexes. The soldiers delight in their slaughter of infants. Even as the women lament, they fight back. For example, the second woman wails 'Owt, owt on thee theife! / My love, my lord, my life, my leife, / did never man or woman greiffe / to suffer such torment' (329–32). She strikes her assailant, vowing, 'But yet wroken [avenged] I will bee' (333), and tells him to take her blows to Herod: 'Have here on, two, or three. / Beare the kinge this from me; and that I yt him sennd' (334–6). When another child is killed, the woman cradling the infant reveals that she is not the mother, but the nurse, and that this child is Herod's son: 'Owt, owt, owt, owt! / You shalbe hanged, the rowte. / ... / This child was taken to me / to looke to ... / Hee was not myne, as you shall see; hee was the kinges sonne. / ... Theeves, ye shall be hanged hye, / ... / For to the kinge I will anon / to playne upon you all' (377–92). When Herod learns that his violence rebounded upon him, he rages at the idiocy of the soldiers who should have easily seen by his son's dress that 'he was a kinges sonne' (412). Then he mewls: 'I wott I must dye soone. Booteles is me to make mone, / for dampned I must bee' (419–21). Just before 'Demon' whisks him away, he wails, 'My legges roten and my armes; / that nowe I see of feindes swarmes – / I have donne so many harmes – / from hell comminge after mee' (422–5). This version makes explicit a subversive aspect of these plays with respect to the existing class system in England.

The Chester Herod, like Kyd's Viceroy and Castile, experiences the death of his own son as a direct consequence of the manner in which he rules. In both instances, the audience witnesses the levelling effect of justice when a nobleman's son is murdered in retribution for a commoner's. The Slaughter plays dramatize God's invocation that vengeance is his; however, they link that divine retribution to the mothers' grief: grief that articulates a system of justice that knows no class distinctions.

'Sweet lovely rose, ill plucked before thy time': The Planctus Hieronimoiae

The Slaughter plays, which have a deep typological relationship with the Passion sequences, are the first in a series of moments that dramatize the monstrous suffering of the innocent, the anguish of their mothers, and the link between the mother's laments and divine retribution. Kyd draws upon this dramaturgy, refracting female lament through Horatio's three mourners: Bel-imperia, Isabella and Hieronimo. Whether he did so consciously or drew on associations that were part of his imaginative lexicon, these parallels show that Kyd understood the dramatic power of the *Planctus Mariae*, especially its ability to engender in an audience not only compassion for the victim, but also a sense of moral and emotional outrage wherein reparation feels necessary and urgent.[20] This is the effect of the series of laments beginning with Bel-imperia's cries in 2.5 when Horatio is attacked, through Hieronimo's vow in 4.3 to 'pursue revenge, / For nothing wants but acting of revenge' (28–9).

Bel-imperia, unlike the Virgin Mary in every other respect, is, however, like the Mary of the Corpus Christi Plays in that she is present when Horatio is assaulted, and her outcry echoes that of Mary's. As four men, like the four torturers of Jesus – Lorenzo, Balthazar, Pedringano and Serberine – hang Horatio in the arbour and then stab him, Bel-imperia cries, 'O save his life and let me die for him!' (2.4.55), echoing the Virgin's cries under the cross in the Chester *Passion* while her son is tortured (also by being hung and stabbed) by four 'Judeus's': 'Alas, theeves, why doe ye soe? / Slayes ye mee and lett my sonne goe. / For him suffer I would this woe / and lett him wend awaye' (261–3). Both women show courage and devotion. Bel-imperia exclaims, 'O save him, brother! Save him Balthazar! / I loved Horatio, but he loved not me!' (2.4.56–7). Until now, Bel-imperia's motives have been ambiguous. When she first expresses her love for Horatio, it is mingled with her desire to avenge Andrea, so much so that she resolves her confusion by conflating love and revenge (1.4.64–8). In her willingness to die for Horatio, Bel-imperia attests to her love and also acknowledges her part in Horatio's death. This mingling of love and vengeance drives the plot of Kyd's play, as it does the Mystery cycles.[21]

Following the murder Lorenzo looks up at Horatio's lifeless body and quips: 'Although his life were still ambitious proud, / Yet is he at the highest now he is dead' (2.4.59–60). In its cruel wit, he evokes the fixation on the height of the cross in the Mysteries, which may have suggested it to Kyd.[22]

In the York *Crucifixion* four soldiers repeat the word 'height' as they complain about their orders to raise Jesus high for people to see. When they finally accomplish their task, the third soldier exclaims, 'He weyes a wikkid weght. / So may we all foure saie, / Or he was heued on heght / And raysed in þis array' (213–16). The word 'array' is a sadistic pun, for it carries several meanings, from the literal: that he has been 'raised in this manner', which was arduous for the soldiers and excruciatingly painful for Jesus; to an ironic comment on Jesus's lack of clothing; to the figurative sense that he has been elevated in status, which is the same play on words as Lorenzo's. Similarly, in the Chester *Passion*, four Judeus's turn their work of arranging Jesus on the cross into a competitive game. They brag about their skill in stretching him to fit while rhyming and punning on the word 'height'. The second Judeus says, 'Fellowe, be this light, / nowe were his feete dight, / this gamon went on right / and up he should be raysed' (201–4). The third Judeus puns back, 'That shall be donne in hight / anon in your sight, / for, by my trouth I plight / I sarve to be praysed' (205–8), and the fourth wants them to 'see / howe I have stretched his knee' (209–10). The first Judeus brings the game to a close, again emphasizing the height of the cross: 'Yea helpe nowe that hee / on height raysed bee' (213–14). This last line mocks the height of Jesus in the same manner as the York torturers and Kyd's Lorenzo.

Lorenzo's vicious wit underscores the brutality of the murderers, for whom killing is sport, contrasting them with the innocent victim. With breathtaking economy, Kyd uses a single line to develop the same contrast dramatized in the drawn out scenes of Jesus's torture in the Corpus Christi cycles. Lorenzo's smug remark also taps into the tensions of a stratified society with an increasingly wealthy and aspiring middle class. The nature of Horatio's threat to the class structure of Kyd's play (and his society) is not substantially different than that which Jesus poses to the ruling powers in the Corpus Christi plays, which satirized contemporary nobility in the figures of Herod and Pilate.[23] Like the Slaughter plays, Kyd emphasizes the monstrous nature of Horatio's murder by contrasting Bel-imperia's womanly courage with the cowardice of the conniving noblemen and their mean accomplices. Lorenzo's heartless pun on Horatio's freshly stabbed and bleeding body hanging high on a tree may also have reminded Kyd's audience of the Doomsday Christ with his bleeding wounds, an image that once perched above the Rood-lofts in churches throughout England.

Having established the horrific nature of the crime, Kyd shifts the focus to the agon of mourning, which underscores the unbearable sorrow of the bereft and their inability to obtain justice. Upon finding Horatio's body, Hieronimo laments, echoing Mary in the N-Town *Burial*. As Joseph of Arimethea and Nicodemus remove Jesus's body from the cross and place him in Mary's lap, she embraces him and laments: 'A Mercy Mercy myn owyn son so dere / Þi blody face now I must kysse / Þi face is pale with-owtyn chere / of meche joy now xal I mysse / Þer was nevyr modyr Þat sey this / so here sone dyspoyled with so gret wo' (1144–9). Like Mary he expresses his wretchedness and lost joy: 'Ay me most wretched, that have lost my joy / In leesing my Horatio, my sweet boy!' (2.5.32–3). When Isabella joins him in the arbour, Hieronimo implores her help: 'Here Isabella help me to lament / for sighs are stopped, and all my tears are spent' (2.5.36–7), echoing Mary, who in the Towneley *Crucifixion* asks the three

Marias to lament with her: 'Madyns, make your mone, / And wepe, ye wyfes, euerichon / With me, most wrich in wone' (418–20). Like Mary and the holy women of the Crucifixion sequences he emphasizes the inhumanity and injustice of the murderers: 'What savage monster ñot of human kind / Hath here been glutted with thy harmless blood? / ... / O wicked butcher, whatso'er thou wert, / How could thou strangle virtue and desert?' (2.5.19–31). In the Towneley *Crucifixion*, Maria wails: 'Alas, my lam so mylde, / Whi will thou fare me fro, / Emang thise wulfes wylde / That wyrke on the this wo?' (410–13). Hieronimo's lyric of the flower crystallizes this juxtaposition of innocence and worthiness laid waste by butchery and deceit: 'Sweet lovely rose, ill plucked before they time, / Fair worthy son, not conquered but betrayed, / I'll kiss thee now, for words with tears are stayed' (2.5.46–8). The tender plant cropped too soon is a common motif of Marian lament: Mary exclaims in the York *Death of Christ*, 'Allas, Þat Þis blossome so bright / Vntrewly is tugged to Þis tree' (137–8) and in the Towneley *Crucifixion* 'Thi face with blode is red, / Was fare as floure in feylde' (329–30).

The Virgin's grief drives her mad, and she longs for death to end her sorrow: 'Mi sorrow it is so sad, / No solace may me safe; / Mowrnyng makys me mad, / None hope of help I hafe; / I am redles and rad / For ferd that I mon rafe; / Noght may make me glad / To I be in my grafe' (Towneley *Crucifixion*, 396–403). Mary never takes her eyes from her son's torn and bleeding body, calling first to death and then to God to let her die and to end her woe: 'Alas, ded, thou dwellys to lang! / Whi art thou hyd fro me? / ... / Good lord, graunte me my boyn / and let me lyf no more!' (Towneley *Crucifixion*, 461–80). Like the Virgin, Hieronimo and Isabella hold the image of Horatio's bloody corpse forever in their thoughts. Their unbearable pain drives them mad and both wish for death.[24] Just as Mary suffers with and for Jesus, so Hieronimo and Isabella suffer and sacrifice their lives in seeking justice for their murdered son.

Hieronimo vows revenge in the first flush of his grief, but it is not until his laments have twice been answered, seemingly by heaven, that he takes action. Until then he proceeds carefully, despite his anguish and Isabella's distress, and in the face of mounting evidence, to 'learn by whom all this was brought about' (2.5.63). Hieronimo stumbles upon the first piece of evidence as he weeps his eyes into 'fountains fraught with tears' (3.2.1), denouncing the world as a 'mass of public wrongs' (3.2.3) before turning to prayerful interrogation: 'O sacred heavens, if this unhallowed deed / … / Shall unrevealed and unrevenged pass, / How should we term your dealing to be just, / If you unjustly deal with those that in your justice trust?' (3.2.5–11). As he wavers between despair and forbearance, Bel-imperia's letter 'falleth' in his path. Upon perusing the evidence, he realizes that he must put away thoughts of suicide: his love for Horatio, 'behoves [he] be revenged' and therefore he must 'live t'effect thy resolution' (3.2.45–7). Wary that the letter might be intended to entrap him, he determines 'to confirm this writ' (3.2.49).

The collaborating evidence arrives again when Heaven seems to hear Hieronimo's cries. In the scene following Pedringano's execution, Hieronimo appears alone onstage, his 'exclaims … surchar[ing] the air' (3.7.3). Echoing the York Maria who asks, 'To whome nowe schall I make my mone / Sen he is dede?' (*Resurrection*, 209–10), Hieronimo implores 'Where shall I run to breath abroad my woes?' (3.7.1). Like the mourning of Ceres and Proserpine, Hieronimo's powerful exclaims strip the landscape, rendering it barren, just as his inability to obtain justice destroys his family's fertility in the plucking of his son too soon (3.7.6–9), yet 'still tormented is [his] tortured soul' (10). His 'broken sighs / … / Beat at the windows of the brightest heavens, / Soliciting for justice and revenge' (3.7.11–14), but he finds 'the place impregnable' (3.7.17).

Yet Hieronimo's prayerful laments appear to be answered, when, in the next moment the hangman enters with Pedringano's letter to Lorenzo, providing corroborating evidence of Bel-imperia's accusations. It is as if Proserpine the mourning goddess of vegetation and Queen of the underworld has heard his laments (or as indicated by the play's framing device, predetermined the outcome). Here, and throughout the play, Proserpine conjures associations with the Virgin Mary, Empress of Hell and Queen of Heaven, who hears the prayers of the faithful, judging and protecting the souls of their loved ones. Hieronimo interprets this serendipitous arrival of evidence as a sign from heaven: 'Till now, and now I feelingly perceive, / They did what heaven unpunished would not leave' (3.7.55–6). Armed with seemingly divine vindication, Hieronimo does not seek revenge, but justice: 'I will go plain me to my lord the king, / And cry aloud for justice through the court, / Wearing the flints with these my withered feet, / And either purchase justice by entreats / Or tire them all with my revenging threats' (3.7.69–73). But he cannot get justice: 'Nor aught avails it me to menace them / Who, as a wintry storm upon a plain, / Will bear me down with their nobility' (3.13.36–8). This simile comparing the nobility with a wintry storm again links the absence of justice on earth with the cycle of mourning and renewal over which Proserpine (and Mary) reign.

Isabella becomes a resonant embodiment of Proserpine and the Virgin Mary when she enacts the barren landscape of Hieronimo's laments in her destruction of the bower: 'Since neither piety nor pity moves / The king to justice or compassion, / I will revenge myself upon this place / Where thus they murdered my beloved son' (4.2.2–5). Here, Isabella invokes both the devotional purpose of meditating on the Virgin's sorrows as well as its underlying ethos of (divine) vengeance. Like Ceres, whose mourning for her abducted daughter, Proserpine, made the earth barren, Isabella's mourning for Horatio renders the bower infertile (4.2 14–15). Isabella transforms the bower into a tomb, a permanent memorial to her son. As she imagines passersby remarking, 'There, murdered, died the son of Isabel' (4.2.22), she sees her son's ghost soliciting 'with his wounds' (4.2.24), like the Doomsday Christ, 'Revenge on her that should revenge his death' (4.2.25). She curses the tree on which he died 'from further fruit' (4.2.35), and her womb 'for his sake' (4.2.36), becoming an inversion of the Virgin Mary whose womb produced blessed fruit. In the Chester *Passion* Marye wails in anguish as she looks up at her son bleeding on the cross: 'Think one, my fruyte, I fostred thee / and gave thee sucke upon my brest' (245–6). The Virgin Mary's grief may also have suggested to Kyd the manner of Isabella's death. In the York *Death of Christ* the Virgin laments as she watches her son die, 'Allas sone, sorowe and si3te, / Þat me were closed in clay / A swerde of sorowe me smyte, / To dede I were done Þis day' (157–60). Her grief pierces her in the breast as she wishes for death to end her pain. Similarly, out of 'sorrow and despair' (4.2.27), Isabella stabs herself: 'with this weapon I wound the breast / The hapless breast that gave Horatio suck' (4.2.37–8). She sacrifices herself to urge Hieronimo to avenge Horatio's death, a frantic act that is a devastating critique of a society in which both justice and the comforts of mourning and burial ritual are out of reach.

These scenes of anguished mourning develop sympathy for Isabella and Hieronimo, deepening the outrage against Lorenzo and Balthazar. Andrea's outbursts guide the audience in experiencing a growing sense of urgency in the need for retribution. In place of the drawn-out scenes of Jesus's suffering in the Corpus Christi plays, Kyd dramatizes Hieronimo's heroic suffering in his drawn-out search for clues to the murder. The playwright asks us not only to respond compassionately, but also to make judgements, attending to cause and effect in scenes that contrast the pitiable condition of the grieving parents with the machinations and negotiations of an aristocratic class concerned with maintaining the status quo. Critics demonstrate how these scenes contrast Hieronimo's methodical, cautious gathering of evidence, despite his anguish, with the recklessness and indifference of the nobility to the lives of those beneath them.[25] The Viceroy on hearsay alone is prepared to execute Alexandro, his most loyal and respected advisor. Lorenzo mistakenly concludes that Serberine has betrayed him, and rashly arranges for the deaths of both Pedringano and Serberine. In contrast,

Hieronimo exhausts every avenue to obtain justice. As Lorna Hutson argues, the class system impedes Hieronimo's suit: 'Kyd skilfully and plausibly hints that political considerations – the impending alliance of Spain and Portugal planned in the marriage of Balthazar to Bel-imperia – render Hieronimo inaudible at court, and prevent awareness of anything so inconvenient as an arraignment of the Prince of Portugal for murder now that a peace treaty has been signed' (284). Castile is implicated as well. No one in the court scene (3.12) is aware that Horatio is dead, and they are all too ready to believe Lorenzo's absurd explanation that Hieronimo's 'distract' and 'lunatic' manner (3.12.87) comes from pride and covetousness in 'having to himself' (3.12.85) the ransom due Horatio. Two scenes later when Castile urges a public peace between Lorenzo and Hieronimo, he either does not hear, wilfully chooses not to hear, or already knows that Horatio has been murdered. He doesn't blink when Lorenzo says, 'But what's a silly man distract in mind, / To think upon the murder of his son? / Alas, how easy is it for him to err!' (3.14.87–9). This juxtaposition of Hieronimo's suffering and the court's indifference shows that the play's central dilemma is not a simple opposition between justice and revenge, but more significantly the problem of obtaining justice in a stratified society.

'Why then I'll fit you': Hieronimo's Ethic of Mourning and Revenge[26]

At the conclusion of his 'Tragedy of Suleiman, the Turkish Emperor', Hieronimo pulls aside the curtain and '*shows his dead son*', urging his viewers to 'look on this spectacle' (4.4.88), as he mourns over Horatio for the last time. The public nature of his lament and the presence of the dead body evoke Catholic burial ritual.[27] At a time in England when such Catholic practices were being actively suppressed, this allusion would have been highly charged.[28] With a single line of verse, Kyd then transports his audience from funeral ritual to Doomsday play when Hieronimo points to Horatio's wounds and intones: 'From forth these wounds came breath that gave me life; / They murdered me that made these fatal marks' (4.4.95–6). Just as father and son appear together here, so, in the mystery of the Trinity, the Father who is also the Son appears in the Corpus Christi Judgement plays where Christ appears and shows his freshly bleeding wounds: 'Here may ye se my woundys wide / That I suffred for youre mysdede / Thrugh harte, hede, fote, hande, and syde, / Not for my gilte bot for youre nede' (Towneley *Judgment*, 576–80).[29] Jesus continues, enumerating the injustices he suffered. When he completes his catalogue of the crimes against him, he asks his onstage audience, which is comprised of the good and bad souls who were gathered at the sounding of God's trumpet: 'Say man, what suffered thou for me?' (607). He then pronounces rewards and punishments. Notably, among the 'bad' are those who were indifferent to the sufferings of the poor, sick, and needy. In the world of the Judgement plays, justice knows no rank. As Deus of the N-Town *Doomsday* declares: 'Ffor this xal be þe day of tene / Nowther pore ne ryche of grett renowne / ne all þe develys in helle þat bene / Ffrom þis day ȝow hyde not mowne / Ffor all ȝour dedys here xal be sene / Opynly in Syght' (17–22). Hieronimo's play similarly exposes everyone's deeds as the aggrieved father catalogues the crimes against his son and explains their punishment to his astonished audience. Michael Neill points out that Hieronimo's manner of addressing the nobility here is insolent.[30] Yet, this is another indication that Kyd's audience has been transported (like Andrea and Revenge) via the echoes of Doomsday to an imaginative space, much like purgatory, where justice and equality reign. Hieronimo's account conflates past and present, just as the Judgement plays encapsulate the fullness of time in their enactment of reciprocal justice: 'He shrieks; I heard, and yet methinks I hear, / His dismal outcry echo in the air / ... / Speak, Portuguese, whose loss resembles mine. / If thou canst weep upon thy Balthazar, / 'Tis like I wailed for my Horatio' (4.4.107–15). Hieronimo plays upon the symbiotic relationship between fathers and sons, Jesus and God, with deadly seriousness. As he tells the Viceroy, 'I will not trust thee with my life, / Which I this day have offered to my son' (4.4.158–9).

Hieronimo's theatre of reciprocal sacrifice evokes the moment in the Judgement plays when the bad souls are punished for their indifference to the suffering of others. None in Hieronimo's onstage audience – the King, the Viceroy, and even Castile – had the imaginative capacity to feel compassion for him when his son was murdered. They were deaf to his complaints and blind to his grief. As the Jesus of the Towneley *Judgment* tells his audience, echoing Matthew 25.40: 'Ye harde thaym noght, youre eeres was hid, / Youre help to thaym was not at hame, / To me was that vnkyndnes kyd, / Therefor ye bere this bitter blame; / To the lest of myne when ye oght dyd, / To me ye dyd the self and same' (692–7). Kyd uses the morality play structure to explore and expose the weaknesses of these three noblemen, a device that implicitly aligns them with Pedringano, whose greed made him vulnerable to Lorenzo's devious plots.[31] Likewise, the Viceroy's wrath made him susceptible to Villupo's machinations, while the King's and Castile's sense of aristocratic superiority – their class pride – rendered them indifferent to their magistrate's suffering.

The Spanish Tragedy explores the problem of mourning at a time of painful religious uncertainty. But it is also a tragedy of class inequity. It is a play about a virtuous, aspiring family of the middling sort that meets with tragedy when the ruling class conspires, consciously or not, to keep it in its place. Class struggle is at the heart of both the Corpus Christi plays and *The Spanish Tragedy*'s dramas of retribution.[32] And, like the Corpus Christi plays in which the mournful cries of unnamed mothers have the power to destroy tyrants, Kyd's Doomsday play punishes rulers for their failure to be moved to justice and compassion.

Kyd crystallizes the shards of the past and the anxieties and fears of the present into a daring exploration of the problem of justice in a stratified society wrestling with religious, economic and social change. Purgatory, above all, promises justice – if not in this life then in the next.[33] Whether or not individual Englishwomen and men believed in purgatory, their society had been steeped for centuries in the promise articulated in its Christian topography. Banning the word could not erase the promise. Like the Corpus Christi pageants, Kyd's play manifests this promise in performance. His Hieronimo, like the God of the Judgement, produces a drama of retribution, and like the Doomsday Christ, explains to his shocked onstage audience what it means. And, as they watched kings, viceroys, and dukes, who had ruled indifferently, Kyd's audience, like Andrea, found in the ending 'spectacles to please [its] soul' (4.5.12).

The ritualistic tone of the final scene, noted by G. K. Hunter (103–4), combined with its evocation of the Corpus Christi Doomsday Christ, invites an allegorical reading, suggesting that the nobility has wrought its own destruction. For, as Isabella's destruction of the bower implies, the court rendered itself infertile when it failed to be concerned with justice. As in the Corpus Christi plays, the one who was wrongly judged returns to judge those who wronged him. Hieronimo cleverly uses the nobility's primary sin, pride (with which Lorenzo had impugned him) against them. As Lorna Hutson argues:

> Hieronimo's carefully scripted intrigue dictates a causally plotted course of action which his actors – the murderous noblemen – *are bound to follow, even to their deaths*. This fantasy of classical dramatic plotting as retribution for class injustice is brilliantly conceived, as Hieronimo turns aside Prince Balthazar's repeated expressions of nervous hesitation by appealing to the snob value of tragedy ... [They] are so beguiled by their faith in tragedy's aristocratic credentials that they enact upon one another the just punishment for murder that it was once Hieronimo's task, as Spain's Knight Marshall, to dispense as part of every citizen's legal right. (285–6)

The relationship of the Corpus Christi plays to Kyd's dramaturgy illuminates without resolving perhaps the knottiest question of *The Spanish Tragedy*: what do we mean when we attempt to distinguish between revenge and justice by saying that vengeance belongs to God? For in both the Corpus Christi pageants and *The Spanish Tragedy* whatever distinction might be possible is collapsed in the theatrical performance. Kyd lived during an age of Doomsday Plays, an age in which both Catholics and Protestants were publically tortured and put to death 'in the name of God', an age in which, only a year or so before Kyd's play took the stage, one of God's anointed put another of God's anointed to death. And within two generations, Kyd's prescient theatre became a terrifying reality when the English parliament performed its own version of a Doomsday play: the execution of Charles I for treason against the commonwealth.

8

The Spanish Tragedy: Resources for Teaching

Leslie Drury

Iconic in its time, Thomas Kyd's *The Spanish Tragedy* had a traceable impact. Repeatedly staged, printed, imitated, and mocked in the decades following its writing, the play elicited active responses to its language, themes, and dramaturgy. The aim of this chapter is to support educators and students as they explore their own active responses to the play, with resources that can be used in the classroom setting to focus discussion around important topics. As with the play editions in the Arden Early Modern Drama series, the chapter is designed with students at late secondary, college, and university levels in mind. The suggested approaches in this chapter are likely to be of most use for students' first contact with this play but should be helpful to students with a range of experience and abilities in discussing early modern drama. The approaches can be used progressively but are readily available as individual activities. The hope is that the suggested activities will serve as a starting point, which teachers can tailor to their own curriculum needs. Resources range from online features, academic articles, and group discussion topics, including both general and close readings of key issues. Suggested activities are for teaching approaches in a classroom setting, but can also be used for individual study.

The resources that follow are grouped into three key themes: First readings, Considering performance, and Judgement and justice. It is a select list of topics for engaging with the play, chosen to suit a discussion-group setting. The final portion of the chapter is a Select Annotated Bibliography, divided by subject.

First readings

As with many early modern texts in the classroom, ensuring that students are able to engage with the play text on a basic level is of utmost importance. For students struggling with Kyd's language, the opportunity to see a performance can be invaluable. Unfortunately, there are currently no full-length film versions of *The Spanish Tragedy*. There is, however, a full-length audio recording. Librivox.org provides free volunteer-based audio recordings of public domain books and there is a multi-contributor version of *The Spanish Tragedy* available, released in 2012.[1] The contributors have produced a clear and well-performed reading: an excellent resource for helping students follow the play. There is also a five-part posting on YouTube of 'Scenes from a reading of Thomas Kyd's play' by filmmaker Alex Cox, starring Derek Jacobi and adapted for the cinema by Tod Davies.[2] This reading is abridged and the filming was impromptu, so the sound quality can be poor at times, but it is nevertheless a reading from a high profile, professional cast. Both of these online recordings of the play can be used either for individual study or, time allowing, in the classroom. The LibriVox cast takes particular care to give distinctive characteristics to the various roles, so is helpful for students struggling to distinguish Kyd's many characters. The reading also presents male roles through female voices, providing opportunities to discuss with students how casting changes affect their interpretations.

Activity: The murder map and the mechanics of revenge

A valuable introductory in-class activity is to discuss and 'map out' the sequence of murders in the play. Beginning with Andrea's death, which is among the play's first information, students can then 'map' the chronological sequence of deaths by creating a flow-chart which shows the connections between these events. For reference, the on-stage deaths in order are: Horatio (stabbed and hanged), Serberine (shot), Pedringano (hanged, legally), Isabella (suicide by stabbing), Lorenzo (stabbed by Hieronimo), Balthazar (stabbed by Bel-imperia), Bel-imperia (suicide by stabbing), Castile (stabbed by Hieronimo), Hieronimo (suicide by stabbing).

For each death, students can then be prompted to discuss the following questions:

- Who has died?
- Who has done the killing? (In several cases the answer would be 'suicide'.)
- What motivated them to do this killing?
- What has this death set in motion?
- How might this scene affect an audience's view of the person responsible for the death?

For an abbreviated example of how this functions in a classroom discussion, we can look at Horatio's murder. Technically murdered by Lorenzo, Balthazar, Serberine and Pedringano, the murder is motivated by Horatio's relationship to Bel-imperia – due to his lower social status and Balthazar's thwarted wishes to woo Bel-imperia. Horatio's death is a major catalyst for several events: his parents' grief will eventually lead to Isabella's suicide and Hieronimo's revenging actions, Bel-imperia's grief and her immediate imprisonment lead to her commitment to the revenge scheme, and the need to cover up the murder leads to Lorenzo orchestrating Serberine and Pedringano's deaths. For many audience members, this scene might cement Balthazar and particularly Lorenzo, with his callous remarks in regard to Horatio's hanged body (2.4.60–61), as villains worthy of retribution.

In the classroom, repeatedly asking for clarification and further details will greatly benefit students in discussion. For example, further elaboration might have students add that Balthazar also seems to bear a grudge against Horatio for his battlefield capture, something also exacerbated by Horatio's lower social status. As we reach the final deaths in the play, the accretion of rationales for the death may increase; Bel-imperia, for instance, has two dead lovers and injustices done against herself as rationales for her murderous actions.

Discussing these deaths will help students new to the play to identify major plot points and key characterizations. This activity also has benefits for a better thematic understanding of the play. Seeing the domino-like effect of the deaths in the play helps students to grasp how the chain of vengeance and the social ties between family, friends, and lovers leads inexorably to the play's bloody conclusion.

Another value in this approach is the further considerations generated by the students themselves. For example, Pedringano's death could segue into a discussion about social inequalities in the play; the pattern of Isabella and Bel-imperia's suicides can lead students to discuss female agency and representation. The activity empowers students to make their own connections, beginning the process of closer dramatic analysis.

Activity: Exploring online resources

The University of Warwick has a resource website for 'Elizabethan and Jacobean Drama' which is an 'open-access resource on the page and stage history of five Jacobethan [*sic*] playwrights and nine of their plays', including Thomas Kyd. This provides an invaluable tool for students to explore close reading and other online resources.

The section concerning Kyd and *The Spanish Tragedy* includes an interactive text analysis activity of Hieronimo's opening speech in Act 3, Scene 12, in which students can listen to a recording of the passage and mouse over underlined words to reveal expanded discussion of characters mentioned and difficult or unfamiliar words.[3] The 'analysing' activity link guides the user through a series of key questions regarding the passage, such as, 'Who does Hieronimo speak as? The Knight Marshal of Spain? A father bereft of his son?', and includes topics for further study. This activity will be particularly useful for students less familiar with close reading as it guides them from initial questions of identifying the speaker and immediate context, through to motivations, implications, stylistic elements and topics for further study.

The resource can also be used for broader discussions of both the play and Kyd's historical context as it includes background for the play, performance history, audio and video recordings of lectures, and a bibliographic database. The interactive timeline is especially useful as an active tool for the classroom, allowing the user to select multiple categories that are shown on the timeline simultaneously. For example, selecting both 'Life of Kyd' and 'Political and Social' allows students to see what 'world' events were happening contemporaneously with the play. In doing so, students can note that in the years just prior to *The Spanish Tragedy* there are multiple military engagements between England and Spain both in Europe and in the Americas. Though a teacher would need to de-emphasize too causal a connection between these events and the militarized Spanish setting in the play, allowing students to discuss cultural contexts such as views of foreign powers can help them see how contemporary issues translated thematically to the stage.

Further in-depth discussion could entail encouraging students to find articles on the play which discuss the same topics as those in the links they have found. This can present an additional opportunity for students to engage with the academic potential of online databases, using appropriate search terms to discover articles or books which elaborate on the patterns they are noticing. For example, a search on Google Scholar for 'The Spanish Tragedy' and 'xenophobia' provides a number of hits leading to valuable scholarly reading. If students are new to searching for their own sources it may be helpful to allow them to initially do a standard internet search, such as on Google.com, and discuss with them the insufficiency of the results presented by the main results page – which will usually be dominated by online study guides, though they may be able to see hits from academic sources as well.

The Warwick resource allows students to explore academically but within the online environment that many of them will prefer. Exploration of the play through this website also provides opportunities to discuss adequate referencing and the reliability of sources. To emphasize this, a teacher might have students do the above activities – with the students assuming the reliability of the source simply because they're being introduced to it within class – and then ask them to explain how they can trust the information on this web page. After looking through the available pages, students might point out that the website itself is presented by a known university, the main page for the 'Thomas Kyd' subsection of the website has a sidebar that has university-affiliated academics as the creators, and the introduction page 'The Spanish Tragedy' and 'Performance History' both have citations for their academic sources.[4] This step will reinforce that students should be evaluating sources appropriately and the necessity of citations in their own work will be organically bolstered.

Please see 'First readings' in the annotated bibliography for cited sources and further reading.

'For nothing wants but acting of revenge!': Considering performance in *The Spanish Tragedy*

Given that *The Spanish Tragedy* was 'one of the first and longest-lasting Renaissance box-office hits', there is a wonderful opportunity in classroom strategies for engaging with the dramatic text as a piece written for performance.[5] Emphasizing performance in in-class discussions can have distinct benefits. Characters that students might initially dismiss as long-winded can become immediate and emotive when seen brought to life by an actor. The scant stage directions that early modern texts give when read on the page, such as 'they stab him' (2.4.54), cannot convey the visceral response elicited when watching an actor be believably attacked. Grasping the important role that performance has when studying early modern drama helps students to become engaged. Creating that livelier link to the language on the page also encourages analysis. By emphasizing performance students can come to see both how stagecraft is integral to literature of the early modern stage and why Kyd's first audiences found this play so compelling.

Activity: Staging a scene

The suggested activities in the following section consider the impact of performance in Act 2, Scene 4. The three considered approaches to the scene – a modern filmed version, in-class performance, and a reconstruction of the scene's original stagings – serve to help students analyse the ways that the specificities of each performance can help to bring out dramatic nuances. While it is not necessary to do all three activities together, comparison between them benefits student understanding.

The Shakespearean London Theatres (ShaLT) project has released a film version of Act Two, Scene Four and the first portion of Scene Five, which can be found both on their website and via their YouTube channel. The project aims to 'tell[ ] the illustrated story of the playhouses, entrepreneurs, audiences, actors and dramatists that made up th[e] founding theatrical industry' in London between the 1570s and 1642.[6] To better understand the world in which playwrights such as Kyd were operating, it is well worth looking through the various resources the ShaLT webpage offers, including: filmed scenes, interviews, and an interactive map of the London theatres.

This filming encompasses the wooing of Horatio and Bel-imperia, the murder of Horatio, and the discovery of the body by Hieronimo. Beyond the opportunity to see professional actors in the roles, the film is particularly compelling. There is performative charm in the flirtation between Horatio and Bel-imperia, menace in the actions of Balthazar and Lorenzo, and poignant grief in Hieronimo's discovery. Kate Sissons gives elegant life to the character of Bel-imperia, showing her melancholy doubt and amorous aggression. The modernized and pared-down performance presents an opportunity for students to consider how directorial and acting choices interact with the text they already know. Below are potential considerations for students to discuss more fully, broken down into the three key stages of the scene – wooing, murder, and discovery.

Initial questions raised might be in regard to casting and costume. How do the look, speech, and mannerisms of each actor affect what you think of that character? What does their clothing and styling seem to imply about them? Students might note that the sophistication of the dress and speech of the actors playing Horatio and Bel-imperia can at times seem at odds with the naivety of their flirtation. How does this dichotomy affect how we feel about the wooing as we watch it progress? Though we know that the scene will turn violent, is there anything in the first portion that foreshadows this?

Pedringano is the only character who speaks directly to the camera. Why might they have chosen him to do this? What effect does this have on the delivery of his lines?

The murder of Horatio in this adaptation is worth particularly discussing with students. The murder avoids gore, opting instead for actors' bodies shielding the stabs, a cut-in shot which focuses on Horatio's feet at the moment of his hanging, and a focused shot on the overturned bench to signify the moment of hanging. There is no stage blood, but the hanged body is shown in full shot after Bel-imperia has been dragged away. Why might one choose to show the murder in this way? What sort of reactions does it produce? How do the actors make clear what is happening?

Finally, Hieronimo's speech, though cut short from that in the text, raises several points of discussion for students. In what may be a difficult speech for new readers to grasp on the page, the progression from denial to recognition in the scene is particularly clear. The use of the flashlight in particular contributes to a focused progression of recognition: first shone toward the viewer and upon the space before the arbour, then on the body of the as yet unidentified hanged man, it finally rises to the face of the now recognized son. The light tracks Hieronimo's own ability to 'see' the truth of the murder before him, reinforcing his verbal progress toward recognition. The flashlight is also the final image of this film, as Hieronimo drops it in shocked grief. How does such a final shot affect how we feel about what we've seen? Does this final image connect to any of the themes of the play which have been discussed?

As can be seen from these brief suggestions for discussing the filmed scene, a performance of the drama can open up interpretative possibilities and make it easier for students to consider the choices the text offers. A second suggested activity is that students take up the directing and the acting of the scene themselves. In doing so, students will again be able to consider the range of choices a dramatic text entails, and are empowered to emphasize some textual details over others, further encouraging critical and close textual engagement. The activity also playfully reflects Kyd's own schooling as 'the performance of plays, often in Latin, was part of the curriculum', as students can be told.[7] There are several further reasons why this scene is valuable for students to act out: it's a pivotal scene in the play; it contrasts short but powerful speeches by several characters with Hieronimo's long speech; and it has several stage directions and physical actions, allowing students to step into an active role as 'director'.

A model for the acting of this scene in an impromptu class session would be to assign certain students the acting roles and then have a student, or a panel of the remaining students, play the role of 'director', discussing with the actors how to position themselves and enact stage directions in between lines. A reading of the wooing, likely avoiding the actual kissing, provides opportunity for students to see how much erotic tension can be present. The class can see this either through the positive chemistry of the two student actors or through an alternative awkwardness, either outcome reinforcing the intensity of the interaction. The murder portion of the scene allows students to discuss how they would want to represent violent action and what it takes to make a character seem villainous. The discovery by Hieronimo, in a passage probably the most difficult for the classroom amateur, will allow students to consider what makes the sequence of his lines sensible and compelling. After students have hashed out the scene to their satisfaction, you might ask them to reflect comparatively with the ShaLT version. What did they choose to do differently? What effect did each change have for an audience's interpretation and view of each character and the scene as a whole?

A third way of considering the performance of the scene is through a description of the likely contemporary stage practice. This is provided in Martin White's book *Renaissance Drama in Action: An Introduction to Aspects of Theatre Performance*.[8] In his chapters, White examines various aspects of early modern performance, such as the playing conditions of the different theatres. The chapter 'Palaces of pleasure: outdoor playing spaces and theatre practice' provides a thorough discussion of the physical parameters and acting specifications of the outdoor theatres, the places in which Kyd's tragedy would have been so successful.[9] This chapter ends with a case study on *The Spanish Tragedy* Act 2, Scene 4, which intersperses the lines of the scene with in-depth analysis of likely stage setup, props, implicit character actions, and thematic implications in the language and metre of the lines.[10] The one stage action not elaborated on is the stabbing of Horatio; White focuses instead on the likely actions of the hanging. He also includes illustrative contemporary woodcuts to aid discussion of the likely staging of the arbour. Students can use White's case study as an illustration of contemporary theatre practice and also comparatively, alongside the approaches to the staging of Act 2, Scene 4 already discussed. Allowing students to see how stagecraft and performance can be an integrative part of textual analysis, White's close readings are particularly valuable.

Activity: Violence as spectacle

For a play widely known for its aggressive on-stage portrayal of violence, many students may not appreciate the role visible violence has when they experience it from the page. Stagecraft in Kyd's time meant that scenes of mutilation and death could be very realistic and its role in the play engages with early modern views of public execution as spectacle and violence as entertainment. As Clara Calvo and Jesús Tronch note, '[p]ractically all of the[ ]deaths or near-deaths occur in front of others, who watch them as the crowds watched the public executions in early modern London'.[11] The scope of these considerations is beyond simple entertainment; staged violence is deeply connected to the play's central concerns of state authority and the enactment of just judgement in the play. There are several critical works that would be a good starting place for more advanced students to learn about early modern expectations of realistic stage violence and its connection to the thematic concerns of the play. In his book *Early Modern Tragedy and the Cinema of Violence*, Stevie Simkin includes the chapter 'Spectacles of Death', which discusses early modern staging practicalities, audience expectations of realism based on their familiarity with execution and death, and meaningful parallels with modern cinema.[12] Citing the work of Andrew Gurr and others on stage practice, Simkin discusses plays which included a prop of a severed head and the use of animal blood and organs to realistically simulate mutilation and death.[13] James Shapiro's chapter '"Tragedies naturally performed": Kyd's Representation of Violence, *The Spanish Tragedy* (c. 1587)' and Molly Smith's book *Breaking Boundaries: Politics and Play in the Drama of Shakespeare and his Contemporaries* both examine the link between state executions, events generally witnessed by the London public, and the representation of such violence in the play.[14] Both of these arguments address the play's repeated descriptions and stagings of violence, providing destabilizing readings regarding the boundaries between state violence, staged violence, and reality.

Besides examining the realism of violent stagings of the time, helping more advanced students understand the play's violence as entertainment serves to reinforce their analytical interest, helping to remove the sometimes adversarial relationship students have with early modern dramatic texts. By asking students to consider the place violence has in our own entertainment models, alongside similarities and differences to early modern theatregoers, discussion can foster a more pertinent understanding of the play as a staged activity. Modern stagings embracing violence offered in the play text have been reviewed as 'blood-soaked', eliciting comparison with the film *Saw*.[15] The parallel with traditional slasher movies is in many ways apt, but increasingly relevant comparisons can be drawn with films outside the horror genre. Quentin Tarantino's films, for example, are known for their violence, both realistic and stylized; the two-part film *Kill Bill* has been critically discussed as a revenge tragedy and the more recent *Django Unchained* presents a similar combination of a revenging protagonist who triumphs over his enemies in a blood-soaked finale.[16] The televised adaptation *Game of Thrones* is presently a cultural touchstone in which deep and compellingly shocking violence is key.[17] For many students the appeal of *The Spanish Tragedy* may not be far from their own preferred entertainment.

Please see 'Considering performance' in the annotated bibliography for cited sources and further reading.

'Let me be judge': Judgement and justice

Issues of judgement – whether through the officially sanctioned channels of state justice or through personal enactments of revenge – are central to the play's themes and actions. The two suggested activities below allow students to participate in actions of judgement in order to build their understanding of how judgement is related to justice, vengeance, or both. The suggested activities in this section focus on having students work through the processes of judgement in the play.

Activity: Character trials

The first suggested activity involves having students stage debate-style trials for the main characters of the play. If students have made the 'murder map' suggested above, this activity can begin by dividing the play characters according to who might generally seem good or bad. Dividing them between Andrea's friends and his enemies will simplify this process. The activity can then successfully be undertaken in one of two ways, depending on the needs of the student group. The first option is to stage a pro et contra trial, in which one half of the class builds arguments in support of the division of characters and the other half argues against it. Alternatively, groups can be assigned particular characters and asked to generate both the pro and contra arguments. If the class does the former, students who are arguing for the division of the characters will have the weight of much of the play in their favour, so it is important to push them to fully support their rationale with textual evidence. Similarly, the second group needn't convince everyone that, for example, Lorenzo is a model of virtue, but rather that his actions do engage with a kind of reason. Encourage students to consider things such as extenuating circumstances, socio-historical context, apportioning of guilt for the crime, psychological states and characters' relationships to build their arguments. For example, a contradictory reading of Lorenzo might argue that, within the gendered and familial relationships of the time, his control of Bel-imperia as a brother might be justified. This of course brings into the conversation the difficult issue of an argument that justifies the subjugation of a woman, but having students directly address such problems is invaluable. Similarly, a subversive reading of Bel-imperia's actions might point out that her suicide implicates her as being morally in the wrong within the Judeo-Christian tradition. Students that are assigned these contradictory roles will find that there are compelling arguments which complicate the moral judgements they assumed about the play. Indeed, what I have been calling 'contradictory' readings of the characters in the play are in fact integrated readings of these characters and their motivations. Once the debate has been made fully, class discussion can be turned to understanding how all of the debate-generated evidence from the play contributes to a more complete reading that is complex, often ambiguous, and much more meaningful now the students have put forth the exploratory effort. In this exercise, the examination of the more minor characters can provide some of the liveliest debate about moral relativity and ambiguous judgements. Many students may find Pedringano a much more sympathetic character when they consider his social class as a motivation in his crimes and his ultimately pitiful end: tricked into complicity in his death by a man to whom he has shown allegiance. Though students may ultimately deem the division of characters as appropriate, the exercise allows them to explore the complexity and moral ambiguity of these varied characters and to question any absolute judgements passed within the play.

Activity: Layers of judgement

Developing student judgements of the play further, a second activity can focus on points in which judgement is passed explicitly within the play. By discussing the nature of these judgements in detail, students can explore the problematic relationship between judgement and justice, according to its 'abundance of adjudications' yet 'scarcity of justice'.[18]

As students consider the various 'judges' and judgements passed in the play, they might ask the following questions:

- Who is the judge and on whom do they pass judgement?
- What gives them authority to pass judgement? For example, Hieronimo has, in certain cases, authority to pass judgement as Knight Marshall, power which is derived from the King. Andrea will supplicate to Proserpine to pass judgements on his friends and enemies (4.5.13–16).
- Does the judgement seem fair and appropriate in nature and scale?

- How does this judgement affect our larger view of the processes of justice in the play?

Judgements that might be discussed are varied in circumstance and outcome, so these questions are starting points only when considering the intersection of judgement and justice in a given case.

Instances of judgement in the play which could be discussed include:

- The judgement of Andrea in the underworld (1.1.32–85)
- The King of Spain's decision in the dispute between Lorenzo and Horatio over Balthazar (1.2.152–97)
- The Viceroy of Portugal's impromptu judgement of Alexandro after Villuppo's false accusation (1.3.55–95)
- Hieronimo presiding as Knight Marshall over Pedringano's sentencing and hanging (3.6)
- Hieronimo's *Vindicta Mihi* speech, in which he considers his revenging intent, and his treatment of the three supplicants who come to him as Knight Marshall (3.8)
- Isabella's 'revenge' on the arbour and her suicide (4.2)
- Hieronimo's reveal of his revenging plot, as he explains the play-within-a-play and commits suicide (4.4.7–196)
- Andrea's judgement of his friends and enemies (4.5.1–44)

These various cases of judgement in the play allow students to examine both officially sanctioned 'justice' and privately enacted revenge. Both involve judgement and punishment but, as students will discover in their discussions, Kyd's play problematizes both the authority and the justness of both forms of judgement. Hanging over all such judgements in the play is the question that Hieronimo himself asks of the 'sacred heav'ns': 'How should we term your dealings to be just, / If you unjustly deal with those that in your justice trust?' (3.2.10–11). Gods, Kings, government officials, and private citizens all participate in and complicate the role that judgement plays in this world and the next.

By considering the role that the underworld gods and Andrea have in the layers of judgement occurring in the play, students can better understand the relationship between the play's frame and central acts. Examining these passages will also help students to strengthen their close reading skills, as the language, particularly in the passages regarding the underworld, is figurative and contains classical allusions.

Once students have clarified the layers of authority in the play, the destabilized judgements they have developed in the previous exercise can be recalled. By comparing the problematized authority of the judge with the problematized justness of the judgement itself, students will be able to see the precarious relationship of justice to personal judgement Kyd has created.

Please see 'Judgement and justice' in the annotated bibliography for cited sources and further reading.

Select annotated bibliography

The following annotations are grouped by subject: suggested single play editions, anthologies, the three key subjects discussed in this chapter – First readings, Considering performance, and Judgement and justice – and additional thematic groupings of criticism for further study. Suggested reading has been limited to what would be most valuable in initial engagements with criticism, so students working on research papers will wish to make further inquiries for suitable secondary sources.

Single editions

Kyd, Thomas, *The Spanish Tragedy: Authoritative Text, Sources and Contexts, Criticism*, ed. by Michael Neill (London: W. W. Norton, 2014)
This Norton Critical Edition provides a well-rounded presentation of material for studying the play. Includes an introduction, play text with glosses in footnotes, texts of sources for the play, and a selection of abridged criticism on the play.

Kyd, Thomas, *The Spanish Tragedy*, ed. by Clara Calvo and Jesús Tronch (London: Bloomsbury, 2013)
This entry in the Arden Early Modern Drama series is perhaps the most detailed in its scholarly presentation of the play, with a lengthy critical introduction and footnotes providing glosses and further explanatory notes.

Kyd, Thomas, *The Spanish Tragedy*, ed. by J. R. Mulryne (London: Bloomsbury, 2013)
With introduction and notes by Andrew Gurr, this New Mermaids edition of the play includes glosses, editorial notes, and further explanatory notes as footnotes.

Kyd, Thomas, *The Spanish Tragedy*, ed. by David Bevington (Manchester: Manchester University Press, 1996)
This Revels Student Edition includes critical introduction with glosses and explanatory notes as footnotes. The 1602 additions to the play are included at the end of the text.

Anthologies

English Renaissance Drama: A Norton Anthology, ed. by David Bevington and others (London: W. W. Norton, 2002)
This collection offers a large selection of drama and provides a general critical introduction with a section on shared themes and a timeline that sets 'authors and texts' with 'contexts'.

The play has a brief critical introduction and glosses are given as footnotes.

Five Revenge Tragedies, ed. by Emma Smith (London: Penguin Classics, 2012)
This collection sets Kyd's play in genre context alongside *Hamlet, Antonio's Revenge, The Tragedy of Hoffman,* and *The Revenger's Tragedy.* Provides a general introduction to the genre of revenge tragedy, a chronology which sets the plays against theatrical and historical backgrounds, and brief author biographies. The play text itself is set out simply on the page with endnotes provided.

Four Revenge Tragedies, ed. by Katharine Eisaman Maus (Oxford: Oxford University Press, 1995)
Providing context within genre, the collection also includes *The Revenger's Tragedy, The Revenge of Bussy D'Ambois,* and *The Atheist's Tragedy.* Introduction focuses on making thematic links within the genre, particularly highlighting the moral ambivalence of private vengeance and its commentary upon the stratified and changing social structure of Elizabethan England. Textual glosses for the play are provided in endnotes.

Four Revenge Tragedies: The Spanish Tragedy, The Revenger's Tragedy, 'Tis Pity She's a Whore, The White Devil, ed. by Janet Clare and others (London: Methuen Drama, 2014)
This New Mermaids Anthology brings together prior editions of the selected plays and provides genre context for *The Spanish Tragedy*. General introduction explores shared themes within the genre and glosses on the play text are provided as footnotes.

The Oxford Anthology of Tudor Drama, ed. by Greg Walker (Oxford : Oxford University Press, 2014)
This collection features a wide range of drama from the period of the long Tudor century (1485–1603), emphasizing continuity between medieval and renaissance drama with a

general introduction for the collection. The play includes an introduction and thorough footnotes.

Six Renaissance Tragedies, ed. by Colin Gibson (London: Macmillan, 1997)

Providing context within genre, the collection also includes *The Tragical History of Doctor Faustus, The Revenger's Tragedy, The Duchess of Malfi, The Changeling,* and *'Tis Pity She's a Whore.* General introduction provides shared thematic elements of the selected plays and contextualizes plays within the individual playing houses of London's theatre scene. The play has a brief introduction covering the text's authorship, history and sources. Textual glosses are provided as end notes. Appendix I addresses the 1602 additions with a brief critical introduction and provides the text of the 'Painter Scene' of 3.12.

Renaissance Drama: An Anthology of Plays and Entertainments, ed. by Arthur F. Kinney (Oxford: Blackwell Publishing, 2005)

This collection offers a wide range of dramatic pieces. Includes general historical and cultural introduction, brief biographies of authors, chronology of historical and dramatic events of note, and maps of London and Britain with 'Places of importance in Renaissance Literature'. Gives a brief critical introduction to the play and footnotes provide glosses on difficult words.

First readings

For many students useful initial engagement with criticism of the play will be provided by the critical introduction to the chosen play edition. The secondary works below have been selected as having broad introductory engagement with *The Spanish Tragedy,* Kyd's works, and revenge tragedy as a genre.

Bowers, Fredson Thayer, *Elizabethan Revenge Tragedy 1587–1642* (Gloucester, MA: Peter Smith, 1959)

This work aims to cover the shared attributes of plays that fall within this genre and survey their development in the period. *The Spanish Tragedy* is given particular attention.

The Cambridge Companion to English Renaissance Tragedy, ed. by Emma Smith and Garrett A. Sullivan Jr (Cambridge: Cambridge University Press, 2010)
Part 1 of this book includes essays covering a variety of themes in relation to English Renaissance tragedy, with a chapter devoted to 'Tragedy and Revenge'. The second half includes readings of particular plays, including Gregory M. Colón Semenza's chapter '*The Spanish Tragedy* and Metatheatre' (pp. 153–62), which argues that the mechanism of the play's consideration of the morality of judgement is through its metatheatrical framings.

Clare, Janet, *Revenge Tragedies of the Renaissance* (Tavistock, Devon: Northcote House Publishers, 2006)
A survey style approach to the genre, this book is useful for general study and contextualizing the play, including an introduction which traces the cultural and legal ramifications of revenge in the era and the development of the dramatic form. The book also provides a section on *The Spanish Tragedy*, giving a brief background and analysis of the play. Includes additional study aids such as relevant photographs from performances, a 'Biographical and Historical Outline' (pp. ix–xi), and suggested further reading.

Cox, Alex (dir.), 'Spanish Tragedy Part I' (2008). Available online: https://www.youtube.com/watch?v=DDuvqnsKXl8 (accessed 1 March 2015)
Abridged impromptu filming of round table reading of the play by professional cast.

Erne, Lukas, *Beyond* The Spanish Tragedy: *A Study of the Works of Thomas Kyd* (Manchester: Manchester University Press, 2001)
Looks more broadly at Kyd's works, focusing predominantly

on the dramatic with the aim to provide a comprehensive review and update to scholarship on Kyd. There are four chapters devoted to in-depth analysis of *The Spanish Tragedy*: Introduction; Origins; Revenge; Additions, Adaptations, and Modern Stage History. Also provides 'Thomas Kyd's Life and Works: A Chronology' which includes the afterlife of his publications and later revival performances.

Hadfield, Andrew, *The English Renaissance 1500–1620* (Oxford: Blackwell Publishers, 2001)

This Blackwell Guide to Literature provides an encyclopaedic approach to key writers, texts, and concepts, including entries for Thomas Kyd and *The Spanish Tragedy*. Also of interest are a chronology of 'significant dates and events', general introduction to the era, and topics such as 'Attitudes to other nations and cultures' or 'Women, Gender and Queer Reading'.

Hill, Eugene, 'Revenge Tragedy', in *A Companion to Renaissance Drama*, ed. by Arthur Kinney (Oxford: Blackwell Publishing, 2002), 326–35

Provides a general discussion of the play with a useful in-depth discussion of the sexual innuendo in the wooing portion of 2.4.

Hillman, Richard, 'Thomas Kyd, *The Spanish Tragedy*', in *The Oxford Handbook of Tudor Drama,* ed. by Thomas Betteridge and Greg Walker (Oxford: Oxford University Press, 2012), 566–83

Provides a survey of common themes in the critical afterlife of the play and contextualizes the play within contemporary European religio-politics.

Revenge Tragedy, ed. by Stevie Simkin (London: Palgrave, 2001)

Simkin's introduction (pp. 1–23) briefly traces extra-legal revenge in the Western tradition and connects the plays of the genre and the essays in this collection through key themes.

Those studying *The Spanish Tragedy* will be particularly interested in Molly Easo Smith's chapter 'The Theatre and the Scaffold: Death as Spectacle in *The Spanish Tragedy*' (pp. 71–87) and Katherine Eisaman Maus's chapter '*The Spanish Tragedy*, or, The Machieval's Revenge' (pp. 88–106).

Shakespearean London Theatres (2013). Available online: http://shalt.dmu.ac.uk/films.html (accessed 1 March 2015)
Website provided by the ShaLT project, which aims to 'tell [ ] the illustrated story of the playhouses, entrepreneurs, audiences, actors and dramatists that made up th[e] founding theatrical industry' in London between the 1570s and 1642. Includes filmed scenes, interviews, and an interactive map of the London theatres.

Smith, Emma, 'The Spanish Tragedy', *Not Shakespeare: Popular Elizabethan and Jacobean Theatre* podcast series (2009). Available online: http://podcasts.ox.ac.uk/series/not-shakespeare-elizabethan-and-jacobean-popular-theatre (accessed 1 March 2015)
In a six-lecture podcast series released by the University of Oxford, the first lecture addresses key issues in Kyd's play and provides context through parallels that make it relevant to a modern group of students. This lecture does not presume the listener has read the play, but familiarity with the period of literature is helpful.

'The Spanish Tragedy' (2012). Available online: https://librivox.org/the-spanish-tragedy-by-thomas-kyd/ (accessed 1 March 2015)
Free volunteer-based audio recording of the play.

'The Spanish Tragedy, Act II Scene 4' (2013). Available online: https://www.youtube.com/watch?v=-PdwrQdcs1Y&feature=youtu.be (accessed 1 March 2015)
A film version of Act Two Scene Four and the first portion of Scene Five released by the Shakespearean London Theatres (ShaLT) project.

'Thomas Kyd', *Elizabethan and Jacobean Drama* (last revised 2012). Available online: http://www2.warwick.ac.uk/fac/arts/ren/elizabethan_jacobean_drama/kyd/ (accessed 1 March 2015)

Interactive 'open-access resource on the page and stage history of five Jacobethan [*sic*] playwrights and nine of their plays' which includes *The Spanish Tragedy* and a close reading exercise for Hieronimo's first speech in Act 3, Scene 12.

Considering performance

Hobgood, Allison P., *Passionate Playgoing in Early Modern England* (Cambridge: Cambridge University Press, 2014)

Chapter 'Emotional Afterlives in *The Spanish Tragedy*' examines the way in which Kyd, particularly through Hieronimo's management, cultivates a genre that is dependent on an affective relationship with the audience.

Shapiro, James, '"Tragedies naturally performed": Kyd's Representation of Violence, *The Spanish Tragedy* (c. 1587)', in *Staging the Renaissance: Reinterpretations of Elizabethan and Jacobean Drama*, ed. by David Scott Kastan and Peter Stallybrass (London: Routledge, 1991), 99–113

Examines the boundary between the spectacle of state punishment and that of the staged violence in the theatre, with Kyd's play being unusual in its portrayal of state-sanctioned violence.

Simkin, Stevie, *Early Modern Tragedy and the Cinema of Violence* (London: Palgrave Macmillan, 2006)

Examines early modern drama and twentieth-century film in parallel. Chapter 'Spectacles of Death' particularly addresses *The Spanish Tragedy* within the context of audience expectations of realism based on their familiarity with execution and death.

Smith, Molly, *Breaking Boundaries: Politics and Play in the*

Drama of Shakespeare and his Contemporaries (Aldershot: Ashgate, 1998)

Chapter 'Theatre and Punishment: Spectacles of Death and Dying on the Stage' considers the broken boundary between public execution and the stage, connecting *The Spanish Tragedy*'s focus on hanging to contemporary punitive practice. The book provides the context for examining these same trends in other drama, but the portion of analysis on *The Spanish Tragedy* can also be found in: 'The Theater and the Scaffold: Death as Spectacle in The Spanish Tragedy', SEL 32 (2) (1992): 217–32, and in *Revenge Tragedy*, ed. Stevie Simkin (London: Palgrave, 2001), cited above.

Tweedie, Eleanor M., '"Action Is Eloquence": The Staging of Thomas Kyd's Spanish Tragedy', *Studies in English Literature, 1500–1900* 16 (2) (1976): 223–39

Encourages imagining the arrangement of actors' bodies, important stage properties, and set pieces as a crucial part of Kyd's emblematizing and emphasizing of the key concerns of the play.

White, Martin, *Renaissance Drama in Action: An Introduction to Aspects of Theatre Practice and Performance* (London: Routledge, 1998)

Chapter 'Palaces of pleasure: outdoor playing spaces and theatre practice' provides a thorough discussion of the physical parameters and acting specifications of the outdoor theatres, ending with a case study on *The Spanish Tragedy* Act 2, Scene 4.

Judgement and justice

Chickera, Ernest D., 'Divine Justice and Private Revenge in "The Spanish Tragedy"', *The Modern Language Review* 57 (2) (1962): 228–32

Examines revenge as a mode of fulfilling God's justice.

Hamlin, William M., *Tragedy and Scepticism in Shakespeare's England* (London: Palgrave Macmillan, 2005)
Chapter '*The Spanish Tragedy:* Doom and the Exile of Justice' addresses the play's use of problematized justice and indecision as centrally focused upon doubt.

Hammersmith, James P., 'The Death of Castile in *The Spanish Tragedy*', in *Renaissance Plays: New Readings and Rereadings*, ed. by Leonard Barkan (Evanston, IL: Northwestern University Press, 1985), 1–16
Examines the death of the seemingly innocent Castile as a form of broader poetic justice, rather than individual retributive justice.

Henke, James T., 'Politics and Politicians in "The Spanish Tragedy"', *Studies in Philology* 78 (4) (1981): 353–69
Provides a defence of the monarchs of the play as just rulers, with a consideration of Hieronimo's extra-legal path of revenge.

Feminist readings

Findlay, Alison, *A Feminist Perspective on Renaissance Drama* (Oxford: Blackwell Publishers, 1999)
Chapter 'Revenge Tragedy' considers revenge as a feminine mode and female characters as particularly driving revenge in the play.

Whigham, Frank, *Seizures of the Will in Early Modern English Drama* (Cambridge: Cambridge University Press, 1996)
Chapter 'Forcing Divorce in *The Spanish Tragedy*' examines imbalances of power in gender and social rank, with particular analysis given to the sexual coercion of Bel-imperia.

Religion and death

Anderson, Thomas P., *Performing Early Modern Trauma from Shakespeare to Milton* (Aldershot: Ashgate, 2006)
Section 'Exhuming the Dead in *The Spanish Tragedy*' examines how changes in the rituals of commemoration create a schism between the past, present, and future.

Döring, Tobias, *Performances of Mourning in Shakespearean Theatre and Early Modern Culture* (London: Palgrave Macmillan, 2006)
Chapter 'Pathologies of Mourning' subchapter 'Translating Tradition: *The Spanish Tragedy* and *Titus Andronicus*' considers 'pathologies of mourning' in both plays as fathers denied proper mourning turn to violence.

Rist, Thomas, *Revenge Tragedy and the Drama of Commemoration in Reforming England* (Aldershot: Ashgate, 2008)
Chapter '"Outrage Fits": Revenge and the "Melodrama" of Mourning in *The Spanish Tragedy, Titus Andronicus* and *Hamlet*' reconsiders prior critical arguments that the play is anti-Catholic as a whole, arguing that the aesthetic of revenge and mode of commemoration in the play is against the Reformation.

Watson, Robert N., *The Rest is Silence: Death as Annihilation in the English Renaissance* (London: University of California Press, 1994)
Chapter 'Religio Vindicis: Substitution and Immortality in *The Spanish Tragedy*' examines the complicating of the general portrayal of revenge as a means of seeking to cure death 'by destroying its immediate agent' (p. 44).

Languages: Latin and foreign vernaculars on stage

Dillon, Janette, *Language and Stage in Medieval and Renaissance England* (Cambridge: Cambridge University Press, 1998)

Considers non-vernacular languages in *The Spanish Tragedy*, with the use of Latin and foreign vernaculars being central to characterization and thematic movement in the play, particularly as it reaches its conclusion in the 'fall of Babel' of the multi-language staging of *Soliman and Perseda*.

Mazzio, Carla, *The Inarticulate Renaissance: Language Trouble in an Age of Eloquence* (Philadelphia: University of Pennsylvania Press, 2009)

Chapter 'Disarticulating Community: Nation, Law, and History in *The Spanish Tragedy*' spends extended time discussing the linguistic confusion of the play, particularly exemplified by the *Soliman and Perseda* playlet, within national, legal and other terms.

Mulryne, J. R., 'Nationality and Language in Thomas Kyd's *The Spanish Tragedy*', in *Travel and Drama in Shakespeare's Time*, ed. by Jean-Pierre Maquerlot and Michèle Williams (Cambridge: Cambridge University Press, 1996), 87–105

Contextualizes the situation of views on Spain and thus the use of the social setting and language in the play.

Language: Style and rhetoric

Baker, Howard, *Induction to Tragedy: A Study in the Development of Form in* Gorboduc, The Spanish Tragedy *and* Titus Andronicus (New York: Russell & Russell, 1965)

Argues in the chapter '*The Spanish Tragedy, Titus Andronicus* and Senecanism' that the 'structural characteristics' of the play are not adequately explained by pointing to Kyd's indebtedness to the Senecan model of drama but instead is more fully understood through 'native poetical forms' and dramatic traditions (p. 107).

Barish, Jonas A., '*The Spanish Tragedy,* or The Pleasures and Perils of Rhetoric', in *Elizabethan Theatre*, ed. by John Russell Brown and Bernard Harris (London: Edward Arnold, 1966), 59–86

A stylistic analysis of the language of the play, this chapter examines Kyd's adoption and transformation of standard rhetorical tropes and poetic precedents.

Clemen, Wolfgang, *English Tragedy Before Shakespeare: The Development of Dramatic Speech*, trans. by T. S. Dorsch (London: Methuen, 1961)

This broader study includes a chapter on Kyd (pp. 100–12) which focuses almost entirely on *The Spanish Tragedy* and provides an analysis of the style and structure of the speeches in the play.

NOTES

Introduction

1 All quotations from *The Spanish Tragedy* in this volume are from *The Spanish Tragedy, by Thomas Kyd*, ed. Clara Calvo and Jesús Tronch, Arden Early Modern Drama (London: Bloomsbury, 2013).

2 Ashley H. Thorndike, 'The Relations of *Hamlet* to Contemporary Revenge Plays', *Modern Language Association* 17.3 (1902): 125–222 (125).

3 For discussion of this disappearance from the theatre and also from general critical appreciation, see Malin and Semple in these pages.

4 The phrase is Dr Johnson's, from his *Preface to Shakespeare* (1765). For more on the development, see Peter Womack, 'Secularizing *King Lear*: Shakespeare, Tate and the Sacred', in *Shakespeare Survey* 55 (2002): 96–105.

5 A. C. Bradley, *Shakespearean Tragedy: Lectures on Hamlet, Othello, King Lear and Macbeth* (Macmillan, 1904; London: Penguin, 1991), 40.

6 Bradley, 40.

7 Ken Jackson and Arthur Marotti, 'The Turn to Religion in Early Modern English Studies', in *Criticism* 46.1 (2004): 167–90.

8 Janette Dillon, *The Cambridge Introduction to Early English Theatre* (Cambridge: Cambridge University Press, 2006), 1–3.

9 Calvo and Tronch, *The Spanish Tragedy*, 127, note 90.

10 For more on this mediation, see Thomas Rist, '"Those Organnons by which it Moves": Shakespearean Theatre and the Romish Cult of the Dead', in *Shakespeare Survey* 69 (2016).

11 King Lear states: 'Nothing will come of nothing' (*King Lear*, 1.1.90). See *William Shakespeare: The Complete Works*, ed. Stanley Wells and Gary Taylor (Oxford: Clarendon Press, 1995), 945. The classical original is *nihil fit ex nihilo*.

12 Emile Durkheim, *The Elementary Forms of the Religious Life* (London: George Allen and Unwin, 1915; repr. 1964), 366.

13 See Charles Parker, 'Diseased Bodies, Defiled Souls: Corporality and Religious Difference in the Reformation', in *Renaissance Quarterly* 67.4 (Winter 2014): 1265–97.

14 I render 'revenge' as 'retribution' here because the latter is 'more nearly equivalent' to modern meanings. See Ronald Broude, 'Revenge and Revenge Tragedy in Renaissance England', *Renaissance Quarterly* 28.1 (Spring 1975): 38–58 (39).

15 See also Thomas Rist, *Revenge Tragedy and the Drama of Commemoration in Reforming England*, Studies in Performance and Early Modern Drama (Aldershot and Burlington, VT: Ashgate, 2008).

16 See Thomas Rist, 'Catharsis as "Purgation" in Shakespearean Drama', in *Shakespearean Sensations: Experiencing Literature in Early Modern England*, ed. Katharine Craik and Tanya Pollard (Cambridge: Cambridge University Press, 2013), 138–56.

17 *The Taming of the Shrew*, Induction 1, 7 and Induction 2, 127–32, in *The Oxford Shakespeare*, 27 and 29.

18 On the imaginative traditions, see Jacques Le Goff, *The Birth of Purgatory*, trans. by Arthur Goldhammer (Chicago: University of Chicago Press, 1984). Lorna Hutson usefully introduces Purgatory's resonances in early modern justice in *The Invention of Suspicion: Law and Mimesis in Shakespeare and Renaissance Drama* (Oxford: Oxford University Press, 2007), 265. For discussion of Purgatory in the play, see Tom Rutter in these pages, where he also notes the traditions not entirely conforming to doctrine, especially of the Council of Trent (p. 160–1).

19 See Marissa Greenburg, 'The Tyranny of Tragedy: Catharsis in England and *The Roman Actor*', in *Renaissance Drama* 39 (2011): 163–96 (170–2). This quotation and the information of the next sentence are from this source.

20 Michel Foucault, *Discipline and Punish: The Birth of the Prison*, trans. Alan Sheridan (New York: Random House, 1991), 9.

21 Bruce Gordon and Peter Marshall, eds., *The Place of the Dead: Death and Remembrance in Late Medieval and Early Modern Europe* (Cambridge: Cambridge University Press, 2000).

22 See Robin McKie, 'Return of the Damned after 400 Years', *The Guardian*, 11 January 2004, available online: http://www.theguardian.com/uk/2004/jan/11/artsandhumanities.research (accessed 1 September, 2015).

23 Saintly iconography is also in the Viceroy's desire to give up his crown to 'live a life / In ceaseless prayers' (3.16.32–3); in 'all the saints do sit soliciting' (4.1.34), it mingles with the wider spiritual circulation by solicitation.

24 On the religious drama of blood, see Andrea Stevens, *Inventions of the Skin: The Painted Body in Early English Drama, 1400–1642* (Edinburgh: Edinburgh University Press, 2013), 51–2.

25 See also Gordon Braden, *Renaissance Tragedy and the Senecan Tradition: Anger's Privilege* (New Haven, CT: Yale University Press, 2005).

26 See *Christopher Marlowe, The Complete Plays*, ed. Frank Romany and Robert Lindsey (London: Penguin, 2003), 303 (3.6.33–6).

27 John Bossy, 'The Social History of Confession in the Age of Reformation', in *Transactions of the Royal Historical Society* 25 (1975): 21–38 (21). Confession is 'purgation' on 22.

28 On these historical points and their sources, see Romany and Lindsey, eds., ix–x and xxxiv.

29 See Stevie Simkin in this volume (p. 92).

30 See Rist, *Revenge Tragedy*, 1–2.

31 See Eamon Duffy, *Saints, Sacrilege and Sedition: Religion and Conflict in the Tudor Reformations* (London: Bloomsbury, 2012), 35–7; also *The Stripping of the Altars: Traditional Religion in England, 1400–1580* (New Haven and London: Yale University Press, 1992), 593.

32 See Paul Koudounaris, *Heavenly Bodies: Cult Treasures and*

Spectacular Saints from the Catacombs (London: Thames and Hudson, 2013).

33　Emblematic understanding of Tyburn's Tree is visible in Robert Southwell's execution speech. See Dennis Flynn, *John Donne and the Ancient Catholic Nobility* (Bloomington and Indianapolis: Indiana University Press, 1995), 105.

34　See Stephen Greenblatt, *Shakespearean Negotiations: The Circulation of Social Energy in Renaissance England* (Berkeley: University of California Press, 1988), 65.

35　Statistics and quotation from Molly Smith, 'The Theatre and the Scaffold: Death as Spectacle', in *The Spanish Tragedy*, in *Revenge Tragedy*, ed. Stevie Simkin (Basingstoke: Palgrave, 2001); and John Carey, 'Donne's Apostasy', in *John Donne's Poetry*, ed. Donald Dickson (New York and London: W. W. Norton, 2007), 212.

36　See, prominently, Marvin Carlson, *The Haunted Stage: The Theatre as Memory Machine* (Ann Arbor: University of Michigan Press, 2003).

Chapter 1

1　Thomas Heywood, *An Apology for Actors* (London: Nicholas Okes, 1612), E3r–E4v.

2　The earliest evidence of performance comes from 1592; however, it is likely that the play was performed several times before this record. *The Spanish Tragedy* was printed twice in 1592, with subsequent editions in 1594, 1599, 1602, 1603, 1610, 1615, 1618, 1623 and 1633.

3　Michael Hattaway, *Elizabethan Popular Theatre: Plays in Performance* (London: Routledge/Kegan Paul, 1982), 103. For a discussion of the possible court performance, see Lukas Erne, *Beyond The Spanish Tragedy: A Study of the Works of Thomas Kyd* (Manchester: Manchester University Press, 2008), 126–7. See also Frank Marcham, *The King's Office of the revels 1610–1622: Fragments of Documents in the Department of Manuscripts, British Museum* (Great Britain: Office of the

Revels, 1925), 10–11. Interestingly, in the list handwritten on the scrap of Revels office waste, reprinted in Marcham, *The Spanish Tragedy* appears immediately after 'The Tradgedy of Ham'.

4 The five passages from the 1602 quarto, which expanded on Hieronimo's madness to exploit popular interest in the tragic hero, have been the source of much critical speculation and, often, praise. For example, Boas remarks that the passages are 'steeped in passion and wild, sombre beauty' and that they 'fully deserved their great popularity'; see Frederick S. Boas, ed., *The Works of Thomas Kyd* (Oxford: Clarendon Press, 1901), xiii, lxxxvii. For more on the Additions, see Eric Griffin's chapter in this volume.

5 For an overview of the critical debates on *1 Hieronimo* and its relationship to Kyd's play see Erne, *Beyond*, 14–46.

6 For more on these European performances and adaptations see Boas, xcix–ciii; Erne, *Beyond*, 119–42. Boas's edition also includes Ayrer's 1615 German adaptation.

7 See also Boas, 393.

8 For more on allusions to and lampoons of *The Spanish Tragedy* see Boas, lxxviii–ciii; Arthur Freeman, *Thomas Kyd: Facts and Problems* (Oxford: Clarendon Press, 1967), 131–9; Rebekah Owens, 'Parody and *The Spanish Tragedy*', *Cahiers Élisabéthains* 71 (2007): 27–36.

9 See Tom Rutter's essay in this volume.

10 Thomas Heywood, *The Fair Maid of the West, Parts I and II*, ed. Robert K. Turner Jr. (Lincoln: University of Nebraska Press, 1967), 5.1.110–15. Clem opens his speech with Castile's reassuring line to Bel-imperia (3.14.111), a line habitually quoted in the period.

11 Francis Beaumont, *The Knight of the Burning Pestle*, ed. Michael Hattaway (London: A&C Black, 2000), 5.278–9.

12 All references to Jonson's works are to *The Cambridge Edition of the Works of Ben Jonson*, ed. David Bevington et al., 7 vols (Cambridge: Cambridge University Press, 2012) and it is hereafter referred to as the Cambridge *Jonson*. In sum, Jonson referenced *The Spanish Tragedy* in seven of his plays.

13 *Cambridge Jonson*, IV, 1.5.40–51.

14 *Cambridge Jonson*, I, 165–7.

15 *Cambridge Jonson*, IV, 79–80.

16 *Cambridge Jonson*, VI, 2.5.82. For a full discussion of works that quote 'Hieronimo, beware; go by, go by' see Boas, 406; Thomas Kyd, *The Spanish Tragedy, with The First Part of Jeronimo*, ed. Emma Smith (London: Penguin, 1998), 133–59.

17 Nathan Field, *A Woman is a Weather-cocke: A new comedy, as it was acted before the King in White-Hall* (London: William Jaggard, 1612), C4r.

18 Lording Barry, *Ram-Alley: Or merrie-trickes a comedy diuers times here-to-fore acted* (London: G. Eld, 1611), I1r.

19 Thomas Tomkis, *Albumazar: A comedy presented before the Kings Maiestie at Cambridge, the ninth of March. 1614* (London: Nicholas Okes, 1615), D1r–D1v.

20 Thomas Dekker, *1603. The Wonderfull Yeare* (London: Thomas Creede, 1603), E4r.

21 Thomas Dekker, *The Seven Deadly Sinnes of London* (London: Edward Allde and S. Stafford, 1606), F5v. Elsewhere in the pamphlet, Dekker references Hieronimo's 'What outcries pluck me' speech and entrance with a naked sword in order to make a bawdy joke (D4r).

22 See Hattaway, 115.

23 Thomas Andrew, 'The Unmasking of a Feminine Machiavell' (London: Simon Stafford, 1604), B1r.

24 Ibid., D2v–E1r.

25 Anthony Scoloker, 'Daiphantus, or the Passions of Love' (London: T. Creed, 1604), D3r, E4v, F1r.

26 'Hockley in the Hole'. EBBA 20138, Magdalene College, Pepys Ballads 1.294–5.

27 'The Spanish Tragedy, Containing the lamentable Murders of Horatio and Bellimperia: With the pitifull Death of old Hieronimo'. EBBA 30246, British Library, Roxburghe 1.364–5.

28 Smith, *The Spanish Tragedy*, 133.

29 Richard Brathwaite, *The English Gentlewoman* (London: B. Alsop and T. Fawcet, 1631), H3v.

30 See also William Prynne in *Histriomastix* (London: Edward Allde, 1633), fol. 556; also Smith, *The Spanish Tragedy*, 141–3.

31 Thomas Randolph, *A pleasant comedie, entituled Hey for honesty, down with knavery* (London, 1651), 2.4.14.

32 James Shirley, *Changes, or Love in a Maze, A comedie* (London: George Purslowe, 1632), H3v.

33 Thomas Rawlins, *The Rebellion* (London: I. Okes, 1640), I2r.

34 Ibid., I2v.

35 Charles Cotton, *Burlesque upon burlesque, or, The scoffer scoft* (London: Henry Brome, 1675), A2r.

36 Samuel Pepys, *The Diary of Samuel Pepys*, ed. John Warrington, 3 vols (London: J. M. Dent & Sons, 1953), III, 179.

37 Gerard Langbaine, *An Account of the English Dramatick Poets* (Oxford: L. L., 1691), 535. In the entry for 'William Smith', Langbaine here disagrees with Edward Philips and William Winstanley who, in *Theatrum Poetarum* (1675) and *The Lives of the Most Famous English Poets* (1687) had attributed the play to Smith (489).

38 Peter Whalley, *An Enquiry into the Learning of Shakespeare* (London: T. Waller, 1748), 48.

39 Richard Grant White, *Memoirs of the life of William Shakespeare* (Boston: Little, Brown, and Co., 1865), 411.

40 Robert, Dodsley, ed. *A Select Collection of Old Plays*, 2 (London, 1744). Richard Farmer, *An Essay on the Learning of Shakespeare* (Basil: J. J. Tourneisen, 1800. First publ. 1766), 51, 79.

41 August Wilhelm von Schlegel, *A Course of Lectures on Dramatic Art and Literature*, trans. John Black, II (London: Baldwin, Cradock and Joy, 1815), 277.

42 Ibid., 276–7.

43 John Payne Collier, *History of English Dramatic Poetry to the Time of Shakespeare and Annals of the Stage to the Restoration*, 3 (London: John Murray, 1831), 209.

44 John M. Manly, *Specimens of the Pre-Shakespearean Drama*, 2 (New York: Dover, 1967. First publ. 1897). Josef Schick, *The Spanish Tragedy* (London: J. M. Dent & Sons, 1898).

45 See Peter Malin's discussion in this volume.

46 Lopez, 49.

47 Regarding flaws see, for example, W. W. Greg, 'Review of *The Works of Thomas Kyd* by Frederick S. Boas', *The Modern Language Quarterly* 4.3 (December 1901): 185–90.

48 Boas, xxxi.

49 Ibid., xxxii.

50 Ibid., xxxvii.

51 Ibid., xxxv–xxxvi.

52 Ibid., xxxiii–xxxiv.

53 Ibid., xxxv.

54 Ibid., xxxix.

55 Ibid., xxxix.

56 William Allan Neilson, *The Chief Elizabethan Dramatists: Excluding Shakespeare* (Boston and New York: Houghton Mifflin Co, 1911), 870.

57 Quoted in Ronald Schuchard, *Eliot's Dark Angel: Intersections of Life and Art* (Oxford: Oxford University Press, 1999), 46.

58 T. S. Eliot, 'Hamlet and His Problems', in *Selected Essays* (London: Faber and Faber, 1951), 142.

59 T. S. Eliot, 'Seneca in Elizabethan Translation', in *Selected Essays* (London: Faber and Faber, 1951), 80–2.

60 For a discussion of Eliot's quotation of Hieronimo in the poem, and his writings on early modern drama in general, see Steven Matthews, *T. S. Eliot and Early Modern Literature* (Oxford: Oxford University Press, 2013), 105–9.

61 Howard Baker, *Induction to Tragedy: A Study in a Development of Form in Gorboduc, The Spanish Tragedy, and Titus Andronicus* (New York: Russell & Russell, 1965. First publ. 1939), 116–18. Baker contests some of the arguments put forward by John William Cunliffe in his PhD thesis, *The Influence of Seneca on Elizabethan Tragedy: An Essay* (1893).

62 Ibid., 109.

63 Ibid., 115.

64 See Eugene Hill, 'Senecan and Vergilian Perspectives in *The Spanish Tragedy*', *ELR* 15 (1985): 143–65, and Hunter, 'Seneca', 1967. Bowers considers the Senecan material in the play and broadly concurs with Baker that, while the influence is certain, its extent has been overstated (73–5, 83–4).

65 Fredson Bowers, *Elizabethan Revenge Tragedy: 1587–1642* (Gloucester, MA: Peter Smith, 1959. First publ. 1940), 65.

66 Ibid., 109. Bowers lays out the Kydian formula in some detail, 71–3.

67 Ibid., 101.

68 Ibid., 65.

69 Bowers, 66; Boas, xxxii–xxxiii.

70 Bowers, 67–8.

71 Ibid., 68.

72 Ibid., 70.

73 Ibid., 78.

74 Ibid., 80.

75 Ibid., 82.

76 Ibid., 71, 81.

77 Moody E. Prior, *The Language of Tragedy* (New York: Columbia University Press, 1947), 48.

78 Ibid., 49.

79 Ibid., 50–1.

80 Ibid., 59.

81 William Empson, '*The Spanish Tragedy*', *Nimbus* 3 (1956): 16–29. The article is reprinted in *Elizabethan Drama: Modern Essays in Criticism*, ed. R. J. Kaufmann (London: Oxford University Press, 1978), 60–80. All references are to this later edition. Empson, 60.

82 Ibid., 60.

83 Ibid., 60.

84 Ibid., 61.

85 Ibid., 168.
86 Ibid., 70.
87 Empson, 79; Bowers, 70–81.
88 Empson, 68.
89 Alfred Harbage, 'Intrigue in Elizabethan Tragedy', in *Essays on Shakespeare and Elizabethan Drama in Honor of Hardin Craig*, ed. Richard Hosley (London: Routledge/Kegan Paul, 1963), 37–44. Harbage, 37.
90 Ibid., 43–4.
91 Ibid., 40, 43.
92 S. F. Johnson, '*The Spanish Tragedy*, or Babylon Revisited', in *Essays on Shakespeare and Elizabethan Drama in Honor of Hardin Craig*, ed. Richard Hosley (London: Routledge/Kegan Paul, 1963), 24.
93 Ibid., 25, 36.
94 Ibid., 28.
95 Ibid., 31. See also Eleanor Prosser, *Hamlet and Revenge* (Stanford: Stanford University Press, 1967), 49.
96 Ibid., 34.
97 Prosser, 44–8.
98 Ibid., 51–2.
99 Philip Edwards, *Thomas Kyd and Early Elizabethan Tragedy* (London: Longmans, 1966), 5.
100 Ibid., 21.
101 Ibid., 40.
102 Ibid., 26.
103 Ibid., 26.
104 Ibid., 34.
105 Ibid., 32.
106 Ibid., 32.
107 Ibid., 39.
108 Ibid., 41.
109 Freeman, vii.

110 Ibid., 56.
111 Ibid., 80.
112 Ibid., 86–9.
113 Ibid., 84.
114 Ibid., 83–5.
115 Ibid., 84.
116 Ibid., 93, 98.
117 Ibid., 95, 100.
118 Ibid., 101.
119 Ibid., 23.
120 Peter B. Murray, *Thomas Kyd* (New York: Twayne Publishers, 1969), 31.
121 Ibid., 64.
122 Ibid., 41–2.
123 Ibid., 41.
124 Ibid., 42.
125 Ibid., 150.
126 Ibid., 46.
127 Ibid., 48.
128 Ibid., 29.
129 Ibid., 146.
130 Ibid., 152.
131 Harriett Hawkins, 'Fabulous Counterfeits: Dramatic Construction and Dramatic Perspectives in *The Spanish Tragedy*, *A Midsummer Night's Dream*, and *The Tempest*', *Shakespeare Studies* 6 (1970): 51–65. The article is reprinted in Harriett Hawkins, *Likenesses of Truth in Elizabethan and Restoration Drama* (Oxford: Clarendon Press, 1972), 27–50. All references are to this later edition. Hawkins, *Likenesses*, 28.
132 Hawkins, *Likenesses*, 44.
133 Ibid., 31.
134 Ronald Broude, 'Time, Truth, and Right, *The Spanish Tragedy*', *Studies in Philology* 68.2 (1971): 130–45 (131).

135 Ibid., 137–8.

136 Ibid., 145.

137 Donna B. Hamilton, '*The Spanish Tragedy*: a speaking picture', *English Literary Renaissance* 4 (1974): 203–17 (208).

138 Ibid., 217.

139 Eleanor M. Tweedie, '"Action Is Eloquence": The Staging of Thomas Kyd's *Spanish Tragedy*', *Studies in English Literature, 1500–1900* 16.2. (1976): 223–39 (225).

140 Ibid., 223, 239.

141 Carol McGinnis Kay, 'Deception through Words: A Reading of *The Spanish Tragedy*', *Studies in Philology*, 74.1. (1977): 20–38 (20).

142 Ibid., 38.

143 Joel B. Altman, *The Tudor Play of Mind: Rhetorical Inquiry and the Development of Elizabethan Drama* (London: University of California Press, 1978), 6.

144 Ibid., 270.

145 Ibid., 274.

146 Ibid., 281–2.

147 Hattaway, 102.

148 Ibid., 101.

149 Ibid., 101–2.

150 Ibid., 111.

151 Ibid., 106.

152 Ibid., 116.

153 Ibid., 127–8.

154 Gordon Braden, *Renaissance Tragedy and the Senecan Tradition: Anger's Privilege* (London: Yale University Press, 1985), 209.

155 Ibid., 206.

156 Ibid., 207.

157 Ibid., 205.

158 Braden, 208. See also Hamilton, 216–17.

159 Ibid., 213.
160 Ibid., 214–15.

Chapter 2

1 F. S. Boas, 'The Spanish Tragedie after Three Centuries', The Lodestone (Lent 1922): 52–3 (52) (Birkbeck College, University of London, archive).

2 B. D. Watters, 'The Spanish Tragedie', The Lodestone (Lent 1922), 82–5 (83) (Birkbeck College archive); H. G., 'The Spanish Tragedie', Observer, 11 December 1921.

3 J. H. Lobban, 'Prologue to The Spanish Tragedy', The Spanish Tragedy, Birkbeck College, December 1931, programme (Birkbeck College archive).

4 Thomas Kyd, The Spanish Tragedy, ed. Clara Calvo and JesúsTronch, Arden Early Modern Drama (London: Bloomsbury, 2013), 66. All references to the play are to this edition.

5 All statistics derived from: Martin Wiggins, in association with Catherine Richardson, British Drama 1533–1642: A Catalogue (Oxford: Oxford University Press, 2012–), 2 (2012), 369–75.

6 Ben Jonson, The Alchemist, ed. F. H. Mares, The Revels Plays (London: Methuen, 1967), 4.7.71; 4.3.24; 4.7.55.

7 Thomas Dekker, The Seven Deadly Sinnes of London, ed. H. F. B. Brett-Smith (Oxford: Blackwell, 1922), 54. N. B. Where I have quoted from old-spelling editions, as here, I have lightly modernized both spelling and punctuation for the sake of clarity and consistency.

8 See 3.11.0.1, 3.11.8 SD, 3.12A.165.1–2, 3.13.122–30.

9 Duncan Salkeld, Madness and Drama in the Age of Shakespeare (Manchester: Manchester University Press, 1993), 123.

10 Thomas May, The Heir, in A Select Collection of Old English Plays, ed. Robert Dodsley, 4th edn, rev. by W. Carew Hazlitt, 15 vols (London: Reeves and Turner, 1874–6), XI (1875), 501–84 (514).

11 Thomas Rawlins, *The Rebellion*, in *Old English Plays*, XIV (1875), 1–92 (82).

12 Rebekah Owens, 'Parody and *The Spanish Tragedy*', *Cahiers Élisabéthains* 71 (2007): 27–36 (32).

13 Andrew Gurr, *The Shakespearian Playing Companies* (Oxford: Clarendon Press, 1996), 427. The evidence that Richard Fowler played Hieronimo is circumstantial but compelling. See Gerald Eades Bentley, *The Jacobean and Caroline Stage*, 7 vols (Oxford: Clarendon Press, 1941–68), II (1941; repr. 1966) for biographical details on Fowler, 439–40, and extract from Edmund Gayton, 690–1.

14 See Lukas Erne, *Beyond 'The Spanish Tragedy': A Study of the Works of Thomas Kyd* (Manchester: Manchester University Press, 2001), 134–5.

15 The only other production to use the archaic spelling was Nevill Coghill's in 1937.

16 Photographs supplied by Birkbeck College archive; records from 1931–2, 26–7.

17 S. R. L., 'An Elizabethan Melodrama', *Morning Post*, 12 December 1931.

18 All quotations from: 'College Play', *The Wykehamist* 672 (30 March 1926): 202–3 (Winchester College archive).

19 *The Spanish Tragedy*, Christ Church, Oxford, March 1932, programme (Christ Church archive).

20 F. S. Boas, '*The Spanish Tragedy* at Christ Church', letter, *The Times*, 9 March 1932.

21 'Elizabethan Tradition Revived', *Manchester Guardian*, 8 March 1932.

22 'Of Oxford Summer Diversions', *St Edmund Hall Magazine* 4.2 (December 1937): 11–12 (St Edmund Hall archive).

23 *The Spanish Tragedie*, St Edmund Hall, Oxford, July 1937, programme (Oxford, Bodleian Library, MS.Eng.misc.c.1013, fol. 48).

24 'College Notes', *St John's College: 1952*, 3–5 (3) (St John's College [Oxford] archive).

25 See Arden edn, 69.

26 *The Spanish Tragedy*, Vandyck Theatre, Bristol, July 1968, programme (University of Bristol Theatre Collection, BDD/PG/000229).

27 Michael Billington, '*Spanish Tragedy* in Oxford', *Guardian*, 29 November 1973.

28 Alan Halliday quoted in Humphrey Carpenter, *OUDS: A Centenary History of the Oxford University Dramatic Society 1885–1985* (Oxford: Oxford University Press, 1985), 212.

29 Emma Smith, 'Performing Relevance / Relevant Performances: Shakespeare, Jonson, Hitchcock', in *New Directions in Renaissance Drama and Performance Studies*, ed. Sarah Werner (Basingstoke: Macmillan, 2010), 147–61 (150).

30 Frank Dibb [F. W. D.], '*The Spanish Tragedy*', *The Oxford Times*, 30 November 1973.

31 The intervening Oxford production, by Worcester College Buskins in 1979, is unrecorded in the college archive and was apparently not reviewed.

32 Rebekah Owens, '*The Spanish Tragedy*', *ROMARD* 49 (2010), 137–9 (138).

33 '*The Spanish Tragedie*', www.dailyinfo.co.uk/reviews/feature/The_Spanish_Tragedie (accessed 15 August 2013). Could 'KLew' be the booming Kate Lewin offering her own review, or just a fan?

34 Nancy Napper Canter, '*The Spanish Tragedy*', *The Tab Cambridge*, www.cambridge.tab.co.uk/2012/11/09/the-spanish-tragedy (accessed 15 August 2013).

35 Emrys Jones, 'Stage-Managing Revenge', *Times Literary Supplement*, 15 October 1982, 1131.

36 Amanda Gunther, '*The Spanish Tragedy* at the Mobtown Players', *DC Metro Theater Arts*, http://dcmetrotheaterarts.com/2014/07/12/spanish-tragedy-mobtown-players1/ (accessed 11 August 2014).

37 Harry Keyishian, 'An Interview with Ron Daley, Director of *The Spanish Tragedy*', *Shakespeare Bulletin* 4.3 (May/June 1986): 11. Daley's production was preceded by *1 Hieronimo*, which at least provided the narrative background omitted in the framing device.

38 Richard Proudfoot, 'Kyd's *Spanish Tragedy*', *Critical Quarterly* 25.1 (Spring 1983): 71–6 (73).

39 Tony Howard, '*The Spanish Tragedy*', *RORD* 21 (1978): 64–6 (65).

40 Kevin Quarmby, '*The Spanish Tragedy*', *British Theatre Guide*, www.britishtheatreguide.info/reviews/spanishtragedy-rev (accessed 15 August 2013).

41 Eoin Price, '*The Spanish Tragedy*', *ROMARD* 49 (2010); 139–42 (140).

42 Robert Hurwitt, '*The Spanish Tragedy* Review: Complicated Revenge', *SFGate*, www.sfgate.com/performance/article/The-Spanish-Tragedy (accessed 15 August 2013).

43 '*The Spanish Tragedy*', http://felttiptheatrecompany.com/productions-2/pre-felt-tip/the-spanish-tragedy-by-thomas-kyd/ (accessed 19 February 2014).

44 Andrew James Hartley, 'Social Consciousness: Spaces for Characters in *The Spanish Tragedy*', *Cahiers Élisabéthains* 58 (October 2000): 1–14.

45 Matthew A. Everett, 'Theatre Pro Rata's *Spanish Tragedy* Gracefully Navigates a Clunky Script', *Twin Cities Daily Planet*, www.tcdailyplanet.net/news/2010/03/15/review-spanish-tragedy-theatre-pro-rata-4-12-stars (accessed 15 August 2013).

46 Michael Billington, '*Spanish Tragedy* in Oxford', *Guardian*, 29 November 1973; 'Sweet Revenge', *Guardian*, 24 September 1982.

47 John Barber, 'The Pre-*Hamlet* Bloodbath', *Daily Telegraph*, 24 September 1982.

48 Nicholas de Jongh, '*The Spanish Tragedy*', *Plays and Players*, December 1982, 24–5 (24).

49 Sheldon P. Zitner, '*The Spanish Tragedy* and the Language of Performance', in *The Elizabethan Theatre XI*, ed. A. L. Magnusson and C. E. McGee (Port Credit: Meany, 1990), 75–93 (78).

50 M. D., '*The Spanish Tragedy*', *Daily Telegraph*, 14 December 1931.

51 B. A. Young, '*The Spanish Tragedy*', *Financial Times*, 30 November 1973.

52 Don Chapman, '*Spanish Tragedy* Fails to Thrill', *Oxford Mail*, 28 November 1973.

53 Eoin Price, '*The Spanish Tragedy*', *ROMARD* 50 (2011): 107–11 (110).

54 For my full review of this production see http://bloggingshakespeare.com/reviewing-shakespeare/spanish-tragedy-lazarus-theatre-company-blue-elephant-theatre-camberwell-london-2013/ (accessed 3 February 2016)

55 Alastair Macaulay, 'A Grievous Attack of Nobility', *Financial Times*, 9 May 1997.

56 RSC, *The Spanish Tragedy*, dir. Michael Boyd, archive DVD, recorded Swan Theatre 19 May 1997 (Shakespeare Centre Library, Stratford-upon-Avon).

57 Sarah Hemming, 'A Sparkling Evening in Hell', *Financial Times*, 10 December 1997.

58 Paul Taylor, 'More Matter, Less Art', *Independent*, 10 May 1997.

59 Charles Spencer, 'RSC's Triumph over Tragedy', *Daily Telegraph*, 9 May 1997.

60 Michael Boyd quoted in Liz Gilbey, 'A Colossus of a Play', *Plays International*, May 1997, 13.

61 Benedict Nightingale, 'First to Cry for Revenge', *The Times*, 9 May 1997.

62 '*Spanish Tragedy*: Script Reading', September 2008, YouTube.com, http://tinyurl.com/SpanTrag (accessed 7 August 2013)

63 'The Spanish Tragedy', http://www.gameshow.org.uk/the-spanish-tragedy.html (accessed 28 February 2014).

Chapter 3

1 Geoffrey Aggeler, 'The Eschatological Crux in *The Spanish Tragedy*', *Journal of English and Germanic Philology* 86.3 (1987): 319.

2 Charles A. Hallett and Elaine S. Hallett, *The Revenger's Madness* (Lincoln: University of Nebraska Press, 1980).

3   Peter Sacks, 'Where Words Prevail Not: Grief, Revenge, and Language in Kyd and Shakespeare', *English Literary History* 49 (1982): 576–601.

4   Tom McAlindon, *English Renaissance Tragedy* (Basingstoke: Macmillan, 1986): 55.

5   Catherine Belsey, *The Subject of Tragedy: Identity and Difference in Renaissance Drama* (London and New York: Routledge, 1985).

6   Graham Holderness, *The Shakespeare Myth* (Manchester: Manchester University Press, 1988).

7   Terence Hawkes, *That Shakespeherian Rag: Essays on a Critical Process* (London: Routledge, 1986).

8   Stephen Greenblatt, *Renaissance Self-Fashioning* (Chicago: Chicago University Press, 1980) and *Shakespearean Negotiations* (Oxford: Clarendon Press, 1988).

9   Steven Mullaney, *The Place of the Stage: License, Power and Play in Renaissance England* (Ann Arbor, MI: University of Michigan Press, 1988).

10 C. L. Barber, *Creating Elizabethan Tragedy: The Theater of Marlowe and Kyd,* ed. Richard P. Wheeler (Chicago and London: University of Chicago Press, 1988).

11 Anthony B. Dawson, 'Madness and Meaning: *The Spanish Tragedy*', *Journal of Dramatic Theory and Criticism* 2.1 (Fall 1987): 55.

12 Katharine Eisaman Maus, *Inwardness and Theater in the English Renaissance* (Chicago: University of Chicago Press, 1995): 35.

13 Frank Whigham, *Seizures of the Will in Early Modern English Drama* (Cambridge: Cambridge University Press, 1996): 3, 22.

14 Richard Hillman, *Self-Speaking in Medieval and Early Modern English Drama: Subjectivity, Discourse, and the Stage* (Basingstoke: Macmillan, 1997).

15 Robert N. Watson, *The Rest Is Silence: Death as Annihilation in the English Renaissance* (Berkeley, LA and London: University of California Press, 1999): 322.

16 James Shapiro, '"Tragedies naturally performed": Kyd's

Representation of Violence', in *Staging the Renaissance: Reinterpretations of Elizabethan and Jacobean Drama*, ed. David Scott Kastan and Peter Stallybrass (Routledge: New York, 1991): 100.

17 Jonathan Bate, 'The Performance of Revenge: *Titus Andronicus* and *The Spanish Tragedy*', in *The Show Within: Dramatic and Other Insets: English Renaissance Drama (1550–1642)*, ed. Francois Laroque, 2 vols (Montpellier: Université Paul-Valery, 1992), vol. 2: 275.

18 Molly Smith, 'The Theater and the Scaffold: Death as Spectacle in The Spanish Tragedy', *Studies in English Literature, 1500–1900* 3.22 (Spring 1992): 217–32.

19 Sandra Clark, *Renaissance Drama* (Cambridge: Polity Press, 2007): 132–3.

20 Timothy A. Turner, 'Torture and Summary justice in *The Spanish Tragedy*', *Studies in English Literature* 53.2 (Spring 2013): 277.

21 Katharine Eisaman Maus, ed., *Four Revenge Tragedies* (Oxford: Oxford University Press, 1995): xvi.

22 Andy Mousley, *Renaissance Drama and Contemporary Literary Theory* (London: Macmillan, 2000): 66.

23 Lukas Erne, *Beyond 'The Spanish Tragedy': A Study of the Works of Thomas Kyd* (Manchester: Manchester University Press, 2002).

24 See Arthur Freeman, *Thomas Kyd: Facts and Problems* (Oxford: Oxford University Press, 1967): 176.

25 D. H. Craig, 'Authorial Styles and the Frequencies of Very Common Words: Jonson, Shakespeare, and the Additions to *The Spanish Tragedy*', *Style* 26.2 (1992): 199–220.

26 Hugh Craig, 'The 1602 Additions to *The Spanish Tragedy*' in *Shakespeare, Computers and the Mystery of Authorship*, ed. Hugh Craig and Arthur F. Kinney (Cambridge: Cambridge University Press, 2009): 162–80.

27 Brian Vickers, 'Shakespeare and Authorship Studies in the Twenty-first Century', *Shakespeare Quarterly* 62 (2011): 111.

28 Douglas Bruster, 'Shakespearean Spellings and Handwriting in the Additional Passages Printed in the 1602 *Spanish Tragedy*',

Notes & Queries 60.3 (2013): 420–4; J. Dover Wilson, 'Bibliographical Links between the Three Pages and the Good Quartos', in *Shakespeare's Hand in 'The Play of Sir Thomas More'*, ed. Andrew F. Pollard et al. (Cambridge: Cambridge University Press, 1923): 113–41.

29 Emma Smith, 'Author v. Character in Early Modern Dramatic Authorship: The Example of Thomas Kyd and *The Spanish Tragedy*', *Medieval and Renaissance Drama in England* 11 (1999): 140.

30 David Cutts,'Writing and Revenge: The Struggle for Authority in Thomas Kyd's The Spanish Tragedy', *Explorations in Renaissance Culture* 22 (1996): 147.

31 Marguerite A. Tassi, *The Scandal of Images: Iconoclasm, Criticism, and Painting in Early Modern English Drama* (Selinsgrove, PA: Susquehanna University Press, 2004): 128.

32 Carol Thomas Neely, *Distracted Subjects: Madness and Gender in Shakespeare and Early Modern Culture* (Ithaca, NY and London: Cornell University Press, 2004): 33.

33 Joost Daalder, 'The Role of "Senex" in Kyd's *The Spanish Tragedy*', *Comparative Drama* 20.3 (Fall 1986): 251–2.

34 Robert S. Miola, 'Another Senecan Echo in Kyd's *The Spanish Tragedy*', *Notes & Queries* 33.3 [231] (September 1986): 337.

35 Eugene Hill, 'Senecan and Vergilian Perspectives in *The Spanish Tragedy*', *English Literary Renaissance* 15 (1985): 149.

36 Gordon Braden, *Renaissance Tragedy and the Senecan Tradition: Anger's Privilege* (New Haven, CT and London: Yale University Press, 1985): 200.

37 John Kerrigan, *Revenge Tragedy: Aeschylus to Armageddon* (Oxford: Clarendon Press, 1997): 171.

38 Lorna Hutson works with the same understanding in her study of *The Spanish Tragedy* in her book *The Invention of Suspicion* (2007): 280.

39 Thomas Rist, *Revenge Tragedy and the Drama of Commemoration in Reforming England* (Aldershot: Ashgate, 2008).

40 '*Vindicta Filia Temporis:* Three English Forerunners of the

Elizabethan Revenge Play', published in the *Journal of English and Germanic Philology* 72 (1973): 489–502.

41 '"Now Shall I See the Fall of Babylon": *The Spanish Tragedy*', in *Shakespeare Yearbook* 1 (1990): 106–13 and 'Hieronimo Agonistes: Kyd's use of Hieronimo as sanctified revenger in *The Spanish Tragedy*', *Journal of Evolutionary Psychology* 15 (1994): 161–5.

42 The Babylonian references were first noted by S. F. Johnson, '*The Spanish Tragedy,* or Babylon Revisited', in *Essays on Shakespeare and Elizabethan Drama in Honor of Hardin Craig*, ed. Richard Hosley (Columbia: University of Missouri Press, 1963): 23–36.

43 J. R. Mulryne, 'Nationality and language in Thomas Kyd's *The Spanish Tragedy*', in *Travel and Drama in Shakespeare's Time*, ed. Jean-Pierre Maquerlot and Michel Willems (Cambridge: Cambridge University Press, 1996): 92.

44 Andrew Hadfield, 'A Handkerchief Dipped in Blood in *The Spanish Tragedy:* An Anti-Catholic Reference?', *Notes & Queries* 46.2 (1999): 197.

45 The story goes that members of the crowd of spectators 'dipped handkerchiefs in the sprayed blood' (see Hadfield, *op. cit.*, 197).

46 Frank Ardolino, '*Corrida* of blood in *The Spanish Tragedy*: Kyd's Use of Revenge as National Destiny', *Medieval and Renaissance Drama in England* 1 (1984): 37–49.

47 In his exhaustive study *Images of Englishmen and Foreigners in the Drama of Shakespeare and his Contemporaries* (Rutherford, NJ: Fairleigh Dickinson University Press, 1992): 78.

48 Frank Ardolino, *Apocalypse and Armada in Kyd's Spanish Tragedy* (Sixteenth Century Essays and Studies, vol. 29) (Kirksville, MO, 1995).

49 Frank Ardolino, '"Now Shall I See the Fall of Babylon": The *Spanish Tragedy*', *Shakespeare Yearbook* 1 (1990): 106–13.

50 Previously argued in his 1990 essay '"In Paris? Mass, and well remembered!": Kyd's *The Spanish Tragedy* and the English Reaction to the St. Bartholomew's Day Massacre', *Sixteenth Century Journal* 21.3 (1990): 401–9.

51 Steven Justice, 'Spain, Tragedy, and *The Spanish Tragedy*', *Studies in English Literature, 1500–1900* 25.2 (Spring 1985): 271–88; Eugene Hill, *op. cit.*, note 35.

52 Eric Griffin, 'Ethos, Empire, and the Valiant Acts of Thomas Kyd's tragedy of "the Spains"', *English Literary Renaissance* 31.2 (March 2001): 202.

53 Eric Griffin, 'Nationalism, the Black Legend, and the Revised Spanish Tragedy', *English Literary Renaissance* 39.2 (Spring 2009): 337.

54 Carla Mazzio, 'Staging the Vernacular: Language and Nation in Thomas Kyd's *The Spanish Tragedy*', *Studies in English Literature, 1500–1900* 38.2, Tudor and Stuart Drama (Spring 1998): 208.

55 Barbara Fuchs, 'Sketches of Spain: Early Modern England's "Orientalising" of Iberia', in *Material and Symbolic Circulation between Spain and England, 1554–1604*, ed. Anne. J. Cruz (Aldershot: Ashgate, 2008): 63.

56 J. W. Lever, *Tragedy of State: a Study of Jacobean Drama* (London: Methuen, 1971).

57 James R. Siemon, 'Sporting Kyd', *English Renaissance Drama* 24.3 (1994): 554.

58 Christopher Crosbie, '*Oeconomia* and the Vegetative Soul: Rethinking Revenge in *The Spanish Tragedy*', *English Literary Renaissance* 38.1 (January 2008): 33.

59 Linda Woodbridge, *English Revenge Drama: Money, Resistance, Equality* (Cambridge: Cambridge University Press, 2010): 237.

60 James J. Condon, 'Setting the Stage for Revenge: Space, Performance, and Power in Early Modern Revenge Tragedy', *Medieval & Renaissance Drama in England* 25 (January 2012): 63.

61 Brian Sheerin, 'Patronage and Perverse Bestowal in *The Spanish Tragedy* and *Antonio's Revenge*', *English Literary Renaissance* 41.2 (Spring 2011): 249.

62 Ian McAdam, '*The Spanish Tragedy* and the Politico-Religious Unconscious', *Texas Studies in Literature and Language* 42.1 (Spring 2000): 46.

63 Frank Ardolino, *Thomas Kyd's Mystery Play: Myth and Ritual in 'The Spanish Tragedy'* (New York: Peter Lang, 1985): 10.

64 Philip Edwards, 'Thrusting Elysium into Hell: the originality of *The Spanish Tragedy*', in *Elizabethan Theatre XI*, ed. A. L. Magnusson and C. E. McGee (Port Credit, Ontario, 1990): 118.

65 Edwards, 'Thrusting Elysium': 123.

66 William M. Hamlin, *Tragedy and Scepticism in Shakespeare's England* (London and New York: Palgrave Macmillan, 2005): 156, 157.

67 Andrew Sofer, 'Absorbing Interests: Kyd's Bloody Handkerchief as Palimpsest', *Comparative Drama* 34.2 (2000): 129.

68 Alexander Leggatt, '"A Membrane is Broken": Returning from the Dead in *The Spanish Tragedy*', in *Renaissance Go-Betweens: Cultural Exchange in Early Modern Europe*, ed. Andreas Höfele, and Werner von Koppenfels (Berlin: Walter de Gruyter, 2005): 216–17.

69 William E. Engel, *Death and Drama in Renaissance England: Shades of Memory* (Oxford: Oxford University Press, 2002): 1–2.

70 Katharine Maus, Introduction, *Titus Andronicus*, in *The Norton Shakespeare*, ed. Stephen Greenblatt et al. (New York: Norton, 1997): 371.

71 Jordi Coral Escola, 'Vengeance is Yours: Reclaiming the Social Bond in *The Spanish Tragedy* and *Titus Andronicus*', Atlantis 29.2 (December 2007): 70.

72 Lorna Hutson, *The Invention of Suspicion: Law and Mimesis in Shakespeare and Renaissance Drama* (Oxford: Oxford University Press, 2007): 269.

73 Simon Barker and Hilary Hinds, eds, *The Routledge Anthology of Renaissance Drama* (London and New York: Routledge, 2003): 35.

74 Gregory M. Colon Semenza, '*The Spanish Tragedy* and revenge', in *Early Modern English Drama: A Critical Companion*, ed. Garrett A. Sullivan, Jr et al. (Oxford: Oxford University Press, 2006), 55.

75 Frank Ardolino, 'Hieronimo Agonistes: Kyd's use of Hieronimo

as sanctified revenger in *The Spanish Tragedy*', *Journal of Evolutionary Psychology* 15 (1994): 161.

76 Duncan Salkeld, *Madness and Drama in the Age of Shakespeare* (Manchester: Manchester University Press, 1993): 120.

77 Philip Edwards, 'Shakespeare and Kyd' in *Shakespeare, Man of the Theater: Proceedings of the Second Congress of the International Shakespeare Association, 1981*, Kenneth Muir et al. (Newark, DE: University of Delaware Press, 1983): 148–54.

78 See note 17.

79 Stanley Wells, *Shakespeare and Co.* (London: Penguin, 2003): 73–5.

80 Martin Wiggins, *Journeymen in Murder: The Assassin in English Renaissance Drama* (Oxford: Clarendon Press, 1991).

81 Rebekah Owens, 'Parody and *The Spanish Tragedy*', *Cahiers Elisabéthains* 71 (2007): 29.

82 From George W. Bush's address to Congress, 21 September 2001. For further discussion, see Stevie Simkin, *Early Modern Tragedy and the Cinema of Violence* (Basingstoke: Palgrave Macmillan, 2006): 85–7.

83 See in particular Park Chan-wook's so-called vengeance trilogy, *Sympathy for Mr. Vengeance* (2002), *Oldboy* (2003) and *Sympathy for Lady Vengeance* (2005).

Chapter 4

1 I quote Seneca's Latin from the text of Otto Zwierlein (Oxford: Clarendon, 1986). For Studley, see *Elizabethan Seneca: Three Tragedies*, ed. James Ker and Jessica Winston (London: MHRA, 2012), 226. Unattributed translations throughout are my own.

2 *Tottel's Miscellany*, ed. Hyder S. Rollins, rev. edn (Cambridge, MA: Harvard University Press, 1966), 1: 80. (Here and elsewhere I silently normalize orthography for old-spelling texts.) Modern editions of Wyatt's poetry print a slightly different text from manuscript. Wyatt's is the first of numerous

translations of this chorus over the next century and a half; examples are collected by G. K. Hunter, 'Seneca and English Tragedy' (1974), in Hunter, *Dramatic Identities and Cultural Tradition* (Liverpool: Liverpool University Press, 1978), 209–13. Wyatt's version leaves a detectable trace not only in these but elsewhere in English Renaissance poetry as well; see Stuart Gillespie, *English Translation and Classical Reception: Toward a New Literary History* (Oxford: Wiley-Blackwell, 2011), 41–3. Tottel's anthology also contains an anonymous Senecan translation that makes a better fit with its context: lines from a chorus on love in *Phaedra* (295–308) are turned into a Petrarchan sonnet (1:188).

3 Wyatt, *The Complete Poems*, ed. R. A. Rebholz (New Haven, CT: Yale University Press, 1981), 155.

4 John W. Cunliffe, *The Influence of Seneca on Elizabethan Tragedy* (Hamden, CT: Archon, 1965), 126.

5 Baker, *Induction to Tragedy* (Baton Rouge, LA: Louisiana State University Press, 1939), 106–53; Hunter, 'Shakespeare and the Elizabethans: A Case Study in "Influence"', in *Dramatic Identities*, 160–73.

6 Braden, *Renaissance Tragedy and the Senecan Tradition* (New Haven, CT: Yale University Press, 1985); Miola, *Shakespeare and Classical Tragedy: The Influence of Seneca* (Oxford: Clarendon, 1992).

7 Colin Burrow, *Shakespeare and Classical Antiquity* (Oxford: Oxford University Press, 2013), 162–3.

8 At least the profession of English studies. Among classicists the last couple of decades have been an unprecedented time of serious attention to Seneca and Senecan tragedy; a sophisticated and ambitious body of scholarship and criticism now exists, sometimes reaching into reception history. Extensive introductions to it are now available in *Brill's Companion to Seneca*, ed. Gregor Damschen and Andreas Heil (Leiden: Brill, 2014), and *The Cambridge Companion to Seneca*, ed. Shadi Bartsch and Alessandro Schiesaro (Cambridge: Cambridge University Press, 2015).

9 The most comprehensive history of the movement is still Alexander Maclaren Witherspoon, *The Influence of Robert*

Garnier on Elizabethan Drama (New Haven, CT: Yale University Press, 1924); the plays in question dominate the section on England in H. B. Charlton's *The Senecan Tradition in Renaissance Tragedy* (Manchester: Manchester University Press, 1946), originally written to introduce an edition of William Alexander's four *Monarchic Tragedies* (1603–7).

10 Lukas Erne, *Beyond* The Spanish Tragedy (Manchester: Manchester University Press, 2001), 211.

11 For Kyd's practice here in its broad early modern context, see Susanna Braund, 'Haunted by Horror: The Ghost of Seneca in Renaissance Drama', in *A Companion to the Neronian Age*, ed. Emma Buckley and Martin T. Dinter (Oxford: Blackwell, 2013), 425–43.

12 Eugene D. Hill, 'Senecan and Vergilian Perspectives in *The Spanish Tragedy*', *English Literary Renaissance* 15 (1985): 162.

13 Miola, 'Another Seneca Echo in *The Spanish Tragedy*', *Notes and Queries* 231 (1986): 337.

14 Boyle, *Tragic Seneca* (London: Routledge, 1997), 29. For an unprecedentedly ambitious analysis of this kind of rhetoric – what Shakespeare's Bottom calls 'Ercles' vein' – and of its historical and conceptual importance, see Christopher D. Johnson, *Hyperboles* (Cambridge, MA: Harvard University Department of Comparative Literature, 2010), 279–333.

15 The contemporary consensus that the authorship of eight of the Senecan tragedies (*Hercules Oetaeus* and *Octavia* aside) has been settled makes the dating of those plays to the time of Caligula and Nero reasonably secure. Reopening the authorship question has, however, recently been proposed, to attribute at least some of the plays to Seneca the elder (c. 55 BC–37 AD); some possible topical allusions could well be to the reign of Augustus, whose press has of course been much more favourable. The consequences of that could be extremely interesting. See Frederick M. Ahl, 'Coping with the Canonical Oedipus', in *Edipo classico e contemporaneo*, ed. Francesco Citti and Alessandro Iannucci (Hildesheim: Olms, 2012), 15–20. Early modern scholars were in fact seriously divided on the question of authorship (and hence dating); see

Roland Mayer, 'Personata Stoa: Neostoicism and Senecan Tragedy', *Journal of the Warburg and Courtauld Institutes* 57 (1994): 151–74; Jan Machielsen, *Martin Delrio: Demonology and Scholarship in the Counter-Reformation* (Oxford: Oxford University Press, 2015), 137–59.

16 Burckhardt, *The Civilization of the Renaissance in Italy*, trans. S. G. C. Middlemore (New York: Harper & Row, 1958), 25.

17 *Elizabethan Critical Essays*, ed. G. Gregory Smith (Oxford: Oxford University Press, 1904), 1:177.

18 Greville, *A Dedication to Sir Philip Sidney*, in *The Prose Work of Fulke Greville, Lord Brookes*, ed. John Gouws (Oxford: Clarendon, 1986), 133.

19 *Justus Lipsius'* Concerning Constancy, ed. and trans. R. V. Young (Tempe, AZ: ACMRS, 2011), 197.

20 Maus, ed., *Four Revenge Tragedies* (Oxford: Oxford University Press, 1995), xiv–xviii.

21 Hakluyt, *Discourse of Western Planting*, ed. David B. Quinn and Alison B. Quinn (London: Hakluyt Society, 1993), 60–1; cited by Hill, 153–6. Hakluyt gleefully describes the Spanish heir apparent as 'the weak son by his sister's daughter', but he did in fact live to reign as Philip III and produce his own male heir – and through his daughter to become posthumously the grandfather of Louis XIV of France. Dynastic history is full of surprises.

22 Eric Griffin, 'Ethos, Empire, and the Valiant Acts of Thomas Kyd's Tragedy of "the Spains"', *English Literary Renaissance* 31 (2001): 204, heightening Hill's 'the beauty, the glory of empire' (p. 151). See also Griffin, 'Nationalism, the Black Legend, and the Revised *Spanish Tragedy*', *English Literary Renaissance* 39 (2009): 336–70. We have no way of knowing if Kyd had heard of the famous courtesan in Renaissance Rome called Imperia. That apparently was her right name; see G. L. Moncallero, *Imperia de Paris nella Roma del Cinquecento* (Rome: Palombi, 1962).

23 Erne, 91: 'none, to my knowledge, of the innumerable early allusions to Kyd's play takes up its historical relevance'.

24 Emrys Jones, *The Origins of Shakespeare* (Oxford: Clarendon, 1977), 90.

25 Edward Muir, *Ritual in Early Modern Europe* (Cambridge: Cambridge University Press, 1997), 106. Muir is speaking specifically of the Mediterranean world, though that is where *The Spanish Tragedy* is set, as are many other English plays.

26 Fredson Bowers, *Elizabethan Revenge Tragedy* (Princeton, NJ: Princeton University Press, 1940), 78.

27 Kerrigan, *Revenge Tragedy* (Oxford: Clarendon, 1996), 140–1.

28 C. J. Herington: 'after rereading it ... I cannot resist the conjecture that Nero's professor was subjected to some early version of the publish-or-perish rule. ... One would readily attribute so fiendish an innovation to the later Julio-Claudian epoch'; 'Senecan Tragedy', *Arion* 5 (1966): 63–4.

29 'Gifts', Ralph Waldo Emerson, *Essays and Lectures*, ed. Joel Porte (New York: Library of America, 1983), 536. Personal experience with the world of *De Beneficiis* may be sensed behind Tacitus's admiration for the ways of gift-giving among the un-Romanized Germans, who he says give and receive simply for the joy of it, without imposing or incurring any obligation to reciprocate ('nec data imputant nec acceptis obligantur'; *Germania* 21.3).

30 Roy W. Battenhouse, 'Tamburlaine, the "Scourge of God"', *PMLA* 56 (1941): 337–48.

31 See the influential discussion by Bowers, 'Hamlet as Minister and Scourge', *PMLA* 70 (1955): 740–9.

32 Thomas Fortescue, *The Forest, or Collection of Histories* (London, 1571), fol. 43^r (a translation of Pedro Mexía's *Silva de varia lección* [1540]). Similar phrasing concludes Beaumont and Fletcher's *The Maid's Tragedy* (c. 1610): 'on lustful kings | Unlooked-for sudden deaths from God are sent; | But cursed is he that is their instrument' (5.3.293–5).

33 Scott McMillin, 'The Book of Seneca in *The Spanish Tragedy*', *Studies in English Literature* 14 (1974): 206–7.

34 On the distress this chorus caused scholarly commentators, see Mayer, 156, 163, 169, 171.

35 Despite its power, the allusion escaped Cunliffe and seems

not to have been noted in print until Miola, *Shakespeare and Classical Tragedy*, 165–6; see also my 'Herakles and Hercules: Survival in Greek and Roman Tragedy (with a Coda on *King Lear*)', in *Theater and Society in the Classical World*, ed. Ruth Scodel (Ann Arbor, MI: University of Michigan Press, 1993), 257–61.

36 In Seneca: 'mihi gelidus horror ac tremor somnum excutit' (*Troades* 457, cold horror and fear shake my sleep), 'horrore nouo terre populos' (*Medea* 794, terrify the people with new horror), 'Horrore quatior, fata quo uergant timens' (*Oedipus* 206, I shake with horror, fearing where the fates may head), 'tenet horror artus' (*Agamemnon* 508, horror seizes the limbs), etc.

Chapter 5

This research was supported by a Huntington Library Mayers Fellowship, July 2014, San Marino, CA.

1 A. H. de Olveira Marques, *History of Portugal*, 2 vols (New York: Columbia University Press, 1972), II, 307; A. R. Disney, *A History of Portugal and the Portuguese Empire*, 2 vols (Cambridge: Cambridge University Press, 2009) II, 20.

2 Fernand Braudel, *The Mediterranean and the Mediterranean World in The Age of Philip II,* trans. Siân Reynolds, 2 vols (New York: Harper and Row, 1973), II, 1176–85.

3 Eric Griffin, 'Ethos, Empire, and the Valiant Acts of Thomas Kyd's Tragedy of "The Spains"', *English Literary Renaissance* 31 (2001): 192–229.

4 'Introduction', in *The Spanish Tragedy*, Thomas Kyd, Clara Calvo and Jesús Tronch eds. (London: Bloomsbury, 2013), 1.

5 See Calvo and Tronch, 166–7.

6 J. H. Elliott, 'The Spanish Monarchy and the Kingdom of Portugal, 1580–1640', in *Conquest and Coalescence. The Shaping of the State in Early Modern Europe*, ed. Mark Greengrass (London: Edward Arnold, 1991), 55.

7 Kyd may have drawn several names and historical details from

the Italian source, Gerolomo de Conestaggio, *Dell' Unione del Regno di Portugallo alla Corona di Castigilia* (Genoa, 1585), published as *The Historie of the Uniting of the Kingdom of Portugal to the Crowne of Castill* (London, 1600). See also John Poleman, *The part of the booke of Battailes, fought in our age* (London, 1587), y.iii-Bb.iv.

8   H. V. Livermore, *A New History of Portugal*, 2nd edn (Cambridge: Cambridge University Press, 1976), 164–5. Kyd may have known Álvaro de Bazan, Marquês de Santa Cruz, *A discourse of that which happened in the battell fought betweene the two navies of Spaine and Portugall* (London, 1583).

9   Philip Edwards, ed., *The Spanish Tragedy* (Manchester: University of Manchester Press, 1959), xxiv; and Arthur Freeman, *Thomas Kyd: Facts and Problems* (Oxford: Oxford University Press, 1967), 52. See also Lucas Erne, *Beyond the Spanish Tragedy* (Manchester: Manchester University Press, 2001), 56.

10 On Kyd's 'ambition' topos see S. F. Johnson, 'The Spanish Tragedy, or Babylon Revisited', *Essays on Shakespeare and Elizabethan Drama*, ed. R. Hosley (Columbia, MO: University of Missouri Press, 1962), 23–36; Stephen Justice, 'Spain, Tragedy, and *The Spanish Tragedy*', *Studies in English Literature* 25 (1985): 271–88; J. R. Mulryne, 'Nationality and Language in Thomas Kyd's *Spanish Tragedy*', *Langues et Nations au Temps de la Renaissance*, ed. M. T. Jones-Davies (Paris: Université de Paris-Sorbonne, 1991), 67–91; Frank Ardolino, *Apocalypse and Armada in Kyd's Spanish Tragedy* (Kirksville, MO, Sixteenth Century Essays & Studies, 1995).

11 I. Van Langen, *The Explanation of the True and Lawfull Right and Tytle, of the Moste Excellent Prince Anthonie the first of that name, King of Portugal* (Leyden, 1585), 50–1. Van Langen notes among the mediators between Philip II and Dom Antonio one 'Ieronimo de Mendoza', 48–50.

12 G. B., *A Fig of the Spaniard, or Spanish Spirits* (London, 1592), B1; Anon., *A True discourse of the Armie which the King of Spaine caused to be assembled in the haven of Lisbon* (London, 1588), 8–11.

13 Machiavelli, *The Prince*, trans. George Bull (London: Penguin Books, 1961), 119–20.

14 Geoffrey Parker, *The World is Not Enough: The Imperial Vision of Philip II of Spain* (Waco, TX: Baylor University Press, 2001), 9–11.

15 Griffin, 'Ethos, Empire', 199–204.

16 Justice, 'Spain, Tragedy', 274; Mulryne, 'Nationality and Language', 68–9; Eugene Hill, 'Senecan and Virgilian Perspectives in *The Spanish Tragedy*', *ELR* 15 (1985): 143–65 (152–6).

17 Anthony Pagden, *Lords of All the World: Ideologies of Empire in Spain, Britain and France, c. 1500–c. 1800* (New Haven: Yale University Press, 1995), 12–28.

18 Pagden, *Lords of All the World*, 11–12.

19 Griffin, *English Renaissance Drama and the Specter of Spain: Ethnopoetics and Empire* (Philadelphia: University of Pennsylvania Press, 2009), 3, 9, 17–18; Barbara Fuchs, *The Poetics of Piracy: Emulating Spain in English Literature* (Philadelphia: University of Pennsylvania Press, 2013), 1–4, 55–8; Fernand Braudel, *The Structures of Everyday Life*, trans. Siân Reynolds (Berkeley: University of California Press, 1992), 317–18.

20 Blundeville, Thomas (c. 1522–c. 1606?), *Oxford Dictionary of National Biography*, at http://www.oxforddnb.com.proxy.its.virginia.edu/view/article/2718 (accessed 6 February 2016).

21 *M. Blundeville his exercises containing sixe treatises* (London, 1594).

22 Richard Eden trans. *The decades of the newe worlde or west India* (London, 1555), Jiii.ii.r.

23 John M. Headley, 'Campanella, America, and World Evangelization', in *America in European Consciousness, 1493–1750*, Karen Ordahl Kupperman, ed. (Chapel Hill: University of North Carolina Press, 1995), 243–71. According to Pliny, 'Thule' was an island 'six days sail from the Orcades'. See John Warrington, ed., *Everyman's Classical Dictionary* (London: J. M. Dent & Sons, 1969), 507.

24 Francis Bacon, 'Of Prophecies' in *Francis Bacon: A Selection*

of His Works, ed. Sidney Warhaft (Indianapolis: Bobs-Merrill, 1965), 142.

25 Philip Ward, ed., *The Oxford Companion to Spanish Literature* (Oxford: Oxford University Press, 1978), 540.

26 Julio Caro Baroja, 'Religion, World Views, Social Classes and Honor During the Sixteenth and Seventeenth Centuries', in *Honor and Grace in Anthropology*, J. G. Peristany and J. Pitt-Rivers, eds. (Cambridge: Cambridge University Press, 1992), 91–102.

27 Griffin, '"Spain is Portugal / And Portugal is Spain": Transnational Attraction in the Stukeley Plays and *The Spanish Tragedy*', *JEMCS* 10 (2010): 95–116.

28 Pagden, *Lords of All the World*, 13. For Augustinian imperial translation, see Donald R. Kelly, *Versions of History from Antiquity to Enlightenment* (New Haven: Yale University Press, 1991), 142–7. On the immediate context, see William Allen, *An Admonition to the Nobility and People of England and Ireland* (Antwerp, 1588), xlv–xlix.

29 Daniel 2.44 provided the Biblical precedent.

30 Pagden, *Lords of All the World*, 42–3.

31 Peter Finch, *John Dee: The World of an Elizabethan Magus* (New York: Dorset, 1972), 56, 180.

32 Marie Tanner, *The Last Descendant of Aeneas: The Hapsburgs and the Mythic Image of the Emperor* (New Haven: Yale University Press, 1993), 145.

33 Griffin, 'Ethos, Empire', 205–6; Ronald Broude, 'Time, Truth, and Right in *The Spanish Tragedy*', *Studies in Philology* 68 (1971): 130–45; Ardolino, *Apocalypse and Armada, passim*.

34 Hill, 'Senecan and Virgilian Perspectives', 143–4, 164.

35 Richard Hakluyt, *A Discourse of Western Planting*, in *The Original Writings & Correspondence of the Two Richard Hakluyts*, ed. E. G. R. Taylor (London: Hakluyt Society, 1935), 264.

36 See Griffin, 'Ethos, Ethnos', 197–8; Edmund Spenser, *The Faerie Queene* 1.2: 32–5; John Vernon, *The Hunting of Purgatorie to Death* (London, 1562), 101–3. Thomas Rist, *Revenge Tragedy and the Drama of Commemoration in*

Reforming England (Aldershot: Ashgate, 2008), 1–18, recovers Kyd's connection to England's Catholic traditions, demonstrating far more ambivalence than 'reformed' readings have allowed.

37 Miguel de Cervantes, *El cerco de Numancia*, ed. Robert Marrast (Salamanca: Biblioteca Anaya, 1970); Willard King, 'Cervantes' *Numancia* and Imperial Spain', *MLN* 94 (1979): 200–21.

38 Whether a global fifth monarchy was to follow upon Spain's neo-Roman fourth remained open to hermeneutic interpretation. See, for example, Thomas Goodwin, *A Sermon of the Fifth Monarchy* (London, 1654).

39 On the appearance of the additions prior to 1602, see Roslyn L. Knutson, 'Influence of the Repertory System on the Revival and Revision of *The Spanish Tragedy* and *Dr. Faustus*', *English Literary Renaissance* 18 (1988): 257–74 (258).

40 See *Henslowe's Diary*, eds. Foakes and Rickert, 182, 203; Erne, *Beyond The Spanish Tragedy*, 119–20.

41 See Brian Vickers, 'Identifying Shakespeare's Additions to *The Spanish Tragedy* (1602): A New(er) Approach', *Shakespeare* 8 (2012): 1343; Hugh Craig and Arthur F. Kinney, *Shakespeare, Computers, and the Mystery of Authorship* (Cambridge: Cambridge University Press, 2009), 162–80; Warren Stevenson, *Shakespeare's Additions to Thomas Kyd's* The Spanish Tragedy: *A Fresh Look at the Evidence Regarding the 1602 Additions* (Lewiston, Queenston, and Lampeter: Edward Mellen, 2008).

42 E. A. J. Honigmann, 'The First Quarto of *Hamlet* and the Date of *Othello*', *The Review of English Studies, New Series* 44, 174 (1993): 211–19.

43 On 'remembrance' as 'the principal religious context of the genre', see Rist, *Revenge Tragedy*, 2–10.

44 Emma Smith, ed. *The Spanish Tragedie* (London: Penguin Books, 1998), xiv.

45 Paul C. Allen, *Philip III and the Pax Hispanica, 1598–1621: The Failure of Grand Strategy* (New Haven: Yale University Press, 2000), 72–6.

46 Griffin, 'Spain is Portugal', 108–9.

47 Janette Dillon, '*The Spanish Tragedy* and Staging Languages in Renaissance Drama', *Research opportunities in Renaissance Drama* 34 (1995): 15–40 (35).

48 The most obvious examples are the two parts of Thomas Heywood's *If You Know Not Me You Know Nobody* (1605).

49 See José Teixeira (1543–1604), *The Strangest Adventure That Ever Happened* (London, 1601), and *The True History of the Late and Lamentable Adventures of Don Sebastian King of Portugal* (London, 1602).

50 Griffin, 'Nationalism, the Black Legend, and the Revised *Spanish Tragedy*', *English Literary Renaissance* 39 (2009): 336–70 (358–68).

51 Griffin, 'Spain is Portugal', 106–7.

52 Henry Savile, 'Historical Collections', in *The Jacobean Union: Six Tracts of 1604*, ed. Bruce R. Galloway and Brian P. Levack. (Edinburgh: Scottish Historical Society, 1985), 229.

53 On *The Spanish Tragedy*'s 1615 title page, see Griffin, 'Nationalism', 337–9.

54 Alexander Samson, ed., *The Spanish Match: Prince Charles's Journey to Madrid, 1623* (Aldershot: Ashgate, 2006), 1–2.

55 'A Treaty of Perpetual Peace and Alliance … in the Year 1604', in *A General Collection of Treaties* (London, 1732), 132.

56 OED. To make Spanish, imbue with Spanish notions.

57 Jerzy Limon, *Dangerous Matter: English Drama and Politics, 1623/24* (Cambridge: Cambridge University Press, 1986), 1–19; A. A. Bromham and Zara Bruzzi, *The Changeling and the Years of Crisis, 1619–1624: A Hieroglyph of Britain* (London: Pinter, 1990), 8–9.

58 Annabel Patterson, *Censorship and Interpretation: The Conditions of Writing in Early Modern England* (Madison: University of Wisconsin Press, 1984), 85. On the era's 'Spanish plays', see Griffin, 'Copying "the Anti-Spaniard": Post-Armada Hispanophobia in English Renaissance Drama', in *Representing Imperial Rivalry in the Early Modern Mediterranean*, Barbara Fuchs and Emily Weissbourd, eds. (Toronto: University of Toronto Press, 2015), 191–216 (208–9).

59 Griffin, 'Copying "the Anti-Spaniard"', 205–8.

60 Thomas Scott, *Vox Regis* (1624), 15–16.

61 Paula Martin, *Spanish Armada Prisoners* (Exeter: Exeter University Press, 1988), 91–8.

62 Limon, *Dangerous Matter,* 11.

63 'Mythical'. OED. Sense 1b. Known only or principally through myths rather than through verifiable historical facts; belonging to or existing only in myth; fantastical. Sense 1c. Having no foundation in fact; fictitious, imaginary; Sense 4. That has acquired an idealized or exaggerated reputation on the basis of popular rumour.

64 Emma Smith, 'Author v. Character in Early Modern Dramatic Authorship: The Example of Thomas Kyd and *The Spanish Tragedy*', *MaRDIE* 11 (1999): 129–42 (135–9).

65 Erne, *Beyond the Spanish Tragedy,* 14–15.

Chapter 6

1 For recent discussions of Virgil's cultural centrality during the English Renaissance, see David Scott Wilson-Okamura, *Virgil in the Renaissance* (Cambridge: Cambridge University Press, 2010), esp. 15–44, and Colin Burrow, 'Shakespeare and Humanistic Culture', in *Shakespeare and the Classics*, Charles Martindale and A. B. Taylor, eds. (Cambridge: Cambridge University Press, 2004), 11–16.

2 Michael Neill, 'Introduction', in Thomas Kyd, *The Spanish Tragedy*, ed. Michael Neill (New York: Norton, 2014), xxxviii.

3 Eugene D. Hill, 'Senecan and Virgilian Perspectives in *The Spanish Tragedy*', *English Literary Renaissance* 15 (1985): 143–65 (151).

4 Katharine Eisaman Maus, *Inwardness and Theater in the English Renaissance* (Chicago: University of Chicago Press, 1995), 64.

5 Philip Edwards, 'Thrusting Elysium into Hell: The Originality of *The Spanish Tragedy*', in *The Elizabethan Theatre* 11, ed. A. L. Magnusson and C. E. McGee (Ontario: Meany, 1990), 121.

6   Latin text: Virgil, *Eclogues, Georgics, Aeneid 1–6*, trans. by H. R. Fairclough, rev. edn, Loeb Classical Library, 63 (Cambridge, MA: Harvard University Press, 1935), 6.759. English text: Virgil, *The Aeneid: A New Prose Translation*, trans. David West (London: Penguin, 1990), 156. Further references to the *Aeneid* supply the book and line number of Virgil's Latin followed by the page number in West's translation.

7   G. K. Hunter, 'Seneca and English Tragedy', in *Dramatic Identities and Cultural Tradition: Studies in Shakespeare and His Contemporaries* (Liverpool: Liverpool University Press, 1978), 218.

8   Donna B. Hamilton, '*The Spanish Tragedy*: A Speaking Picture', *English Literary Renaissance* 4 (1974): 203–17 (205).

9   *Articles … for the Auoiding of the Diuersities of Opinions, and for the Stablishyng of Consent Touching True Religion* (London, 1571), 8, 11.

10 Jean Calvin, *The Institution of Christian Religion*, trans. Thomas Norton (London, 1561), Book 2, sig. [A8]^v.

11 *The Canons and Decrees of the Council of Trent* (anon. translation) (London, 1687), 28.

12 Lukas Erne, *Beyond 'The Spanish Tragedy': A Study of the Works of Thomas Kyd* (Manchester: Manchester University Press, 2001), 103. See also Clara Calvo and Jesús Tronch, 'Introduction', in Thomas Kyd, *The Spanish Tragedy*, Clara Calvo and Jesús Tronch, eds. (London: Bloomsbury, 2013), 44.

13 The phrase comes from a Privy Council minute recording letters to this effect to the Archbishop of Canterbury, the Lord Mayor of London and the Master of the Revels. See *English Professional Theatre, 1530–1660*, Glynne Wickham, Herbert Berry and William Ingram, eds. (Cambridge: Cambridge University Press, 2000), 94–5.

14 Michael Neill, *Issues of Death: Mortality and Identity in English Renaissance Tragedy* (Oxford: Clarendon Press, 1997), 38; Stephen Greenblatt, *Hamlet in Purgatory* (Princeton: Princeton University Press, 2001); Thomas Rist, *Revenge Tragedy and the Drama of Commemoration in Reforming England* (Aldershot: Ashgate, 2008).

15 Rist, 27–44.
16 Wilson-Okamura, 177; Rist, 31.
17 Rist, 32.
18 Lorna Hutson, *The Invention of Suspicion* (Oxford: Oxford University Press, 2007), 280. See also Erne, 53; Rist, 32–3.
19 Neill, *Issues of Death*, 30.
20 Rist, 33.
21 *The Canons and Decrees of the Council of Trent*, 145.
22 Philip Edwards, 'Introduction', in Thomas Kyd, *The Spanish Tragedy*, ed. Philip Edwards (London: Methuen, 1959), lx.
23 Robert Greene, *Menaphon: Camillas Alarum to Slumbering Euphues, in His Melancholie Cell at Silexdra* (London, 1589), sigs *2^r, **1^r.
24 Greene, *Menaphon*, sigs **1^v, **2^v, **3^r.
25 For a sceptical survey of this controversy, see Emma Smith, 'Ghost Writing: *Hamlet* and the Ur-Hamlet', in *The Renaissance Text: Theory, Editing, Textuality*, ed. Andrew Murphy (Manchester: Manchester University Press, 2000), 177–90.
26 Thomas Nashe, *The Works of Thomas Nashe*, ed. Ronald B. McKerrow (London: Bullen, 1904–10), vol. 4, 448–52.
27 Erne, 53. See also Arthur Freeman, *Thomas Kyd: Facts and Problems* (Oxford: Clarendon Press, 1967), 39–48; G. R. Hibbard, *Thomas Nashe: A Critical Introduction* (London: Routledge and Kegan Paul, 1962), 35.
28 See Hibbard, 27, 36; Lorna Hutson, 'Fictive Acts: Thomas Nashe and the Mid-Tudor Legacy', in *The Oxford Handbook of Tudor Literature 1485–1603*, Mike Pincombe and Cathy Shrank, eds. (Oxford: Oxford University Press, 2009), 720.
29 Greene, *Menaphon*, sigs **3^v, **4^v, A1^r.
30 Thomas M. Greene, *The Light in Troy: Imitation and Discovery in Renaissance Poetry* (New Haven: Yale University Press, 1982), 30, 32.
31 Greene, *Menaphon*, sigs A2v, A1r, [**4]v.
32 Greene, *Menaphon*, sig. A1r; compare 'rownce robel hobble',

Thee First Foure Bookes of Virgil His Aeneis, trans. by
Richard Stanyhurst (Leyden, 1582), 95. Freeman similarly sees
Nashe as suggesting that the translator 'has botched the job,
discrediting and possibly mistranslating the classical original'
(44), although in this reading Nashe attacks the translation for
inaccuracy rather than indecorum.

33 Christopher Marlowe and Thomas Nashe, *The Tragedie of
    Dido Queene of Carthage* (London, 1594).

34 The similarity has also been noted in Geoffrey Aggeler, 'The
    Eschatological Crux in *The Spanish Tragedy*', *Journal of
    English and Germanic Philology* 86 (1987): 319–31 (320).

35 Christopher Marlowe, *Doctor Faustus: A- and B- Texts (1604,
    1616)*, ed. David Bevington and Eric Rasmussen (Manchester:
    Manchester University Press, 1993), A-text, 1.3.60–2.
    Subsequent quotations in the main text are to this edition.

36 Nashe, ed. McKerrow, vol. 4, 450.

37 Saint Jerome's text is actually 'Mihi uindictam': *Nouum
    Testamentum Latine Secundum Editionem Sancti Hiernoymi*,
    John Wordsworth and Henry Julian White, eds. (Oxford:
    Clarendon Press, 1911). I am not arguing for any significance
    in the reversal of word order.

38 Letter to Sir John Puckering (MS. *Harl.* 6849, fols 218–19),
    quoted in Freeman, 181.

39 Margaret Tudeau-Clayton, *Jonson, Shakespeare and Early
    Modern Virgil* (Cambridge: Cambridge University Press, 1998),
    7.

40 Greene, 32–3. Greene translates from *De dignitate et
    augmentis scientiarum* in *The Works of Francis Bacon*, James
    Spedding, Robert Leslie Ellis and Douglas Denon Heath, eds
    (London: Longman, 1857–72), vol. 1, 504.

41 Virgil, *Georgics*, 4.483.

42 Greene, *Menaphon*, sigs. **1^r-**1^v, A2^v.

43 See Bevington and Rasmussen, 70–2.

44 See Calvo and Tronch, 13–14; Bevington and Rasmussen, 1–3.

45 Thomas Dekker, *A Knights Coniuring Done in Earnest:
    Discouered in Iest* (London, 1607), sigs K4^r–L1^r.

Chapter 7

1 Johnston and Rogerson state that 1569 is the last recorded performance of York's Corpus Christi Cycle; According to Lawrence Clopper, 1575 was the final Chester performance; Lumiansky and Mills show that the Chester plays survive in five extant MSS, dating from 1591 to 1607. R. A. Foakes discusses the emergence of London's Red Lion in 1567 and The Theatre in 1576.

2 Thomas Rist, *Revenge Tragedy and the Drama of Commemoration in Reforming England* (Aldershot, England: Ashgate 2008), 15.

3 Eamon Duffy, *The Stripping of the Altars* (New Haven, CT: Yale University Press, 1992), 260.

4 See Chapter Five of my *Female Mourning and Tragedy*.

5 For further discussion of Seneca, see Gordon Braden's and Eric Griffin's chapters in this book. On Garnier, see Lukas Erne's *Beyond the Spanish Tragedy*, especially Chapter 9.

6 On the pervasiveness of the Corpus Christi drama, see Barbara Palmer, 'Early Modern Mobility, Players, Payments, and Patrons', *SQ* 56.3 (Fall 2005): 259–305.

7 C. L. Barber, *Creating Elizabethan Tragedy: The Theater of Marlowe and Kyd*, ed. Richard P. Wheeler (Chicago: University of Chicago Press, 1988), 153–64; cited in Erne, 94N21.

8 Lisa Hopkins, 'What's Hercules to Hamlet?: The Emblematic Garden in *The Spanish Tragedy* and *Hamlet*', *Hamlet Studies* 21.1–2 (Summer–Winter 1999): 114–43 (122).

9 Andrew Sofer, 'Absorbing Interests: Kyd's Bloody Handkerchief as Palimpsest', *Comparative Drama* 34.2 (Summer 2000): 127–53 (142).

10 'This sign will call down vengeance on the whole lot of you!' (my translation).

11 In the Towneley *Scourging* Maria Magdalena gives the curse of revenge: 'This thing shall venyance call / On you holly in fere' (492–3), while in The Chester *Passion* Maria Magadalena curses the Judeuses, less felicitously, 'God, that rules aye the right, / give you mickell mischance' (271–2). Sofer discusses the

Veronica cloth in the N-Town and York cycles, but misses the Third Maria's curse, which occurs in the York 6 lines after the section he quotes.

12 On this dynamic see especially Horacio Sierra, 'Bearing Witness and Taking Action: Audiences and Morality in Renaissance Tragedy and Activist Street Theater', *Comparative Drama*, 48.1/2 (Spring/Summer 2014): 39–57.

13 On Mary as Queen of Hell see my Chapter 2. See also Frances Dolan, *Whores of Babylon* (Ithaca: Cornell University Press, 1999), 102–17.

14 Towneley *Herod* (530–2).

15 I refer collectively to the five different plays depicting the biblical episode of the Slaughter of the Holy Innocents as the 'Slaughter' plays.

16 The integral relationship between female mourning and revenge has a long history that reaches back at least as far as classical Greek tragedy. See my *Female Mourning and Tragedy*. The most troubling aspect of this connection in the Corpus Christi drama is the repeated (and unbiblical) invocations of revenge against the Jews for murdering Mary's innocent child. For a recent discussion see, Maija Birenbaum, 'Affective Vengeance in Titus and Vespasian', *The Chaucer Review* 43.3 (2009): 330–44; Merrall Llewelyn Price, 'Re-membering the Jews: Theatrical Violence in the N-Town Marian Plays', *Comparative Drama* 41.4 (Winter 2007–8): 439–63.

17 I include the Digby *Killing of the Children,* which, though not a cycle play, parallels the other plays, and helps to demonstrate the pervasiveness of the plays and their ideology.

18 The Towneley and the York Slaughter plays, like the Passion sequences, delay the enactment of divine vengeance against the murderers of the innocents until the Judgement.

19 Herod's pleas to 'Mahound' are typical of the evil characters in the Corpus Christi cycles. It is notable, in this regard, that in Hieronimo's 'The Tragedy of Suleiman the Turkish Emperor', Balthazar plays Suleiman, who praises 'holy Muhammad' (4.4.12).

20 See George R. Kaiser, 'The Middle English *Planctus Mariae* and

the Rhetoric of Pathos', in *The Popular Literature of Medieval England*, ed. Thomas J. Heffernan (University of Tennessee 1985).

21 For a persuasive analysis of the symbiotic relationship between love and vengeance in the vegetative soul, see Christopher Crosbie, '*Oeconomia* and the Vegetative Soul: Rethinking Revenge in *The Spanish Tragedy*', *ELR* (2008): 3–33.

22 'The raising [of the cross with Jesus on it] is given considerable prominence ... as an important piece of stage business' in the cycles. R. M. Lumiansky and David Mills, *The Chester Mystery Cycle, Volume 2: Commentary and Glossary* (Oxford, 1986), 252N213–6.

23 Martin Stevens and A. C. Cawley (Volume II, Commentary) note that 'the Wakefield author's portrait of Herod is a commonplace of medieval political thought ... But his portraiture of [the tyrant] has no doubt gained in zest from his own observation of contemporary magnates', among them 'the Duke of Suffolk' (521). Of Pilate they note that he, 'is a caricature of the ruling class; he speaks in the way that *men of cowrte now can* (30), giving preferment to liars, false jurors, and thieves' (547).

24 Kyd's interest in female lamentation as a dramatic form is visible in his *Cornelia*. On its relationship to *The Spanish Tragedy*, see Lukas Erne, *Beyond the Spanish Tragedy* (Manchester, 2001), esp. Chapter 9.

25 G. K. Hunter, 'Ironies of Justice in *The Spanish Tragedy*', *Renaissance Drama* 8 (1965): 89–104. Lorna Hutson, *The Invention of Suspicion* (Oxford 2007), 277–87.

26 In Middle English fitte also means punishment. See York Glossary, s.v. 'fitte' (493).

27 At least as late as 1590 Ecclesiastical Officials reported the performance of Catholic Burial rites in England. See David Cressy, *Birth, Marriage, and Death: Ritual, Religion, and the Life-Cycle in Tudor and Stuart England* (Oxford: Oxford University Press, 1997), 400.

28 On Elizabethan attempts to suppress Catholic practices see Duffy, 565–93.

29 Three of the four have almost identical 'showings' of Jesus' wounds. The N-Town manuscript is incomplete after line 130. It is likely that it also had a showing of the wounds because Jesus' suffering is central to the working of divine retribution in the Judgement plays. All of the judgement plays follow the same essential format in which Jesus shows his wounds, doles out sentences, and the audience witnesses the punishment of the evil and indifferent.

30 Norton, 107N115.

31 See Erne, 88–9 for a reading of the Pedringano-Lorenzo subplot as morality play.

32 The argument of Linda Woodbridge's *English Revenge Drama* (Cambridge 2010) is that the genre of Revenge drama embodied middle class ideas about social equality and contributed to the transformation of English society. See especially page 7.

33 See Hutson, 275–7.

Chapter 8

1 'The Spanish Tragedy' (2012). Available online: https://librivox.org/the-spanish-tragedy-by-thomas-kyd/ (accessed 1 March 2015).

2 Alex Cox (dir.), 'Spanish Tragedy Part I' (2008). Available online: https://www.youtube.com/watch?v=DDuvqnsKXl8 (accessed 1 March 2015).

3 'Thomas Kyd', *Elizabethan and Jacobean Drama* (last revised 2012). Available online: http://www2.warwick.ac.uk/fac/arts/ren/elizabethan_jacobean_drama/kyd/ (accessed 1 March 2015).

4 'The Spanish Tragedy', *Elizabethan and Jacobean Drama* (last revised 2012) Available online: http://www2.warwick.ac.uk/fac/arts/ren/elizabethan_jacobean_drama/kyd/spanishtragedy/ (accessed 1 March 2015). 'Performance History', *Elizabethan and Jacobean Drama* (last revised 2012). Available online: http://www2.warwick.ac.uk/fac/

arts/ren/elizabethan_jacobean_drama/kyd/spanishtragedy/performancehistory/ (accessed 1 March 2015).

5   Thomas Kyd, *The Spanish Tragedy*, ed. by Clara Calvo and Jesús Tronch (London: Bloomsbury, 2013), 1.

6   *Shakespearean London Theatres* (2013). Available online: http://shalt.dmu.ac.uk/films.html (accessed 1 March 2015); (para. 2 of 3). 'The Spanish Tragedy, Act II Scene 4' (2013). Available online: https://www.youtube.com/watch?v=-PdwrQdcs1Y&feature=youtu.be (accessed 1 March 2015).

7   Kyd, 2013: 7.

8   Martin White, *Renaissance Drama in Action: An Introduction to Aspects of Theatre Practice and Performance* (London: Routledge, 1998).

9   White, 109–43.

10   White, 133–43.

11   Kyd, 2013: 17.

12   Stevie Simkin, *Early Modern Tragedy and the Cinema of Violence* (London: Palgrave Macmillan, 2006), 178–97.

13   Simkin, 182.

14   James Shapiro, '"Tragedies naturally performed": Kyd's Representation of Violence, *The Spanish Tragedy* (c. 1587)', in *Staging the Renaissance: Reinterpretations of Elizabethan and Jacobean Drama*, ed. by David Scott Kastan and Peter Stallybrass (London: Routledge, 1991), pp. 99–113. Molly Smith, *Breaking Boundaries: Politics and Play in the Drama of Shakespeare and his Contemporaries* (Aldershot: Ashgate, 1998).

15   Kevin Quarmby, 'The Spanish Tragedy' *British Theatre Guide* (2009). Available online: http://www.britishtheatreguide.info/reviews/spanishtragedy-rev (accessed 1 March 2015); (para. 8 of 8). Matthew Everett, 'Theatre Pro Rata's "Spanish Tragedy" gracefully navigates a clunky script', *TC Daily Planet* (2010). Available online: http://www.tcdailyplanet.net/news/2010/03/15/theater-theatre-pro-ratas-spanish-tragedy-gracefully-navigates-clunky-script (accessed 1 March 2015); (para. 1 of 9). Noah Guiney, '"Spanish Tragedy" Brings Blood and Violence to the NCT', *The Harvard Crimson*

(2010). Available online: http://www.thecrimson.com/article/2010/10/27/play-tragedy-spanish-blood/ (accessed 1 March 2015); (para. 8 of 8).

16 *Kill Bill: Vol. 1 and Vol. 2*, dir. Quentin Tarantino (A Band Apart, 2003/04). *Django Unchained,* dir. Quentin Tarantino (Columbia Pictures, 2012). The argument for *Kill Bill* as revenge tragedy is made by both Simkin (2006: 216) and Lesel Dawson, 'Revenge and the Family Romance in Tarantino's *Kill Bill*', *Mosaic (Winnipeg)*, 47 (5) (2014).

17 *Game of Thrones*, created by David Benioff and D. B. Weiss (HBO, 2011–).

18 William M. Hamlin, *Tragedy and Scepticism in Shakespeare's England* (London: Palgrave Macmillan, 2005), p. 156.

SELECT BIBLIOGRAPHY

Aebischer, Pascale. *Screening Early Modern Drama: Beyond Shakespeare* (Cambridge: Cambridge University Press, 2013)

Aebischer, Pascale and Kathryn Prince, *Performing Early Modern Drama Today* (Cambridge: Cambridge University Press, 2012)

Aggeler, Geoffrey. 'The Eschatological Crux in *The Spanish Tragedy*', *Journal of English and Germanic Philology* 86.3 (1987): 31–31

Ahl, Frederick M. 'Coping with the Canonical Oedipus', in *Edippoclassico e contemporaneo*, ed. Francesco Citti and Alessandro Iannucci (Hildesheim: Olms, 2012), 1–30

Allen, Paul C., *Philip III and the PaxHispanica, 1598–1621: The Failure of Grand Strategy* (New Haven: Yale University Press, 2000)

Allen, William. *An Admonition to the Nobility and People of England and Ireland* (Antwerp, 1588)

Altman, Joel B. *The Tudor Play of Mind: Rhetorical Inquiry and the Development of Elizabethan Drama* (London: University of California Press, 1978)

Andrew, Thomas. 'The Unmasking of a Feminine Machiavell' (London: Simon Stafford, 1604)

Anghiera, Pietro Martire d'. *The decades of the neweworlde or west India conteynyng the nauigations and conquestes of the Spanyardes, with the particular description of the mosteryche and large landes and ilandes lately founde in the west ocean perteynyng to the inheritaunce of the kinges of Spayne*, trans. Richard Eden (London, 1555)

Anon. *Articles ... for the Auoiding of the Diuersities of Opinions, and for the Stablishyng of Consent Touching True Religion* (London, 1571)

Anon. *A True discourse of the Armie which the King of Spaine caused to be assembled in the haven of Lisbon* (London, 1588)

Anon. *The Canons and Decrees of the Council of Trent* (anon. trans.) (London, 1687)

Anon. *The First Part of Jeronimo*, in *The Spanish Tragedie*, ed. by Emma Smith, (London: Penguin Books, 1998), 93–132

Ardolino, Frank. '*Corrida* of Blood in *The Spanish Tragedy*: Kyd's use of Revenge as National Destiny', *Medieval and Renaissance Drama in England* 1 (1984): 37–49

Ardolino, Frank. *Thomas Kyd's Mystery Play: Myth and Ritual in 'The Spanish Tragedy'* (New York: Peter Lang, 1985)

Ardolino, Frank. '"In Paris? Mass, and well remembered!": Kyd's *The Spanish Tragedy* and the English Reaction to the St. Bartholomew's Day Massacre', *Sixteenth Century Journal* 21.3 (1990): 401–9

Ardolino, Frank. '"Now Shall I See the Fall of Babylon": *The Spanish Tragedy*', *Shakespeare Yearbook* 1 (1990): 106–13

Ardolino, Frank. 'Hieronimo Agonistes: Kyd's use of Hieronimo as Sanctified Revenger in *The Spanish Tragedy*', *Journal of Evolutionary Psychology* 15 (1994): 161–5

Ardolino, Frank. *Apocalypse and Armada in Kyd's Spanish Tragedy* (Sixteenth Century Essays and Studies, vol. 29) (Kirksville, MO: Truman State University Press, 1995)

B., G. *A Fig of the Spaniard, or Spanish Spirits, or Spanish Spirits. Wherein are liuelie portaihed the damnable deeds, miserable murders, and monstrous massacres of the cursed Spaniard. With a true rehersal of the late troubles, and troublesome estate of Aragon, Catalonia, Valencia, and Portingall* (London, 1592)

Bacon, Francis. *The Works of Francis Bacon*, ed. James Spedding, Robert Leslie Ellis and Douglas Denon Heath (London: Longman, 1857–72)

Baker, Donald C., John L. Murphy and Louis B. Hall, Jr., eds. *The Late Medieval Religious Plays of Bodleian Mss. Digby 133 and E Museo 160* (Oxford: Oxford University Press, 1982)

Baker, Howard. *Induction to Tragedy: A Study in a Development of Form in* Gorboduc, The Spanish Tragedy *and* Titus Andronicus (Baton Rouge, LA: Louisiana State University Press, 1939)

Barber, C. L. *Creating Elizabethan Tragedy: The Theater of Marlowe and Kyd*, ed. Richard P. Wheeler (Chicago and London: University of Chicago Press, 1988)

Barber, John. 'The Pre-*Hamlet* Bloodbath', *Daily Telegraph*, 24 September 1982

Barish, Jonas A. '*The Spanish Tragedy*; or, The Pleasures and Perils of Rhetoric', in *Elizabethan Theatre*, Stratford-upon-Avon Studies 9 (London: Arnold, 1966): 58–85

Barker, Simon and Hilary Hinds, eds. *The Routledge Anthology of Renaissance Drama* (London and New York: Routledge, 2003)

Baroja, Julio Caro. 'Religion, World Views, Social Classes and Honor During the Sixteenth And Seventeenth Centuries', in *Honor and Grace in Anthropology*, J. G. Peristany and J. Pitt-Rivers, eds. (Cambridge: Cambridge University Press, 1992), 91–102

Barry, Lording. *Ram-Alley: or merrie-trickes A comedy diuers times here-to-fore acted. By the Children of the Kings Revels* (London: G. Eld, 1611)

Bartsch, Shadi and Alessandro Schiesaro, eds. *The Cambridge Companion to Seneca* (Cambridge: Cambridge University Press, 2015)

Bate, Jonathan. 'The Performance of Revenge: *Titus Andronicus* and *The Spanish Tragedy*', in *The Show Within, Dramatic and Other Insets, English Renaissance Drama (1500–1642)* 2 vols (Montepellier: Paul-Valery University Press, 1992), 267–83

Bate, Jonathan. *The Genius of Shakespeare* (London: Picador, 1997)

Battenhouse, Roy W. 'Tamburlaine, the "Scourge of God"', *PMLA* 56 (1941): 337–48

Bazan, Álvaro de, Marquês de Santa Cruz. *A Discourse of that which Happened in the Battell Fought betweene the two Navies of Spaine and Portugall* (London, 1583)

Beadle, Richard, ed. *The York Plays* (London: Edward Arnold, 1982)

Beaumont, Francis. *The Knight of the Burning Pestle*, ed. Michael Hattaway (London: A&C Black, 2000).

Belsey, Catherine. *The Subject of Tragedy: Identity and Difference in Renaissance Drama* (London and New York: Routledge, 1985)

Bentley, Gerald Eades. *The Jacobean and Caroline Stage*, 7 vols (Oxford: Clarendon Press, 1941–68), II (1941; repr. 1966)

Billington, Michael. '*Spanish Tragedy* in Oxford', *Guardian*, 29 November 1973

Billington, Michael. 'Sweet Revenge', *Guardian*, 24 September 1982

Birenbaum, Maija. 'Affective Vengeance in Titus and Vespasian.' *The Chaucer Review* 43.3 (2009): 330–44.

Block, K. S., ed. *Ludus Coventriae or The Play Called Corpus Christi* (Oxford: Oxford University Press, 1922; repr. 1960; 1974)

Blundeville, Thomas. *M. Blundevile his exercises containing sixe treatises ... to be read and learned of all yoong gentlemen ... desirous to haue knowledge as well in cosmographie, astronomie, and geographie, as also in the arte of navigation* (London, 1594)

Boas, Frederick S., ed. *The Works of Thomas Kyd* (Oxford: Clarendon Press, 1901)

Boas, F. S. '*The Spanish Tragedie* after Three Centuries', *The Lodestone* (Lent 1922): 52–3 (Birkbeck College, University of London, archive)

Boas, F. S. '*The Spanish Tragedy* at Christ Church', letter, *The Times*, 9 March 1932

Bossy, John. 'The Social History of Confession in the Age of Reformation', in *Transactions of the Royal Historical Society* 25 (1975): 21–38

Bowers, Fredson. *Elizabethan Revenge Tragedy 1587–1642* (Princeton, NJ: Princeton University Press, 1940)

Bowers, Fredson. 'Hamlet as Minister and Scourge', *PMLA* 70 (1955): 740–9

Boyle, A. J. *Tragic Seneca: An Essay in the Theatrical Tradition* (London: Routledge, 1997)

Braden, Gordon. *Renaissance Tragedy and the Senecan Tradition: Anger's Privilege* (London: Yale University Press, 1985)

Braden, Gordon. 'Herakles and Hercules: Survival in Greek and Roman Tragedy (with a Coda on *King Lear*)', in *Theater and Society in the Ancient World*, ed. Ruth Scodel (Ann Arbor, MI: University of Michigan Press, 1993), 245–64

Bradley, A. C. *Shakespearean Tragedy: Lectures on Hamlet, Othello, King Lear and Macbeth* (London: Penguin, 1991)

Brathwaite, Richard. *The English Gentlewoman* (London: B. Alsop and T. Fawcet, 1631)

Braudel, Fernand. *The Mediterranean and the Mediterranean World in The Age of Philip II*, trans. Siân Reynolds, 2 vols, rev. 2nd edn (New York: Harper and Row, 1973 [1966])

Braudel, Fernand. *The Structures of Everyday Life*, trans. Siân Reynolds (Berkeley: University of California Press, 1992)

Braund, Susanna. 'Haunted by Horror: The Ghost of Seneca in Renaissance Drama', in *A Companion to the Neronian Age*, ed. Emma Buckley and Martin T. Dinter (Oxford: Blackwell, 2013), 425–43

Bromham, A. A. and Zara Bruzzi. *The Changeling and the Years of Crisis, 1619–1624: A Hieroglyph of Britain* (London: Pinter, 1990)

Broude, Ronald. 'Time, Truth, and Right in *The Spanish Tragedy*', *Studies in Philology* 68.2 (1971): 130–45

Broude, Ronald. '*Vindicta Filia Temporis:* Three English Forerunners of the Elizabethan Revenge Play', *Journal of English and Germanic Philology* 72 (1973): 489–502

Broude, Ronald. 'Revenge and Revenge Tragedy in Renaissance England', *Renaissance Quarterly* 28.1 (Spring 1975): 38–58

Bruster, Douglas. 'Shakespearean Spellings and Handwriting in the Additional Passages Printed in the 1602 *Spanish Tragedy*', *Notes and Queries* 60.3 (2013): 420–4.

Burckhardt, Jacob. *The Civilization of the Renaissance in Italy*, trans. S. G. C. Middlemore, 2 vols (New York: Harper & Row, 1958)

Burrow, Colin. 'Shakespeare and Humanistic Culture', in *Shakespeare and the Classics*, ed. Charles Martindale and A. B. Taylor (Cambridge: Cambridge University Press, 2004), 11–16

Burrow, Colin. *Shakespeare and Classical Antiquity* (Oxford: Oxford University Press, 2013)

Canter, Nancy Napper. '*The Spanish Tragedy*', *The Tab Cambridge*, available online: www.cambridge.tab.co.uk/2012/11/09/the-spanish-tragedy (Accessed 15 August 2013)

Carey, John. 'Donne's Apostasy', in *John Donne's Poetry*, ed. Donald Dickson (New York and London: W. W. Norton, 2007), 209–25

Carlson, Marvin. *The Haunted Stage: The Theatre as Memory Machine* (Ann Arbor: University of Michigan Press, 2003)

Carpenter, Humphrey. *OUDS: A Centenary History of the Oxford University Dramatic Society 1885–1985* (Oxford: Oxford University Press, 1985)

Cervantes, Miguel de. *El cerco de Numancia*, ed. Robert Marrast (Salamanca: Biblioteca Anaya, 1970)

Chapman, Don. '*Spanish Tragedy* Fails to Thrill', *Oxford Mail*, 28 November 1973

Charlton, H. B. *The Senecan Tradition in Renaissance Tragedy* (Manchester: Manchester University Press, 1946)

Clark, Sandra. *Renaissance Drama* (Cambridge: Polity Press, 2007)

Clopper, Lawrence ed. *Records of Early English Drama: Chester* (Toronto: University of Toronto Press, 1979)

'College Notes', *St John's College: 1952*, 3–5 (St John's College [Oxford] archive)

'College Play', *The Wykehamist* 672 (30 March 1926): 202–3 (Winchester College archive)

Condon, James J. 'Setting the Stage for Revenge: Space, Performance, and Power in Early Modern Revenge Tragedy' in *Medieval & Renaissance Drama in England* 25 (January 2012): 62–82

Conestaggio, GerolomoFranchi di. *The Historie of the Uniting of the Kingdom of Portugal to the Crowne of Castill* (London, 1600)

Cotton, Charles. *Burlesque upon burlesque, or, The scoffer scoft* (London: Henry Brome, 1675)

Coveney, Michael. *The Citz: 21 Years of the Glasgow Citizens Theatre* (London: Nick Hern, 1990)

Craig, D. H. 'Authorial Styles and the Frequencies of Very Common Words: Jonson, Shakespeare, and the Additions to *The Spanish Tragedy*', *Style* 26.2 (1992): 199–220

Craig, Hugh. 'The 1602 Additions to *The Spanish Tragedy*' in *Shakespeare, Computers and the Mystery of Authorship*, Hugh Craig and Arthur F. Kinney, eds. (Cambridge: Cambridge University Press, 2009), 162–80

Craig, Hugh and Arthur F. Kinney. *Shakespeare, Computers, and the Mystery of Authorship* (Cambridge: Cambridge University Press, 2009)

Cressy, David. *Birth, Marriage, and Death: Ritual, Religion, and the Life-Cycle in Tudor and Stuart England* (Oxford: Oxford University Press, 1997)

Crosbie, Christopher. '*Oeconomia* and the Vegetative Soul: Rethinking Revenge in *The Spanish Tragedy*' in *English Literary Renaissance* 38.1 (January 2008): 3–33

Cruz, J., ed. *Material and Symbolic Circulation between Spain and England, 1554–1604* (Aldershot: Ashgate, 2008)

Cunliffe, John William. *The Influence of Seneca on Elizabethan Tragedy: An Essay* (London and New York: Macmillan, 1893)

Cutts, David. 'Writing and Revenge: The Struggle for Authority in Thomas Kyd's *The Spanish Tragedy*', *Explorations in Renaissance Culture* 22 (1996): 147–59

Daalder, Joost. 'The Role of "Senex" in *The Spanish Tragedy*', *Comparative Drama*, 20.3 (Fall 1986): 247–60

Damschen, Gregor and Andreas Heil, eds. *Brill's Companion to Seneca: Philosopher and Dramatist* (Leiden: Brill, 2014)

Dawson, Anthony B. 'Madness and Meaning: *The Spanish Tragedy*', *Journal of Dramatic Theory and Criticism* 2.1 (Fall 1987): 53–67.

De Jongh, Nicholas. '*The Spanish Tragedy*', *Plays and Players*, December 1982, 24–5

Dekker, Thomas. *1603. The Wonderfull Yeare. Wherein is shewed the picture of London lying sicke of the Plague* (London: Thomas Creede, 1603)

Dekker, Thomas. *A Knights Coniuring Done in Earnest: Discouered in Iest* (London, 1607)

Dekker, Thomas. *The Seven Deadly Sinnes of London*, ed. H. F. B. Brett-Smith (Oxford: Blackwell, 1922)

Derrida, Jacques. *Spectres of Marx: The State of Debt, the Work of Mourning and the New International*, trans. Peggy Kamuf (New York and London: Routledge, 1994)

Dibb, Frank [F. W. D.]. '*The Spanish Tragedy*', *The Oxford Times*, 30 November 1973

Dillon, Janette. '*The Spanish Tragedy* and Staging Languages in Renaissance Drama', *Research Opportunities in Renaissance Drama* 34 (1995): 15–40

Dillon, Janette. *The Cambridge Introduction to Early English Theatre* (Cambridge: Cambridge University Press, 2006)

Disney, A. R. *A History of Portugal and the Portuguese Empire*, 2 vols (Cambridge: Cambridge University Press, 2009)

Dolan, Francis E. *Whores of Babylon* (Cornell: Cornell University Press, 1999)

Dollimore, Jonathan. *Radical Tragedy: Religion, Ideology, and Power in the Drama of Shakespeare and his Contemporaries*, 2nd edn (Durham, NC: Duke University Press, 1989)

Dudrap, Claude. 'La "Tragédie Espagnole" face à la critique Élisabéthaine et Jacobéenne', in *Dramaturgie et société:*

Rapports entre l'oeuvre théâtrale, son interprétation et son public aux XVIe et XVIIe siècles, ed. Jean Jacquot, 2 vols (Paris: Éditions du centre nationale de la recherche scientifique, 1968), 2, 607–31

Duffy, Eamon. *The Stripping of the Altars: Traditional Religion in England 1400–1580* (New Haven: Yale University Press, 1992)

Duffy, Eamon. *Fires of Faith: Catholic England under Mary Tudor* (New Haven and London: Yale University Press, 2009)

Duffy, Eamon. *Saints, Sacrilege and Sedition: Religion and Conflict in the Tudor Reformations* (London: Bloomsbury, 2012)

Durkheim, Emile. *The Elementary Forms of the Religious Life* (London: George Allen and Unwin, 1915; repr. 1964)

Edwards, Philip, ed. *The Spanish Tragedy* (Cambridge, MA: Harvard University Press, 1959)

Edwards, Philip. *Thomas Kyd and Early Elizabethan Tragedy* (London: Longmans, 1966)

Edwards, Philip. 'Shakespeare and Kyd' in *Shakespeare, Man of the Theater: Proceedings of the Second Congress of the International Shakespeare Association, 1981*, ed. Kenneth Muir, Jay L. Halio and D. J. Palmer (Newark, DE: University of Delaware Press, 1983), 148–54.

Edwards, Philip. 'Thrusting Elysium into Hell: the originality of *The Spanish Tragedy*', in *Elizabethan Theatre XI*, ed. A. L. Magnusson and C. E. McGee (Ontario: P. D. Meany Publishers, 1990), 117–32

Eliot, T. S. 'Hamlet and His Problems', in *Selected Essays* (London: Faber and Faber, 1951)

Eliot, T. S. 'Seneca in Elizabethan Translation', in *Selected Essays* (London: Faber and Faber, 1951)

'Elizabethan Tradition Revived', *Manchester Guardian*, 8 March 1932

Elliott, J. H. 'The Spanish Monarchy and the Kingdom of Portugal, 1580–1640', in *Conquest and Coalescence: The Shaping of the State in Early Modern Europe*, ed. Mark Greengrass (London: Edward Arnold, 1991)

Emerson, Ralph Waldo. *Essays and Lectures*, ed. Joel Porte (New York: Library of America, 1983)

Empson, William. '*The Spanish Tragedy*', *Nimbus* 3 (1956): 16–29. [The article is reprinted in *Elizabethan Drama: Modern Essays in Criticism*, ed. R. J. Kaufmann (London: Oxford University Press, 1978), 60–80]

Engel, William E. *Death and Drama in Renaissance England: Shades of Memory* (Oxford: Oxford University Press, 2002)

Erne, Lukas. *Beyond 'The Spanish Tragedy': A Study of the Works of Thomas Kyd* (Manchester: Manchester University Press, 2001)

Escola, Jordi Coral. 'Vengeance is Yours: Reclaiming the Social Bond in *The Spanish Tragedy* and *Titus Andronicus*', *Atlantis* 29.2 (December 2007): 59–74.

Everett, Matthew A. 'Theatre Pro Rata's *Spanish Tragedy* Gracefully Navigates a Clunky Script', *Twin Cities Daily Planet*, available online: www.tcdailyplanet.net/news/2010/03/15/review-spanish-tragedy-theatre-pro-rata-4-12-stars (Accessed 15 August 2013)

Farmer, Richard. *An Essay on the Learning of Shakespeare* (Basil: J. J. Tourneisen, 1800 [First publ. 1766])

Field, Nathan. *A Woman is a Weather-cocke: A new comedy, as it was acted before the King in White-Hall* (London: William Jaggard, 1612)

Finch, Peter. *John Dee: The World of an Elizabethan Magus* (New York: Dorset, 1972)

Flynn, Dennis. *John Donne and the Ancient Catholic Nobility* (Bloomington and Indianapolis: Indiana University Press, 1995)

Foakes, R. A. 'Playhouses and Players', in *The Cambridge Companion to English Renaissance Drama*, ed. A. R. Braunmuller and Michael Hattaway (Cambridge: Cambridge University Press, 1990)

Foakes, R. A., and R. T. Ricker, eds. *Henslowe's Diary* (Cambridge: Cambridge University Press, 1961)

Fortescue, Thomas. *The Forest or Collection of Histories ... Done out of French into English* (London, 1571)

Foucault, Michel. *Discipline and Punish: The Birth of the Prison*, trans. Alan Sheridan (New York: Random House, 1991)

Freeman, Arthur. *Thomas Kyd: Facts and Problems* (Oxford: Oxford University Press, 1967)

Fuchs, Barbara. 'Sketches of Spain: Early Modern England's "Orientalising" of Iberia', in *Material and Symbolic Circulation between Spain and England, 1554–1604*, ed. Anne Cruz (Aldershot and Burlington, VT: Ashgate, 2008), 63–71

Fuchs, Barbara. *The Poetics of Piracy: Emulating Spain in English Literature* (Philadelphia: University of Pennsylvania Press, 2013)

Gilbey, Liz. 'A Colossus of a Play', *Plays International*, May 1997, 13

Goodland, Katharine. *Female Mourning and Tragedy in Medieval and Renaissance English Drama* (Aldershot: Ashgate 2006)

Goodwin, Thomas. *A sermon of the fifth monarchy. Proving by invincible arguments, that the saints shall have a kingdom here on earth, which is yet to come, after the fourth monarchy is destroy'd by the sword of the saints, the followers of the lamb* (London, 1654)

Greenblatt, Stephen. *Renaissance Self-Fashioning* (Chicago: Chicago University Press, 1980)

Greenblatt, Stephen. *Shakespearean Negotiations* (Oxford: Clarendon Press, 1988)

Greenblatt, Stephen. *Hamlet in Purgatory* (Princeton, NJ and Oxford: Oxford University Press, 2001)

Greenburg, Marissa. 'The Tyranny of Tragedy: Catharsis in England and *The Roman Actor*', in *Renaissance Drama* 39 (2011): 163–96

Greene, Robert. *Menaphon: Camillas Alarum to Slumbering Euphues, in His Melancholie Cell at Silexdra* (London, 1589)

Greene, Thomas M. *The Light in Troy: Imitation and Discovery in Renaissance Poetry* (New Haven: Yale University Press, 1982)

Greg, W. W. 'Review of *The Works of Thomas Kyd* by Frederick S. Boas', *The Modern Language Quarterly* 4.3 (December 1901): 185–90

Greville, Fulke. *The Prose Work of Fulke Greville, Lord Brookes*, ed. John Gouws (Oxford: Clarendon, 1986)

Griffin, Eric [J.]. 'Copying "the Anti-Spaniard": Post-Armada Hispanophobia in English Renaissance Drama', in *Representing Imperial Rivalry in the Early Modern Mediterranean*, ed. Barbara Fuchs and Emily Weissbourd (Toronto: University of Toronto Press, 2015), 191–216

Griffin, Eric. 'Ethos, Empire, and the Valiant Acts of Thomas Kyd's tragedy of "the Spains"', *English Literary Renaissance* 31.2 (March 2001): 192–229.

Griffin, Eric. *English Renaissance Drama and the Specter of Spain: Ethnopoetics and Empire* (Philadelphia: University of Pennsylvania Press, 2009)

Griffin, Eric. 'Nationalism, the Black Legend, and the Revised

Spanish Tragedy', *English Literary Renaissance* 39.2 (Spring 2009): 336–70

Griffin, Eric.'"Spain is Portugal / And Portugal is Spain": Transnational Attraction in the Stukeley Plays and *The Spanish Tragedy*', *JEMCS* 10 (2010): 95–116

Guiney, Noah. '"Spanish Tragedy" Brings Blood and Violence to the NCT', *The Harvard Crimson* (2010), available online: http://www.thecrimson.com/article/2010/10/27/play-tragedy-spanish-blood/

Gunther, Amanda. '*The Spanish Tragedy* at the Mobtown Players', *DC Metro Theater Arts*, available online: http://dcmetrotheaterarts.com/2014/07/12/spanish-tragedy-mobtown-players1 (Accessed 11 August 2014)

Gurr, Andrew. *The Shakespearian Playing Companies* (Oxford: Clarendon Press, 1996)

Hadfield, Andrew. 'A Handkerchief Dipped in Blood in *The Spanish Tragedy*: An Anti-Catholic Reference?', *Notes & Queries* 46.2 (1999): 197

Hakluyt, Richard, *Discourse of Western Planting*, ed. David B. Quinn and Alison B. Quinn (London: Hakluyt Society, 1993)

Hallett, Charles A. and Elaine S. Hallett. *The Revenger's Madness* (Lincoln: University of Nebraska Press, 1980)

Hamilton, Donna B. '*The Spanish Tragedy*: A Speaking Picture' *English Literary Renaissance* 4 (1974): 203–17

Hamlin, William M. *Tragedy and Scepticism in Shakespeare's England* (London and New York: Palgrave Macmillan, 2005), 155–66

Harbage, Alfred. 'Intrigue in Elizabethan Tragedy', in *Essays on Shakespeare and Elizabethan Drama in Honor of Hardin Craig*, ed. Richard Hosley (London: Routledge/Kegan Paul, 1963), 37–44

Hartley, Andrew James. 'Social Consciousness: Spaces for Characters in *The Spanish Tragedy*', *Cahiers Élisabéthains* 58 (October 2000): 1–14

Hattaway, Michael. *Elizabethan Popular Theatre: Plays in Performance* (London: Routledge/Kegan Paul, 1982)

Hawkes, Terence. *That Shakespeherian Rag: Essays on a Critical Process* (London: Routledge, 1986)

Hawkins, Harriett. 'Fabulous Counterfeits: Dramatic Construction and Dramatic Perspectives in *The Spanish Tragedy*, *A Midsummer Night's Dream*, and *The Tempest*', *Shakespeare*

Studies 6 (1970): 51–65. [The article is reprinted in Harriett Hawkins, *Likenesses of Truth in Elizabethan and Restoration Drama* (Oxford: Clarendon Press, 1972), 27–50]

Hawkins, Thomas. *The Origin of the English Drama: illustrated in its various species, viz., mystery, morality, tragedy, and comedy, by specimens from our earliest writers, with explanatory notes*, 3 vols (Oxford: Clarendon Press, 1773)

Headley, John M. 'Campanella, America, and World Evangelization', in *America in European Consciousness, 1493–1750*, Karen Ordahl Kupperman, ed. (Chapel Hill: University of North Carolina Press, 1995), 243–71

Hemming, Sarah. 'A Sparkling Evening in Hell', *Financial Times*, 10 December 1997

Herington, C. J. 'Senecan Tragedy', *Arion* 5 (1966): 422–71

Heywood, Thomas. *An Apology for Actors* (London: Nicholas Okes, 1612)

Heywood, Thomas. *The Fair Maid of the West, Parts I and II*, ed. Robert K. Turner Jr. (Lincoln: University of Nebraska Press, 1967)

Heywood, Thomas. *If You Know Not Me You Know Nobody*, Part I and Part II (Oxford: Benediction Classics, 2008)

H. G. '*The Spanish Tragedie*', *Observer*, 11 December 1921

Hibbard, G. R. *Thomas Nashe: A Critical Introduction* (London: Routledge/Kegan Paul, 1962)

Hill, Eugene. 'Senecan and Vergilian perspectives in *The Spanish Tragedy*', *ELR* 15 (1985): 143–65

Hillman, Richard. *Self-Speaking in Medieval and Early Modern English Drama: Subjectivity, Discourse, and the Stage* (Basingstoke: Macmillan, 1997)

'Hockley in the hole'. EBBA 20138, Magdalene College, Pepys Ballads 1.294–295

Hoenslaars, A. J. *Images of Englishmen and Foreigners in the Drama of Shakespeare and his Contemporaries* (Rutherford, NJ: Fairleigh Dickinson University Press, 1992)

Holderness, Graham, *The Shakespeare Myth* (Manchester: Manchester University Press, 1988)

Honigmann, E. A. J. 'The First Quarto of *Hamlet* and the Date of *Othello*', *The Review of English Studies, New Series* 44 (174) (1993): 211–19

Hopkins, Lisa. 'What's Hercules to Hamlet?: The Emblematic

Garden in *The Spanish Tragedy* and *Hamlet*.' *Hamlet Studies* 21.1–2 (Summer–Winter 1999): 114–43

Howard, Tony. '*The Spanish Tragedy*', *Research Opportunities in Renaissance Drama* 21 (1978): 64–6

Hunter, G. K. 'Ironies of Justice in *The Spanish Tragedy*'. *Renaissance Drama* 8 (1965): 89–104.

Hunter, G. K. 'Seneca and the Elizabethans: A Case Study in "Influence"', *Shakespeare Survey* 20 (1967): 17–26

Hunter, G. K. *Dramatic Identities and Cultural Tradition: Studies in Shakespeare and his Contemporaries* (Liverpool: Liverpool University Press, 1978)

Hunter, G. K. 'Seneca and English Tragedy', in *Dramatic Identities and Cultural Tradition: Studies in Shakespeare and His Contemporaries* (Liverpool: Liverpool University Press, 1978), 174–213

Hurwitt, Robert. '*The Spanish Tragedy* Review: Complicated Revenge', *SFGate*, available online: www.sfgate.com/performance/article/The-Spanish-Tragedy (Accessed 15 August 2015)

Hutson, Lorna. *The Invention of Suspicion: Law and Mimesis in Shakespeare and Renaissance Drama* (Oxford: Oxford University Press, 2007)

Hutson, Lorna. 'Fictive Acts: Thomas Nashe and the Mid-Tudor Legacy', in *The Oxford Handbook of Tudor Literature 1485–1603*, ed. Mike Pincombe and Cathy Shrank (Oxford: Oxford University Press, 2009), 718–32

Jackson, Ken and Arthur Marotti. 'The Turn to Religion in Early Modern English Studies', *Criticism* 46.1 (2004): 167–90

James I, King of England. *A Treaty of perpetual Peace and Alliance between Philip III. King of Spain, and the Archduke and Archduchess Albert and Isabella on the one side, and James the I. King of England on the other side. Made in the Year 1604*, in *A General Collection of Treaties* (London, 1732)

Johnson, Christopher D. *Hyperboles: The Rhetoric of Excess in Baroque Literature and Thought* (Cambridge, MA: Harvard University Department of Comparative Literature, 2010)

Johnson, S. F. '*The Spanish Tragedy*, or the Babylonian revisited', in *Essays on Shakespeare and Elizabethan drama in Honor of Hardin Craig*, ed. Richard Hosley (London: Routledge/Kegan Paul, 1963)

Johnston, Alexandra F. and Margaret Rogerson, eds. *Records of Early English Drama: York*, 2 vols (Toronto: University of Toronto Press, 1979)

Jones, Emrys. 'Stage-Managing Revenge', *Times Literary Supplement*, 15 October 1982, 1131

Jones, Emrys. *The Origins of Shakespeare* (Oxford: Clarendon, 1996)

Jonson, Ben. *The Alchemist, The Revels Plays*, ed. F. H. Mares (London: Methuen, 1967)

Jonson, Ben. *The Cambridge Edition of the Works of Ben Jonson*, ed. David Bevington et al., 7 vols (Cambridge: Cambridge University Press, 2012)

Justice, Steven. 'Spain, Tragedy, and *The Spanish Tragedy*', *Studies in English Literature, 1500–1900* 25.2 (Spring 1985): 271–88

Kaiser, George R. 'The Middle English *Planctus Mariae* and the Rhetoric of Pathos', in *The Popular Literature of Medieval England*, ed. Thomas J. Heffernan (Knoxville: University of Tennessee Press, 1985)

Kelly, Donald R. *Versions of History from Antiquity to Enlightenment* (New Haven: Yale University Press, 1991)

Ker, James and Jessica Winston, eds. *Elizabethan Seneca: Three Tragedies*, J. Kerr and U. J. Winston, eds. (London: MHRA, 2012)

Kerrigan, John. *Revenge Tragedy: Aeschylus to Armageddon* (Oxford: Clarendon Press, 1997)

Keyishian, Harry. 'An Interview with Ron Daley, Director of *The Spanish Tragedy*', *Shakespeare Bulletin* 4.3 (May/June 1986): 11

King, Willard F. 'Cervantes' *Numancia* and Imperial Spain', *Modern Language Notes* 94 (1979): 200–1

Kirwan, Peter. 'From Script to Stage', in *William Shakespeare and others, Collaborative Plays*, ed. Jonathan Bate and Eric Rasmussen with Jan Sewell and Will Sharpe (Basingstoke: Palgrave Macmillan, 2013), 746–82

Knutson, Roslyn L. 'Influence of the Repertory System on the Revival and Revision of *The Spanish Tragedy* and *Dr. Faustus*', *English Literary Renaissance* 18 (1988): 257–74

Koudounaris, Paul. *Heavenly Bodies: Cult Treasures and Spectacular Saints from the Catacombs* (London: Thames and Hudson, 2013)

Kyd, Thomas. *The Spanish Tragedy*, ed. Philip Edwards (Manchester: University of Manchester Press, 1977 [1959])

Kyd, Thomas. *The Spanish Tragedy, with The First Part of Jeronimo*, ed. Emma Smith (London: Penguin, 1998)
Kyd, Thomas. *The Spanish Tragedy*, ed. Clara Calvo and Jesús Tronch (London: Bloomsbury, 2013)
Kyd, Thomas. *The Spanish Tragedy*, ed. Michael Neill (New York: W. W. Norton, 2014)
Langbaine, Gerard. *An Account of the English Dramatick Poets: Or, Some Observations and Remarks on the Lives and Writings, of All Those that Have Publish'd Either Comedies, Tragedies, Tragi-comedies, Pastorals, Masques, Interludes, Farces, Or Opera's in the English Tongue* (Oxford: L. L., 1691)
Laroque, Francois, ed. *The Show Within: Dramatic and Other Insets: English Renaissance Drama (1550–1642)*, 2 vols (Montpellier: Université Paul-Valery, 1992), vol. 2, 267–84
Leggatt, Alexander. '"A Membrane is Broken": Returning from the Dead in *The Spanish Tragedy*', in *Renaissance Go-Betweens: Cultural Exchange in Early Modern Europe*, ed. Andreas Höfele and Werner von Koppenfels (Berlin: Walter de Gruyter, 2005), 214–30
Le Goff, Jacques. *The Birth of Purgatory*, trans. Arthur Goldhammer (Chicago: University of Chicago Press, 1984)
Lever, J. W. *Tragedy of State: a Study of Jacobean Drama* (London: Methuen, 1971)
Limon, Jerzy. *Dangerous Matter: English Drama and Politics, 1623/4* (Cambridge: Cambridge University Press, 1986)
Lipsius, Justus. *Justus Lipsius' Concerning Constancy*, ed. and trans. R. V. Young (Tempe, AZ: ACMRS, 2011)
Livermore, H. V. *A New History of Portugal*, 2nd edn (Cambridge: Cambridge University Press, 1976)
Lobban, J. H. 'Prologue to *The Spanish Tragedy*', *The Spanish Tragedy*, Birkbeck College, December 1931, programme (Birkbeck College, University of London, archive)
Lopez, Jeremy. *Constructing the Canon of Early Modern Drama* (Cambridge: Cambridge University Press, 2014)
Lumiansky, R. M. and David Mills, eds. *The Chester Mystery Cycle, Volume 1: Text* (Oxford: Oxford University Press, 1974)
Lumiansky, R. M. and David Mills, eds. *The Chester Mystery Cycle: Essays and Documents* (Chapel Hill: University of North Carolina Press, 1983)

Lumiansky, R. M. and David Mills, eds. *The Chester Mystery Cycle, Volume 2: Commentary and Glossary* (Oxford: Oxford University Press, 1986)

Macaulay, Alastair. 'A Grievous Attack of Nobility', *Financial Times*, 9 May 1997

Machiavelli, Niccolò. *The Prince*, trans. George Bull (London: Penguin Books, 1961)

Machielsen, Jan. *Martin Delrio: Demonology and Scholarship in the Counter-Reformation* (Oxford: Oxford University Press, 2015)

Magnusson, A. L. and C. E. McGee, eds. *The Elizabethan Theatre*, 11 (Ontario: P. D. Meany Publishers, 1990)

Malin, Peter. '*The Spanish Tragedy*', available online: http://bloggingshakespeare.com/reviewing-shakespeare/spanish-tragedy-lazarus-theatre-company-blue-elephant-theatre-camberwell-london-2013/ (Accessed 3 February 2016)

Manly, John M. *Specimens of Pre-Shakespearean Drama*, II (New York: Dover, 1967.[First publ. 1897])

Marcham, Frank. *The King's Office of the Revels 1610–1622: Fragments of Documents in the Department of Manuscripts, British Museum* (Great Britain: Office of the Revels, 1925)

Marlowe, Christopher. *Doctor Faustus: A- and B- Texts (1604, 1616)*, ed. David Bevington and Eric Rasmussen (Manchester: Manchester University Press, 1993)

Marlowe, Christopher and Thomas Nashe. *The Tragedie of Dido Queene of Carthage* (London, 1594)

Marshall, Peter, *Beliefs and the Dead in Reformation England* (Oxford and New York: Oxford University Press, 2002)

Martin, Paula. *Spanish Armada Prisoners* (Exeter: Exeter University Press, 1988)

Martindale, Charles and A. B. Taylor, eds. *Shakespeare and the Classics* (Cambridge: Cambridge University Press, 2004)

Maslen, Elizabeth. 'The Dynamics of Kyd's *Spanish Tragedy*', *English* 22, (143) (Summer 1983): 111–25

Matthews, Steven. *T. S. Eliot and Early Modern Literature* (Oxford: Oxford University Press, 2013)

Maus, Katharine Eisaman, ed. *Four Revenge Tragedies* (Oxford: Oxford University Press, 1995)

Maus, Katharine Eisaman. *Inwardness and Theater in the English Renaissance* (Chicago: University of Chicago Press, 1995)

Maus, Katharine. 'Introduction', in *Titus Andronicus*, in *The Norton Shakespeare*, ed. Stephen Greenblatt et al. (New York: Norton, 1997), 371–8

May, Thomas. *The Heir*, in *A Select Collection of Old English Plays*, ed. Robert Dodsley, 4th edn, rev. by W. Carew Hazlitt, 15 vols (London: Reeves and Turner, 1874–6), XI (1875): 501–84

Mayer, Roland. 'PersonataStoa: Neostoicism and Senecan Tragedy', *Journal of the Warburg and Courtauld Institutes* 57 (1994): 151–74

Mazzio, Carla. 'Staging the Vernacular: Language and Nation in Thomas Kyd's *The Spanish Tragedy*', *Studies in English Literature, 1500–1900* 38.2 (Tudor and Stuart Drama) (Spring 1998): 207–32

McAdam, Ian. '*The Spanish Tragedy* and the Politico-Religious Unconscious', *Texas Studies in Literature and Language* 42.1 (Spring 2000): 33–60

McAlindon, Tom. *English Renaissance Tragedy* (Basingstoke: Macmillan, 1986).

McGinnis Kay, Carol. 'Deception through Words: A Reading of *The Spanish Tragedy*', *Studies in Philology* 74.1 (1977): 20–38

McKie, Robin. 'Return of the Damned after 400 Years', *The Guardian*, 11 January 2004

McMillin, Scott. 'The Book of Seneca in *The Spanish Tragedy*', *Studies in English Literature* 14 (1974): 201–8

M. D., '*The Spanish Tragedy*', *Daily Telegraph*, 14 December 1931

Miola, Robert S. 'Another Senecan Echo in Kyd's *The Spanish Tragedy*', *Notes & Queries* 33.3 [231] (September 1986): 337

Miola, Robert. *Shakespeare and Classical Tragedy: The Influence of Seneca* (Oxford: Clarendon, 1992)

Moncallero, G. L. *Imperia de Paris nella Roma nella Cinquecento* (Rome: Palombi, 1962)

Mousley, Andy. *Renaissance Drama and Contemporary Literary Theory*, (London: Macmillan, 2000)

Muir, Edward. *Ritual in Early Modern Europe* (Cambridge: Cambridge University Press, 1997)

Mullaney, Steven. *The Place of the Stage: License, Power and Play in Renaissance England* (Ann Arbor, MI: University of Michigan Press, 1988)

Mulryne, J. R. 'Nationality and language in Thomas Kyd's *The Spanish Tragedy*', in *Travel and Drama in Shakespeare's Time*, ed. Jean-Pierre Maquerlot and Michel Willems (Cambridge: Cambridge University Press, 1996), 87–105

Murphy, Andrew, ed. *The Renaissance Text: Theory, Editing, Textuality* (Manchester: Manchester University Press, 2000)

Murray, Peter B. *Thomas Kyd* (New York: Twayne Publishers, 1969)

Nashe, Thomas. *The Works of Thomas Nashe*, ed. Ronald B. McKerrow, IV (Oxford: Blackwell, 1958)

Nashe, Thomas. 'To the Gentlemen Students of both Universities' in *Menaphon Camillas alarum to slumbering Euphues, in his melancholie cell at Silexedra* (London: Thomas Orwin, 1589)

Neely, Carol Thomas. *Distracted Subjects: Madness and Gender in Shakespeare and Early Modern Culture* (Ithaca, NY and London: Cornell University Press, 2004)

Neill, Michael. *Issues of Death: Mortality and Identity in English Renaissance Tragedy* (Oxford: Clarendon Press, 1997)

Neilson, William Allan. *The Chief Elizabethan Dramatists: Excluding Shakespeare* (Boston and New York: Houghton Mifflin Co., 1911)

Nightingale, Benedict. 'First to Cry for Revenge', *The Times*, 9 May 1997

'Of Oxford Summer Diversions', *St Edmund Hall Magazine* 4.2 (December 1937) 11–12 (St Edmund Hall archive)

Oliveira Marques, A. H. de. *History of Portugal*, 2 vols (New York: Columbia University Press, 1972)

Owens, Rebekah. 'Parody and *The Spanish Tragedy*', *Cahiers Élisabéthains* 71 (2007): 27–36

Owens, Rebekah. '*The Spanish Tragedy*', *Research Opportunities in Medieval and Renaissance Drama (ROMARD)* 49 (2010): 137–9

Pagden, Anthony. *Lords of All the World: Ideologies of Empire in Spain, Britain and France, c. 1500–c. 1800* (New Haven: Yale University Press, 1995)

Palmer, Barbara. 'Early Modern Mobillty, Players, Payments, and Patrons', *SQ* 56.3 (Fall 2005): 259–305

Parker, Charles. 'Diseased Bodies, Defiled Souls: Corporality and Religious Difference in the Reformation', in *Renaissance Quarterly* 67.4 (Winter 2014): 1265–97

Parker, Geoffrey. *The World is Not Enough: The Imperial Vision of Philip II of Spain* (Waco, TX: Baylor University Press, 2001)

Patterson, Annabel. *Censorship and Interpretation: The Conditions of Writing in Early Modern England* (Madison: University of Wisconsin Press, 1984)

Payne Collier, John. *History of English Dramatic Poetry to the Time of Shakespeare and Annals of the Stage to the Restoration*, III (London: John Murray, 1831)

Pepys, Samuel. *The Diary of Samuel Pepys*, ed. John Warrington, 3 vols (London: J. M Dent and Sons, 1953)

Pincombe, Mike and Cathy Shrank, eds. *The Oxford Handbook of Tudor Literature 1485– 1603* (Oxford: Oxford University Press, 2009)

Poleman, John. *The Second Part of the Booke of Battailes, Fought in our Age* (London, 1587)

Price, Eoin. '*The Spanish Tragedy*', *ROMARD* 49 (2010): 139–42

Price, Eoin. '*The Spanish Tragedy*', *ROMARD* 50 (2011): 107.11

Price, Merrall Llewelyn. 'Re-membering the Jews: Theatrical Violence in the N-Town Marian Plays', *Comparative Drama* 41.4 (Winter 2007–8): 439–63

Prior, Moody E. *The Language of Tragedy* (New York: Columbia University Press, 1947)

Prosser, Eleanor. *Hamlet and Revenge* (Stanford, CA: Stanford University Press, 1967)

Proudfoot, Richard. 'Kyd's *Spanish Tragedy*', *Critical Quarterly* 25.1 (Spring 1983): 71–6

Prynne, William. *Histriomastix* (London: Edward Allde, 1633)

Quarmby, Kevin. '*The Spanish Tragedy*', *British Theatre Guide*, available online: www.britishtheatreguide.info/reviews/spanishtragedy-rev (Accessed 15 August 2015)

Randolph, Thomas. *A pleasant comedie, entituled Hey for honesty, down with knavery* (London, 1651)

Rawlins, Thomas. *The Rebellion*, in *A Select Collection of Old English Plays*, ed. Robert Dodsley, 4th edn, rev. by W. Carew Hazlitt, 15 vols (London: Reeves and Turner, 1874–6), XIV (1875), 1–92

Rawlins, Thomas. *The Rebellion* (London: I. Okes, 1640)

Rist, Thomas. 'Catharsis as "Purgation" in Shakespearean Drama', in *Shakespearean Sensations: Experiencing Literature in Early Modern England*, ed. Katharine Craik and Tanya Pollard (Cambridge: Cambridge University Press, 2013), 138–56

Rist, Thomas. *Revenge Tragedy and the Drama of Commemoration in Reforming England*, Studies in Performance and Early Modern Drama (Aldershot: Ashgate, 2008)

Robert, Dodsley, ed. *A Select Collection of Old Plays*, II (London: 1744)

Rollins, Hyder (ed.). *Tottel's Miscellany (1557–1587)*, 2 vols, rev. ed. (Cambridge, MA: Harvard University Press, 1966)

Rowan, D. F. 'The Staging of *The Spanish Tragedy*', in *The Elizabethan Theatre V*, ed. G. R. Hibbard (London: Macmillan, 1975), 112–23

RSC. *The Spanish Tragedy*, dir. Michael Boyd, archive DVD, recorded Swan Theatre 19 May 1997 (Shakespeare Centre Library, Stratford-upon-Avon)

Sacks, Peter. 'Where words prevail not: grief, revenge, and language in Kyd and Shakespeare', *English Literary History* 49 (1982): 576–601

Salkeld, Duncan. *Madness and Drama in the Age of Shakespeare* (Manchester: Manchester University Press, 1993)

Samson, Alexander, ed. *The Spanish Match: Prince Charles's Journey to Madrid, 1623* (Aldershot: Ashgate, 2006)

Savile, Henry. 'Historical Collections', in *The Jacobean Union: Six Tracts of 1604*, Bruce R. Galloway and Brian P. Levack, eds. (Edinburgh: Scottish Historical Society, 1985)

Schick, Josef. *The Spanish Tragedy* (London: J. M. Dent and Co., 1898)

Schlegel, August Wilhelm von. *A Course of Lectures on Dramatic Art and Literature*, trans. John Black, II (London: Baldwin, Cradock and Joy, 1815)

Schuchard, Ronald. *Eliot's Dark Angel: Intersections of Life and Art* (Oxford: Oxford University Press, 1999)

Scoloker, Anthony. 'Daiphantus, or the Passions of Love' (London: T. Creed, 1604)

Scott, Thomas. *Vox Regis* (Utrecht, 1624)

Semenza, Gregory M. Colon. '*The Spanish Tragedy* and Revenge', in *Early Modern English Drama: A Critical Companion*, Garrett A. Sullivan, Jr et al. (Oxford: Oxford University Press, 2006), 50–60

Seneca, Lucius Annaeus. *Tragoediae*, ed. Otto Zwierlein (Oxford: Clarendon, 1986)

Shapiro, James. '"Tragedies naturally performed": Kyd's representation of violence', in *Staging the Renaissance:*

Reinterpretations of Elizabethan and Jacobean Drama, ed. David Scott Kastan and Peter Stallybrass (Routledge: New York, 1991), 99–113

Sheerin, Brian. 'Patronage and Perverse Bestowal in *The Spanish Tragedy* and *Antonio's Revenge*', *English Literary Renaissance* 41.2 (Spring 2011): 247–79.

Shirley, James. *Changes, or Love in a Maze, A comedie* (London: George Purslowe, 1632)

Siemon, James R. 'Sporting Kyd', *English Renaissance Drama* 24.3 (1994): 553–82

Sierra, Horacio. 'Bearing Witness and Taking Action: Audiences and Morality in Renaissance Tragedy and Activist Street Theater', *Comparative Drama*, 48.1/2 (Spring and Summer 2014): 39–57

Simkin, Stevie. *Early Modern Tragedy and the Cinema of Violence* (Basingstoke: Palgrave Macmillan, 2006)

Smith, Emma. 'Author v. Character in Early Modern Dramatic Authorship: The Example of Thomas Kyd and *The Spanish Tragedy*', *MaRDIE* 11 (1999): 129–42

Smith, Emma. 'Ghost Writing: *Hamlet* and the Ur-Hamlet', in *The Renaissance Text: Theory, Editing, Textuality*, ed. Andrew Murphy (Manchester: Manchester University Press, 2000), 177–90

Smith, Gregory, ed. *Elizabethan Critical Essays*, 2 vols (Oxford: Oxford University Press, 1904)

Smith, Molly. 'The Theater and the Scaffold: Death as Spectacle in The Spanish Tragedy', *Studies in English Literature, 1500–1900* 3.22 (Spring 1992): 217–32

Smith, Molly. *Breaking Boundaries: Politics and Play in the Drama of Shakespeare and his Contemporaries* (Aldershot: Ashgate, 1998)

Sofer, Andrew. 'Absorbing Interests: Kyd's Bloody Handkerchief as Palimpsest', *Comparative Drama* 34.2 (2000): 127–53

Spencer, Charles. 'RSC's Triumph over Tragedy', *Daily Telegraph*, 9 May 1997

Spenser, Edmund. *The Faerie Queene*, in *Edmund Spenser's Poetry*, 3rd edn, ed. Hugh Maclean and Anne Lake Prescott (New York: W. W. Norton, 1993)

S. R. L. 'An Elizabethan Melodrama', *Morning Post*, 12 December 1931

Stevens, Andrea. *Inventions of the Skin: The Painted Body in Early English Drama, 1400–1642* (Edinburgh: Edinburgh University Press, 2013)

Stevens, Martin and A. C. Cawley, eds. *The Towneley Plays*, 2 vols. (Oxford: Oxford University Press, 1994)

Stevenson, Warren. *Shakespeare's Additions to Thomas Kyd's* The Spanish Tragedy: *A Fresh Look at the Evidence Regarding the 1602 Additions* (Lewiston, Queenston and Lampeter: Edward Mellen, 2008)

Tanner, Marie. *The Last Descendant of Aeneas: The Hapsburgs and the Mythic Image of the Emperor* (New Haven: Yale University Press, 1993)

Tassi, Marguerite A. *The Scandal of Images: Iconoclasm, Criticism, and Painting in Early Modern English Drama* (Selinsgrove, PA: Susquehanna University Press, 2004)

Taylor, Paul. 'More Matter, Less Art', *Independent*, 10 May 1997

Teixeira, José. *The Strangest Adventure That Ever Happened* (London, 1601)

Teixeira, José. *The True History of the late and lamentable adventures of Don Sebastian King of Portugal* (London, 1602)

The Geneva Bible: A facsimile of the 1560 edition. Intro. Lloyd E. Berry (Madison, WI: University of Wisconsin Press, 1969)

The Spanish Tragedie. St Edmund Hall, Oxford, July 1937, programme (Oxford, Bodleian Library, MS.Eng.misc.c.1013, fol. 48)

'*The Spanish Tragedie*'. Available online: www.dailyinfo.co.uk/reviews/feature/The_Spanish_Tragedie (Accessed 15 August 2015)

The Spanish Tragedy. Vandyck Theatre, Bristol, July 1968, programme (University of Bristol Theatre Collection, BDD/PG/000229)

The Spanish Tragedy. Christ Church, Oxford, March 1932, programme (Christ Church archive)

'The Spanish Tragedy, Containing the lamentable Murders of Horatio and Bellimperia: With the pitifull Death of old Hieronimo'. EBBA 30246, British Library, Roxburghe 1.364–5

Thorndike, Ashley H. 'The Relations of *Hamlet* to Contemporary Revenge Plays', *Modern Language Association* 17.3 (1902): 125–222

Tomkis, Thomas. *Albumazar: A comedy presented before the Kings Maiestie at Cambridge, the ninth of March. 1614. By the Gentlemen of Trinitie Colledge* (London: Nicholas Okes, 1615)

Tudeau-Clayton, Margaret. *Jonson, Shakespeare and Early Modern Virgil* (Cambridge: Cambridge University Press, 1998)

Turner, Timothy A. 'Torture and Summary Justice in *The Spanish Tragedy*' in *Studies in English Literature* 53.2 (Spring 2013): 277–92.
Tweedie, Eleanor M. '"Action Is Eloquence": The Staging of Thomas Kyd's *Spanish Tragedy*', *Studies in English Literature, 1500–1900* 16.2 (1976): 223–39
Van Langen, I. *The Explanation of the True and Lawfull Right and Tytle, of the Moste Excellent Prince Anthonie the first of that name, King of Portugal, concerning his warres, againste Phillip King of Castile, and against his subjectes and adherentes, for the recoverie of his kingdome. Together with a Briefe History of all that hath passed aboute that matter, untill the yeare of our Lord, 1583* (Leyden, 1585)
Vernon [Veron], John [Jean]. *The Hunting of Purgatorie to Death* (London, 1561)
Vickers, Brian. 'Shakespeare and Authorship Studies in the Twenty-first Century', *Shakespeare Quarterly* 62 (2011): 106–42
Vickers, Brian. 'Identifying Shakespeare's Additions to The Spanish Tragedy (1602): A New(er) Approach', *Shakespeare* 8 (2012): 13–43
Virgil. *Thee First Foure Bookes of Virgil His Aeneis*, trans. Richard Stanyhurst (Leyden, 1582)
Ward, Philip, ed. *Oxford Companion to Spanish Literature* (Oxford: Oxford University Press, 1978)
Warrington, John, ed. *Everyman's Classical Dictionary*, rev. 3rd edn (London: J. M. Dent & Sons, 1969)
Watson, Robert N. *The Rest Is Silence: Death as Annihilation in the English Renaissance* (Berkeley, LA and London: University of California Press, 1999)
Watters, B. D. '*The Spanish Tragedie*', *The Lodestone* (Lent 1922): 82–5 (Birkbeck College, University of London, archive)
Wells, Stanely and Gary Taylor, eds. *William Shakespeare: The Complete Works* (Oxford: Oxford University Press, 1994; repr. 1995)
Werner, Sarah, ed. *New Directions in Renaissance Drama and Performance Studies* (Basingstoke: Macmillan, 2010)
Whalley, Peter. *An Enquiry into the Learning of Shakespeare* (London: T. Waller, 1748)
Whigham, Frank. *Seizures of the Will in Early Modern English Drama* (Cambridge: Cambridge University Press, 1996)

White, Martin. *Renaissance Drama in Action: An Introduction to Aspects of Theatre Practice and Performance* (London: Routledge, 1998)

White, Richard Grant. *Memoirs of the Life of William Shakespeare, with an Essay toward the Expression of his Genius, and an Account of the Rise and Progress of the English Drama* (Boston: Little, Brown, and Co., 1865)

Wickham, Glynne, Herbert Berry and William Ingram, eds. *English Professional Theatre, 1530–1660* (Cambridge: Cambridge University Press, 2000)

Wiggins, Martin. *Journeymen in Murder: The Assassin in English Renaissance Drama* (Oxford: Clarendon Press, 1991)

Wiggins, Martin, in association with Catherine Richardson, *British Drama 1533–1642: A Catalogue* (Oxford: Oxford University Press, 2012–), II

Wilson, J. Dover. 'Bibliographical Links between the Three Pages and the Good Quartos', in *Shakespeare's Hand in 'The Play of Sir Thomas More'*, ed. Andrew F. Pollard et al. (Cambridge: Cambridge University Press, 1923), 113–41

Wilson-Okamura, David Scott. *Virgil in the Renaissance* (Cambridge: Cambridge University Press, 2010)

Witherspoon, Alexander Maclaren. *The Influence of Robert Garnier on Elizabethan Drama* (New Haven, CT: Yale University Press, 1924)

Womack, Peter. 'Secularizing *King Lear*: Shakespeare, Tate and the Sacred', *Shakespeare Survey* 55 (2002): 96–105

Woodbridge, Linda. *English Revenge Drama: Money, Resistance, Equality* (Cambridge: Cambridge University Press, 2010)

Wordsworth, John and Henry Julian White, eds. *Nouum Testamentum Latine Secundum Editionem Sancti Hiernoymi* (Oxford: Clarendon Press, 1911)

Wyatt, Thomas. *The Complete Poems*, ed. R. A. Rebholz (New Haven, CT: Yale University Press, 1981)

Young, B. A. '*The Spanish Tragedy*', *Financial Times*, 30 November 1973

Zitner, Sheldon P. '*The Spanish Tragedy* and the Language of Performance', in *The Elizabethan Theatre XI*, ed. A. L. Magnusson and C. E. McGee (Ontario: P. D. Meany Publishers, 1990), 75–93

INDEX

action 3–5, 11–15, 27, 28–9, 36, 38–40, 44–50, 55, 57–8, 67–9, 71, 76–7, 87, 90–2, 98–9, 105–6, 109, 114, 116, 127–8, 133, 149, 153, 156, 162, 174, 177, 180, 188, 194, 200, 204–7, 209–11, 221, 229, 238, 247, 266, 269, 272, 291, 293, 294
additions (1602) 55, 89, 145, 214, 216, 230, 231, 245, 259, 260, 275, 276, 292, 293
afterlife 1, 8, 28, 155–6, 158–60, 162, 167, 218
see also Underworld
Alexander the Great 120, 143, 169, 171–2
Alexandro 7–9, 13–14, 43, 58, 134, 190, 212
Alleyn, Edward 56
ambition 7, 114, 118, 133–5, 147, 256
America ix, 91, 96, 103, 139–41, 201, 257, 278, 282
Andrea *see Ghost*
Andrew, Thomas 26, 232
anger 15, 49, 123–6, 142, 177, 193, 229, 238, 246, 274
Ardolino, Frank 89, 93, 94–5, 100, 107, 121, 247, 249, 256, 258, 272
Aristotle 6
Armada, the 95, 120–1, 134–5, 148, 150, 247, 256, 258, 260, 261, 272, 280, 286
Augustine, St 119, 142, 159
Augustus, Emperor 138, 142–4, 252
authorship 16, 88–92, 145, 216, 245, 246, 252, 253, 259, 261, 276, 291, 293

Babylon 12, 29, 93–4, 142, 145, 247, 256, 272, 277, 283
Baines, Richard 11
Baker, Howard 35, 113, 115, 224, 234, 235, 251, 272
Bale, John 143
Balthazar 5, 7, 23–5, 29, 36, 38, 44–5, 58–9, 74–7, 79, 93, 100, 102, 119, 132–4, 153, 156, 184, 190–2, 194, 199, 200, 204, 212, 266
Barber, C. L. 14, 84, 85, 87, 91, 97, 102, 177–8, 244, 265, 272
Barry, Lording 24, 232, 273
Battle of Alcantara 133–4
Battle of the Three Kings 131
BBC radio productions 79

Beaumont, Francis 148, 231, 254, 273
Beckett, Samuel 77
Bel-imperia 4–6, 22, 25, 33, 35, 38, 40, 43, 45, 56, 58, 62, 66–7, 69, 74, 76, 77, 79, 88, 93, 97–100, 102, 119, 132, 136–7, 153, 156, 160, 167, 177–8, 184–6, 188, 191, 199–200, 204–5, 210, 222, 231
Bible 12, 18, 93, 95, 107, 123, 125, 129–30, 142, 144, 168, 181, 258, 292
Black Legend of Spanish Cruelty 17, 95–6, 121, 142, 248, 253, 260, 281
blood 6–7, 9, 27, 34, 37, 40, 42, 44–5, 50, 61, 70–1, 75, 77, 86, 94, 102, 119, 122, 133–4, 154–5, 159–60, 167, 175, 177–9, 187, 200, 205, 208–9, 229, 242, 247, 249, 265, 269, 272, 273, 280, 281, 291
Blundeville, Thomas 138–9, 257, 274
Boas, Frederick 15, 32–3, 48, 53, 60, 63, 74, 231, 232, 234, 235, 239, 240, 274, 280
body v, 4, 8–9, 23, 33, 58, 62, 77, 86, 90, 102, 141, 154, 159, 161, 176, 178–9, 185–7, 191, 200, 204–5, 229, 251, 260, 292
Boleyn, Anne 112

Borromeo, Charles 10
Bowers, Fredson 35–6, 38, 40, 42, 105, 121, 216, 235, 236, 254, 274
Bower, the 33, 78, 179, 189, 194
Braden, Gordon v, viii, 10, 15, 17, 49–50, 91–2, 97, 111–30, 139, 154, 229, 238–9, 246, 251, 265, 274
Bradley, A. C. 2, 12, 225, 227, 274
Braithwaite, Richard 15
Bridewell 87
Broude, Ronald 12, 46, 93, 104, 228, 237, 258, 275
Burbage, Richard 56
Bush, President George 109, 250

Calvo, Clara (Arden editor) 3, 55, 70, 120, 151, 207, 214, 225, 227, 239, 255, 262, 264, 269, 285
Campanella, Tomasso de 140, 257, 282
Castile 43–5, 94, 100, 103, 120, 132, 134–5, 183, 191, 193, 199, 222, 231, 293
Catharsis 6–7, 9, 228, 280, 289
Catholic 9, 11–14, 16, 46, 92–5, 102–3, 135, 139, 143, 146–7, 158–62, 178, 191, 195, 223, 230, 247, 259, 267, 278, 279, 281
Cervantes, Miguel de 17, 144, 259, 275, 284
Chambers, E. K. 176

character 3–4, 16, 22, 24,
  26, 29, 33, 36–8, 41,
  43–6, 55–6, 58, 67, 70,
  72–9, 99, 90–1, 98, 106,
  115–16, 120, 129, 151,
  154–8, 160, 182, 166,
  167, 180, 198, 200, 201,
  206–7, 209, 209–11,
  222, 224, 242, 246, 261,
  266, 281, 291
Charles I 147, 195
Charon 154
chorus 89, 111–12, 115, 128,
  140, 153, 180, 251, 254
Christianity 1, 9, 17–18, 41,
  92, 100–2, 105, 122–30,
  135, 142, 156, 158,
  162, 166–7, 172–3, 176,
  178–9, 194, 210, 262
Church 60, 63, 80, 93, 149,
  157–8, 176, 186, 240,
  274, 292
class (social) 18, 36, 88, 96–9,
  117, 126, 182–3, 186,
  190–1, 193–4, 211, 258,
  267, 268, 273
classical 3, 17–18, 32–3, 41–2,
  49, 65, 69, 88, 91,
  100–3, 114–15, 118–19,
  123–5, 135, 139, 143
Coghill, Nevill 63–5, 80, 240
Coleridge, Samuel Taylor 89
Collier, John 31, 233, 289
confession 10–12, 136, 145,
  229, 274
Corneille 114
Corpus Christi 18, 175–95,
  265, 266, 274
cosmology 16, 88, 100–4, 108,
  166, 169

Crossman, Richard 62, 80
court 22–3, 29, 48–9, 55–7,
  62, 64–5, 74, 87, 93, 99,
  104, 112, 117, 132,134,
  136–7, 153, 155–6, 189,
  191, 194, 230, 253
Cross 9, 14, 176, 178, 180,
  184–7, 190, 267

dates 95, 120, 135, 172, 218
dead, the 7, 9, 12, 26, 42, 84,
  94, 103, 119, 127, 154,
  158–9, 161–3, 169–70,
  172, 173, 176, 179, 185,
  191, 193, 200, 223, 227,
  229, 249, 285, 286
Dee, John 138, 258, 279
Dekker, Thomas 14, 25–6, 57,
  148, 173–4, 232, 239,
  264, 277
destiny 5, 37, 77, 100, 104,
  157–8, 247, 272
Dodsley, Robert 30, 233, 239,
  287, 289, 290
Doomsday v, 18, 175–95
Dresden 22, 56
Dr Faustus 3, 17, 79, 154,
  166–9, 171–3, 216, 259,
  264, 284, 286
Drury, Leslie vi, viii, 18,
  197–225
Durkheim, Emile 3, 228, 278

Elizabeth I 18, 112
Eliot, T. S. 15, 34–5, 234, 278,
  286, 290
Emotion ix, 15, 17–18, 25, 45,
  55, 59, 63, 74–7, 79,
  116, 153, 161, 176, 184,
  220 *see also* passion

INDEX

Empson, William 15, 37–9, 43, 235, 236, 278
Erne, Lukas 12, 55, 72, 84, 88–9, 91–2, 95, 101, 114–15, 169, 165, 177–8, 190, 194, 217, 230, 231, 240, 241, 245, 252, 253, 256, 259, 261, 262, 263, 265, 267, 268, 279
Euripides 101, 122
excess 25, 30, 103, 106, 126, 135, 141, 284
execution 7–9, 13–14, 41, 49, 67, 86–7, 94, 165, 188, 195, 207–8, 220, 230

feminist 76, 87, 222
Ferdinand II 135
Field, Nathan 24, 232, 279
films 70, 109–10, 123, 209, 219, 269, 280
First Part of Hieronimo The 89, 146, 162, 232, 272, 285
Fletcher, John ix, 148, 254
Ford, John 148
Foucault, Michelle 7, 85, 87, 229, 279
Foxe, John 143

Garnier, Robert 114, 177, 252, 265, 294
gender ix, x, 18, 67, 70, 72, 119, 210, 218, 222, 246, 288
ghost 1–7, 19, 23, 26, 28, 35, 38, 55, 57, 59, 62, 64, 68–70, 76–7, 101–3, 115, 153–6, 160, 162, 166–7, 169, 178, 189, 252, 263, 275, 291
Glasgow Citizens Theatre 60, 70, 80, 276
God 2, 11, 27, 28, 71, 91, 93, 100–1, 107, 110, 124–5, 127, 129, 156–8, 166, 168, 176, 179–80, 182–3, 187, 188, 192, 194–5, 213, 221, 254, 265, 273
Goodland, Katharine v, viii, 5, 14, 18, 175–95, 280
grace 33, 43, 129, 142, 149, 157–8, 171, 242, 258, 269, 273, 279
Greenblatt, Stephen 84, 103, 158, 230, 244, 249, 262, 280, 287
Greene, Robert 23, 163, 169, 173, 263, 264, 280
Greville, Fulke 118, 253, 280
grief 5, 14, 23, 35–8, 54, 59, 61, 74, 100, 106, 108, 122, 145, 153, 163, 176–7, 183, 187, 190, 193, 200, 204–5, 244, 290
Griffin, Eric v, ix, 17, 95, 121, 131–52, 231, 248, 253, 255, 257, 258, 259, 265, 280, 281
Gurr, Andrew 59, 208, 214, 240, 281

Hamlet 1, 28, 30, 34–5, 38, 39–40, 97, 103, 95, 107, 123, 127, 145, 163–4 *see also* Shakespeare
hangman 9, 188

INDEX

Harbage, Alfred 39, 236, 281
Hawkins, Thomas 30–1, 282
Hell 2, 10, 23, 26, 40, 46, 81, 85, 92, 100, 116, 119, 128, 145, 155, 159–61, 164–70, 172–3, 180–3, 189, 192, 243, 249, 259, 261, 266, 278, 279, 282
Henry VIII 13, 112
Henslowe, Philip 21, 151, 259, 279
Heywood, Jasper 125
Heywood, Thomas 21, 23, 125, 128, 230, 231, 260, 282
Hieronimo v, 4–7, 11–15, 17–18, 22–9, 32–3, 35–51, 55–6, 58–60, 62–9, 70–1, 73–4, 76, 78–9, 85–6, 89–91, 93–5, 97–102, 104–7, 115–16, 119–20, 122–4, 127–8, 132, 145–7, 151, 153, 155–6, 159–61, 168, 175, 177–95, 199–201, 204–6, 211–13, 220–2, 231, 232, 234, 240, 241, 247, 247, 249, 266, 272
Hiscock, Andrew ii, vii
Hispanophilia 138, 141–2, 147–8, 151
Hispanophobia 12, 17, 137–8, 141–2, 147–9, 151, 260, 280
'Hockley in the hole' (ballad) 216–27, 232, 282
Homer 101, 169, 171
Hopkins, Lisa ii, vii, 177–8, 263, 283

Horatio 4–6, 11, 13–14, 23–5, 27, 29, 36, 43, 45, 58–9, 62–63, 72, 74–9, 89, 94, 97–8, 100, 102–3, 132, 136, 153, 159–62, 177–9, 184–92, 199–200, 204–5, 207, 212, 232, 292
humanism 85, 101, 138–9, 165 261, 275

icon 8, 29, 54, 55, 79, 96, 135, 176, 197, 229, 246, 292
identity 2, 78, 86, 99, 104, 244, 262, 273, 288
Innocents, the 177, 266
Inns of Court 112
Isabella 6–7, 13, 35, 43, 58, 67, 72, 77, 102, 107, 162, 177–8, 186–90, 194, 199–200, 212, 283

James I of England / James VI of Scotland 25, 97, 146–50, 283
Jesus 129, 177, 179, 184–7, 190, 192–3, 267, 268
Johnson, S. F. 12, 39–40, 43, 236, 247, 256, 283
Jonson, Ben 24, 56, 85, 89, 231, 232, 239, 241, 245, 264, 276, 284, 293
judgement 48, 61, 83, 113, 129, 190, 192–3, 268
justice 2, 6–7, 13, 18, 28, 40–1, 43, 45–9, 87, 95, 98, 100–2, 104–6, 109, 123, 126, 132, 141, 153, 156, 157, 176–7, 181,

183, 186–95, 198, 200, 209, 211–13, 221–2, 228, 245, 248, 257, 267, 283, 284, 293

King Lear 107, 124, 126, 129, 227, 228, 255, 274, 294 *see also* Shakespeare
King's Men, The 56
Kubrick, Stanley 54

Lamb, Charles 89
Legacy 16, 107–10, 112, 129, 263, 283
Librivox 198, 219, 268
Loban, J. H. 54–5, 61, 65, 80, 239, 285
Lord Strange's Men 56
Lorenzo 11, 36, 38, 45, 58, 70, 74–6, 79, 98–100, 108, 119, 132, 184–6, 188, 190–1, 193–4, 199–200, 204, 210, 212, 268
Lucan 32

Macbeth 3, 33, 72, 157, 227, 274 *see also* Shakespeare
Machiavelli 36, 74, 108, 135, 148, 257, 286
madness 14, 23, 25–7, 29, 31, 35, 38–9, 45, 48, 58, 60, 78, 85, 90, 99, 107, 122, 129, 147, 151, 177, 180, 182, 187, 231, 239, 243, 244, 246, 250, 277, 281, 288, 290
Malin, Peter v, ix, 2, 15–16, 53–82, 227, 234, 286
Manly, John 31, 234, 286

Marlowe, Christopher x, 3, 10–11, 17–18, 41, 54, 82, 85, 96, 98, 113, 115–16, 154, 166–8, 171–3, 229, 244, 264, 265, 272, 286 *see also Dr Faustus*; *Tamburlaine*
Marshall, Peter 7, 229, 286
Martyr 13–14
Masefield, John 63
Massinger, Philip 148
May, Thomas 58, 287
Medici, Giuliano di and Lorenzo 95
memory ix, 5, 9, 23, 29, 90, 102–3, 129, 161, 178, 189, 230, 247, 249, 272, 275, 279
Mercury Theatre 60, 65, 80,
Middleton, Thomas 148–9
Milton, John 85, 107, 114, 223
Minos 153, 155
Mirror for Magistrates, The 35
Moors 96, 148
morality 15, 18, 27, 32, 36, 39–41, 48–50, 54, 71, 92, 101, 104, 106–7, 109, 122–3, 126, 155, 180–1, 184, 193, 210–11, 215, 217, 266, 282, 291
mother 43, 72, 108, 176–7, 180–4, 193
mourning v, viii, 18, 86, 100, 159–60, 175–95, 223, 265, 266, 277, 280
mystery 1–2, 19, 38, 57, 93, 100, 176, 185, 192, 245, 249, 259, 267, 272, 276, 282, 285, 286

Nashe, Thomas 166–7, 170–3, 263, 264, 282, 283, 286, 288
nationalism 121, 147, 248, 253, 260, 281
National Theatre, The 60, 69, 74–5, 81
nobility 7, 64, 74, 95, 97–8, 119, 132, 136, 141, 147, 183, 186, 189–90, 192–4, 230, 243, 258, 271, 279, 286
Noyes, Alfred 53

outrage 11, 18, 127, 177, 184, 190, 233

Pagan 17, 92, 94, 100–1, 124–7, 129, 143, 146, 167
Pagden, Anthony 137, 257, 257, 288
parody 9, 11, 13, 25, 108, 231, 240, 250, 288
passion 14, 18, 23, 25–6, 34, 40, 45, 50, 59, 121–2, 125, 156, 167, 176–9, 181, 184, 185, 189–90, 193, 220, 231, 232, 265, 266, 290 *see also* emotion
patience, 6, 24, 73, 92, 121
Pedringano 3, 8–10, 14, 39, 41, 66–7, 70, 87, 108, 184, 188, 193, 199–200, 205, 211–12, 268
Peele, George 96, 113, 171, 173
Pepys, Samuel 15, 29, 60, 232, 233, 282, 289

performance v, vii, viii, ix, 13–16, 18, 21–2, 24–5, 29, 31, 48, 53–82, 87, 96, 98, 101–2, 114, 116, 145, 150, 194–5, 198, 201–7, 209, 213, 217, 218, 220–1, 223, 228, 230, 231, 241, 242, 245, 248, 265, 267, 268, 269, 273, 276, 281, 283, 290, 294, 295
Philip II 120, 131, 133–5, 144–7, 253, 255, 256, 259, 271, 274, 283, 289
Philip III 146–7, 253, 259, 271, 283
Philip IV 147, 149–50
Pilate, Pontius 186, 267
politics v, ix, 2, 16–17, 84, 83, 94, 96–9, 131–52, 208, 218, 220, 222, 260, 269, 285, 291
Pope, the 93
Portugal 2, 44, 93, 94, 96, 101, 120, 131–4, 137–9, 147, 153, 155, 191, 212, 255, 256, 258, 259, 260, 273, 276, 277, 278, 281, 285, 288, 292, 293
postmodern 86, 90
pride 135–6, 139, 155, 168, 191, 193–4
Privy Council 11, 262
Proserpine 101, 153, 156–7, 160, 177, 180, 188–9, 211
Prosser, Eleanor 40, 236, 289
Protestant 7, 12–14, 16, 93–6, 99, 103, 105, 142–8, 157–9, 195

Prynne, William 28, 233, 289
punishment 7, 9, 13–14, 44, 46, 87, 100, 104, 154–5, 158, 160, 181, 192, 194, 212, 220, 221, 267, 268
purgatory 6–7, 9, 92, 103, 128, 158–60, 162, 165, 180, 192, 194, 228, 262, 280, 285
purge 7–8, 160

Randloph, Thomas 28, 233, 289
Rawlin, Thomas 14, 29, 59, 60, 223, 240, 289
Revenge (character) 2–6, 26, 28, 30, 35–6, 38–40, 44, 46, 55, 57, 61–2, 67, 69–72, 75, 78, 104, 115, 153–4, 156–7, 180
Revenge tragedy ix, x, 1, 6, 16, 30, 35–6, 54, 88, 93–4, 97–110, 121–7, 141, 145, 176, 182, 215–25, 228, 229, 230, 235, 241, 243, 244, 245, 247, 248, 249, 250, 254, 258, 259, 262, 265, 266, 267, 270
rhetoric 15–16, 24, 29, 43, 54–5, 58, 67, 71–9, 81, 92, 108–9, 115–16, 125, 133, 148, 156, 224, 225, 238, 252, 267, 271, 273, 284
Rist, Thomas iii, v, ix, 1–19, 93–4, 103, 106, 158–9, 176, 223, 227, 228, 229, 246, 258, 259, 262, 263, 265, 289, 290

rites 10, 102–3, 154, 159, 161, 165, 170, 267
Rowley, William 148
Royal Shakespeare Company ix, 16, 61, 65, 75–9, 81, 243, 290, 291
Rutter, Tom v, x, 5, 17, 92, 128, 152–74, 228, 231

sacrifice 160, 187, 190, 193
scarf 102, 159
Schick, Josef 31–2, 234, 290
Schlegel, August Wilhelm von 31, 233, 290
Scott, Thomas 149–51, 290
scourge of god, the 127, 154, 273
Sebastian I (King) 131, 146
Semple, Edel v, x, 2, 14–16, 21–51, 139, 227
Seneca v, vii, 10, 15, 17, 32, 34–5, 49–50, 70, 91–2, 103, 105, 109–30, 139–41, 143–4, 163–4, 177, 224, 225, 229, 234, 235, 238, 246, 250, 251, 252, 253, 254, 255, 257, 258, 261, 262, 265, 273, 274, 275, 276, 278, 282, 283, 284, 287, 291
Shakespeare, William vii, 1–3, 6, 29, 32, 34, 42, 46, 53–4, 59, 63, 66, 73, 85, 89, 103, 107, 113–14, 122, 129, 132, 145–6, 157, 164, 170, 178, 208 *see also Hamlet*; *King Lear*; *Macbeth*
ShaLT, 204, 206, 219, 269

Shirley, James 14, 28, 233, 291
Sidney, Sir Philip 114, 118, 253, 258
Simkin, Stevie v, x, 5, 14, 16, 83–110, 208, 218, 220, 221, 229, 230, 250,269, 270, 291
slaughter 18, 101, 111, 120, 176–7, 180–4, 186, 266
Soliman and Perseda 12, 89, 96, 224
Sophocles 32
soul 3–6, 8–10, 23, 78, 92, 98, 104, 124, 126, 136, 153, 160, 167, 172, 177, 180, 182, 188–9, 192–4, 228, 248, 267, 276, 288
Southwell, Robert 94, 230
Spain ix, 2, 17, 29, 39, 44–5, 74, 93–7, 101, 102, 119–21, 131–52, 155, 166, 179, 191, 194, 201, 212, 224, 248, 253, 255, 256, 257, 258, 259, 260, 272, 273, 276, 271, 283, 284, 288, 289
Spanish Peace, Somerset House Conference 146
spectacle v, 6–7, 9, 12, 14–15, 17, 25, 30, 51–82, 87, 104, 125, 127, 160, 182, 191, 194, 207–8, 219, 220, 221, 230, 245, 291
Spenser, Edmund 143, 258, 291
St Bartholomew Day Massacre 95, 247, 272
Studley, John 111, 250
suicide 27, 35–6, 43, 64, 107–8, 127, 161–2, 167, 169, 188, 199–200, 210, 212

Tamburlaine 37, 96, 115–17, 127, 254, 273
teaching resources vi, vii, 14, 18, 197–225
theatre ix, x, 2–3, 5–6, 9, 12, 15, 21–2, 26, 28, 33, 38, 44, 48, 53, 56, 60, 63, 65, 68–9, 78–82, 96, 102, 104, 107, 148, 170–2, 175–6, 178, 193, 195, 204, 207–8, 216–17, 219–21, 223, 225, 227, 230, 241, 242, 243, 249, 261, 262, 265, 269, 273, 275, 276, 277, 278, 279, 281, 286, 290, 294, 295
theology 7–8, 101, 157–8, 162
Thorndike, A. H. 1, 226, 292
tomb 168, 179, 189
torture 8, 12, 33, 43–4, 71, 87, 180, 184–6, 188, 195, 245, 293
translation viii, 17–18, 98, 111–12, 114, 125, 128, 143, 144, 155, 164–6, 169, 173, 250, 251, 254, 258, 262, 264, 265, 268
Trinity 176, 192
Tronch, Jesús (Arden editor) 3, 55, 70, 120, 151, 207, 214, 225, 227, 239, 255, 262, 264, 269, 285
tyrant 17, 118–19, 127, 181–2, 193, 267

Underworld, the 18, 23, 26,

68, 92, 100, 127, 153–6, 158–62, 166–7, 169–70, 172–3, 180, 188, 212–13 *see also* afterlife
Universal Monarchy 131, 140, 147
University Productions 25, 53–4, 61–4, 66–7, 70, 80–2, 229, 232–9, 240, 241, 274, 276, 285, 293

victim 18, 71, 104–6, 108, 122, 127, 184, 186
Villuppo 4, 8, 13, 41, 43, 45, 212
violence x, 10, 18, 30, 33, 36, 71, 77, 75, 86–7, 91–2, 113, 127, 183–209, 220, 223, 245, 250, 266, 269, 280, 289, 291
Virgil v, 17–18, 23, 32, 33, 35, 69, 91–2, 112, 143, 153–74, 257, 258, 261, 262, 264, 293, 294

Virgin Mary 176–8, 180, 184, 186–7, 189–90, 266
vengeance 18, 26–7, 36, 38, 67, 71, 91, 99–101, 105–6, 123–6, 141, 160, 168, 175–81, 183, 185, 189, 195, 200, 209, 215, 249, 250, 265, 266, 267, 279

Watch 10
Webster, John 61, 148
Wergild 106
Whalley, Peter 30, 51, 233, 294
Wickham, Glynne 65, 80, 262, 294
wounds 14, 161–2, 176–9, 186, 189, 192, 268,
Wyatt, Thomas 112, 117, 129, 250, 250, 294

YouTube 79, 198, 201, 217, 219, 243, 268, 269